Social Psychology of Globalization

Issue Editors: Chi-yue Chiu, Peter Gries, Carlos J. Torelli and Shirley Y. Y. Cheng

Journal of Social Issues, Vol. 67, No. 4, 2011, pp. 663–676

Toward a Social Psychology of Globalization

Chi-yue Chiu*
Nanyang Technological University

Peter Gries
University of Oklahoma

Carlos J. Torelli
University of Minnesota

Shirley Y. Y. Cheng
Hong Kong Baptist University

In most parts of the world, globalization has become an unstoppable and potent force that impacts everyday life and international relations. The articles in this issue draw on theoretical insights from diverse perspectives (clinical psychology, consumer research, organizational behavior, political psychology, and cultural psychology) to offer nuanced understanding of individuals' psychological reactions to globalization in different parts of the world (Australia, Hong Kong, Japan, Mainland China, Singapore, Switzerland, United States, Taiwan). These articles address the questions of how people make sense of and respond to globalization and its sociocultural ramifications; how people defend the integrity of their heritage cultural identities against the "culturally erosive" effects of globalization, and how individuals harness creative insights from their interactions with global cultures. The new theoretical insights and revealing empirical analyses presented in this issue set the stage for an emergent interdisciplinary inquiry into the psychology of globalization.

At the turn of the century, Albert Bandura (2001) noted that societies today are undergoing drastic social, informational, and technological changes, and that

---

*Correspondences concerning this article should be addressed to Chi-yue Chiu, S3–01C-81, Nanyang Business School, Nanyang Technological University, Nanyang Avenue, Singapore 639798 [e-mail: cychiu@ntu.edu.sg]

This article was supported by a research grant awarded to Chi-yue Chiu by National Science Foundation Grant (NSF BCS 07–43119).*

663

"revolutionary advances in electronic technologies and globalization are trans-forming the nature, reach, speed, and loci of human influence." (p. 12) He invited psychologists to examine the psychological processes that shape personal destinies and the national life of societies in rapidly globalized environments.

However, this important message has not received much attention, and the discipline seems to have remained impassive toward globalization as a topic of psychological inquiry. In June 2011, we found only 32 articles in the *PsycARTI-CLES* database that are indexed with the keyword *globalization*. Among them, only four (Aaker, Benet-Martinez, & Garolera, 2001; Alter & Kwan, 2009; de Oliveria, Braun, Carlson, & de Oliveria, 2009; Pinquart & Silbereisen, 2008) are empirical papers. The seeming apathy over globalization in psychology is unfortunate given that the discipline is well positioned to offer new conceptual and empirical perspectives on issues concerning the social and cultural implications of globalization (Arnett, 2002; Chiu & Cheng, 2007; Hermans & Dimaggio, 2007).

Nonetheless, exciting developments are being made. For instance, theoretical and empirical analyses have been advanced to understand lay people's understanding of the meanings of globalization and social change (Kashima et al., 2009), reactions to the experiential compression of space and time in globalized cultural environments (Chiu, Mallorie, Keh, & Law, 2009), and the impacts of global contacts on international and intercultural relations (Gries, Crowson, & Sandel, 2010).

The objective of this issue is to leverage and promote these developments for the purpose of advancing a psychological science of globalization. The authors in this issue have illustrated with their latest research how social psychology can deepen psychological understanding of several important aspects of globalization. Their conceptual and empirical analyses have offered deep insights into the following issues:

1. How do lay people understand globalization and what are the social and psychological implications of such understanding?
2. What are the negative psychological effects of globalization?
3. What are the social psychological factors that can enlarge or reduce these negative effects?
4. What are the potential psychological benefits of globalization?
5. What are the social psychological factors that can enhance these positive effects and what are the boundaries of such effects?

Lay Perceptions of Globalization

Broadly defined, globalization refers to a process of interaction and integration among the peoples, companies, and governments of different nations. This process is driven by international trade and investment and aided by information technology (Carnegie Endowment for International Peace, 2007). Globalization has led to rapid diffusion of economic, political and cultural practices across national borders, creating optimism in global acceptance of the finest universal values of humanity as well as fear of erosion of local cultural traditions. Globalization has fueled economic developments in both developed and developing countries, but has also intensified both positive and negative interdependence among national and religious cultures.

Although globalization has transformed the cultures and life practices in all countries, the flow of resources, wealth and sociocultural practices between countries is asymmetrical. For instance, the United States has been a major exporter of pop culture, and China has been a main beneficiary of global trade. A productive way to begin the scientific study of the relationship between globalization and psychology is to examine the similarities and differences in the lay perceptions and appraisals of globalization and social change across nations. In this issue, Yang et al. (2011) applied multidimensional scaling to reveal the structure of lay perceptions of 24 objects that are strongly associated with globalization (e.g., McDonald's, global warming) in the United States and three cities in Greater China (Hong Kong, Shanghai, and Taipei). Their results showed that people in these four regions agree that globalization has five major facets: (a) global business enterprises (e.g., Starbucks), (b) information technology (e.g., the Internet), (c) migration of people (e.g., air travel), (d) global disasters (e.g., HIV), and (e) international regulators (e.g., the United Nations). Yang and his colleagues also measured their participants' evaluations of the impacts of these five facets of globalization on the levels of competence and interpersonal warmth in their societies. These evaluations reveal that people in the four regions generally believe that globalization has more positive effects on people's competence than on their warmth. Despite the striking similarity in the perceptions of globalization among Americans and the Chinese, there are regional differences in the perceptions of the cultural impacts of global business. For instance, whereas the Chinese perceived global businesses to have positive impacts on people's warmth and competence, Americans had more varied evaluations of the cultural impacts of global businesses, believing that some global businesses (Hollywood) have more negative impacts than do others (e.g., Disneyland).

Yang et al.'s results are consistent with Kashima et al.'s (2009) observation that people typically believe that a society undergoes a natural course of evolution from a traditional community with relatively low levels of competence and high levels of morality, to a modern society with relatively high levels of competence and low levels of morality. To probe how this folk theory of globalization varies with a country's recent economic experiences, in this issue, Kashima et al. (2011) compared the lay theory of globalization in the People's Republic of China (an Asian country that has experienced an explosive growth in the past two decades due to global trade), Japan (an Asian country that has experienced a slide in its economic status in the global economy) and Australia (a Western-European based economy that has experienced relative steady economic growth). These investigators found that people in all three countries regard their societies to have evolved from more moral but less competent communities to less moral but more competent societies. Despite this similarity in the appraisal of past trends, there are marked country differences in people's future imagination of their societies. Whereas Australians and the Japanese expect the trend described above to continue into the future, the Chinese, encouraged by their recent explosive economic growth, predict their society to be equally moral as now while continuing to become more competent into the future. This result is consistent with Cheng et al.'s (2010) observation that China's unprecedented economic growth has led the Mainland Chinese to expect a more competent China in the future (vs. now; the "better tomorrow effect") and a perception of a more moral China in the past (vs. now; the "good old days effect"). Cheng et al. (2010) also tracked the change of these expectations during the 2008 Beijing Olympics and found that as the Olympics proceeded, the perceived compatibility of competence and warmth/morality increased and the good old days effect diminished. Taken together, the results reviewed above suggest that rapid economic growth and enhanced international status through success in global mega-events (e.g., the Olympics) could promote more optimistic lay theories of social change.

Cultural and Intercultural Implications of Globalization

As Robertson (1992) noted, globalization involves "the compression of the world and the intensification of consciousness of the world as a whole." (p. 8) With the advancement of globalization, many people have experienced an increase in the frequency and intensity of exposure to other cultures. Giddens (1985) also points out that globalization has resulted in experiential compression of time and space; people in global cities frequently experience traditional and modern cultures (and their symbols) at the same time and cultures (and their symbols) from different geographical regions in the same space. A global culture is often characterized as one "of virtuality in the global flows which transcend time and space" (Castells, 1998, p. 350).

Social scientists have different views on the possible cultural impacts of globalization. Some writers believe that exposure to foreign cultures is a profoundly enriching process that opens minds to new experiences, removes cultural barriers, strengthens the cultural diffusion of human rights and democracy, and accelerates cultural change. These writers envision the emergence a multicultural global village, where people from different nation-states and cultural backgrounds can freely exchange their ideas and practices and appreciate those of others. The enthusiasts also envision the rise of cultural cosmopolitanism marked by a zest for wide international experience and acknowledgements of the otherness of those who are culturally different (Appiah, 2006).

In contrast, some scholars believe that increased cultural exposure may incite parochial and exclusionary resistance against foreign cultures (Barber, 1996), as well as collective movements that aim at reaffirming local cultures. These reactions, according to some, could lead to clashes of civilizations (Huntington, 1996). For example, there are concerns in France that American restaurant chains may crowd out French cuisines (a source of national pride for the French) with fast food. There are also concerns over the massive emigration of U.S.-dominated popular culture (e.g., Hollywood movies) to the world. In some countries, the spread of U.S. popular culture and its attendant American values and beliefs has evoked xenophobic anxieties over and incited nationalistic reactions toward the Americanization of world cultures (Chiu & Hong, 2006).

Exclusionary and Integrative Reactions Toward Foreign Cultures

Based on a review of the theoretical discourses in the social sciences, Chiu and Cheng (2007, 2010) propose that when the iconic symbols of the local and global cultures are seen together in a globalized environment, "culture" will become a salient mental category for organizing perceptions; people will attend to the differences between local and foreign cultures, become sensitive to the cultural implications of the inflow of foreign cultures (Chiu et al., 2009). This psychological state can promote both *exclusionary* and *integrative* reactions to foreign cultures.

Table 1 summarizes the major differences between exclusionary and integrative reactions to foreign cultures. Exclusionary reactions are emotional, reflexive responses evoked by perceived threats to the integrity and vitality of one's heritage culture. These reactions could lead to xenophobic, exclusionary behaviors or constructive effort directed to preserve the integrity and vitality of heritage cultures.

People on the receiving end of the global culture are often concerned that globalization will ultimately lead to homogenization of cultures, a seemingly an inevitable trend at first glance. Western nations, representatives of global culture, are generally perceived to be more economically advanced than non-Western ones. Developing countries that aspire to become an industrialized nation may treat Western economic powers as reference nations not only in the domain of economic development, but also in the realm of cultural restructuring. Global culture has been characterized as new, modern, scientific and results-oriented. It privileges consumerism, individualism, competition, and efficiency (Pilkington & Johnson, 2003). These values may be seen as the ones separating advanced societies from economically backward traditional economies. Thus, global culture may become the reference culture for some developing countries that seek to emulate

Table 1. Exclusionary and Integrative Reactions to Global Culture

Exclusionary Reactions	Integrative Reactions
Emotional reactions to fear of cultural contamination/erosion	Goal-oriented reactions geared toward problem solving
Quick, spontaneous, reflexive	Slow, deliberate, effortful
Perceptions of global/foreign cultures: Cultural threats	Perceptions of global/foreign cultures: Cultural resources
High identity salience	Low identity salience
Negative intercultural affect: Envy, fear, anger, disgust, pity	Positive intercultural affect: admiration
Exclusionary behavioral reactions: isolation, rejection, aggression	Inclusionary behavioral reactions: acceptance, integration, synthesis
Accentuated by the need to defend the integrity and vitality of the heritage culture	Accentuated by a cultural learning mindset
Attenuated by the need for cognition	Attenuated by the need for firm answers and cultural consensus

Western economic powers by embracing global values. Consequently, global culture exerts its hegemonic influence on some local cultures via voluntary submission to global culture (van Strien, 1997). Furthermore, globalization has brought rapid changes in consumption patterns and the spread of global "brand-name" goods. An expanding consumerist culture with its attending global marketing strategies such as global advertising tends to exploit similar basic material desires and create similar lifestyles (Parameswaran, 2002).

Fear of global culture's hegemonic influence on the local culture often takes the form of contamination anxiety—the worry that the global culture will contaminate the local culture (Pickowicz, 1991). Such contamination fear was responsible for the closedown of the Starbucks coffee shop in the Imperial Palace Museum in Beijing in 2007. In January 2007, Chenggang Rui, Director and Anchor of *BizChina*, the prime-time daily business show on CCTV International, led an online campaign to have Starbucks removed from Beijing's Forbidden City (the Palace Museum). Rui (2007) made the following remarks in his online article:

> The Forbidden City is a symbol of China's cultural heritage. Starbucks is a symbol of lower middle class culture in the west. We need to embrace the world, but we also need to preserve our cultural identity. There is a fine line between globalization and contamination. . . . But please don't interpret this as an act of nationalism. It is just about we Chinese people respecting ourselves. I actually like drinking Starbucks coffee. I am just against having one in the Forbidden City.

This article has attracted more than half a million readers and inspired more than 2700 commentaries, mostly of which are written in Chinese and are sympathetic to Rui's cause. In July 2007, Starbucks closed its shop in the Forbidden City.

Attacking the contaminants is not the only exclusionary response to contamination anxiety; another exclusionary response is to quarantine or isolate the erosive effects of global culture to selected life domains so that these effects can be prevented from spreading to other life domains, particularly those domains that are tied to the identity of local culture. For example, although modernization and Westernization often arrive in one package, Hong Kong Chinese distinguish between modernization and Westernization, with modernization involving acquisition of specific skills and competencies that have fueled the economic development in the West, and Westernization involving adoption of the Western social-moral values. Hong Kong Chinese welcome modernization and its attendant instrumental values (e.g., power and creativity) more than they do Western moral values (e.g., individuality and uniqueness; Fu & Chiu, 2007). This strategy shelters the core moral values in Chinese culture from the erosive effects of globalization, resulting in the differential rates of cultural change in different life domains (Cheung et al., 2006).

In contrast to exclusionary responses, integrative responses are reflective mental processes that facilitate the use of ideas from foreign cultures as means or resources to further one's valued goals. Individuals view the newly arrived foreign cultures as intellectual resources that complement their heritage culture for achieving valued goals. Individuals with multicultural experiences can flexibly switch their cultural frames in response to the changing cultural demands in the environment—they retrieve culturally appropriate interpretive frames and behavioral scripts depending on whether they interact with a member of the ingroup or outgroup culture (Chiu & Hong, 2005). They are willing to appropriate ideas from foreign cultures to generate creative solutions to a problem (Leung & Chiu, 2010; Leung Maddux, Galinsky & Chiu, 2008; Maddux & Galinsky, 2009). Creative synthesis of ideas from diverse cultures has led to product innovations in local and global markets. One example is Starbucks Coffee Singapore's introduction of a range of handcrafted snow-skin mooncakes—*Caramel Macchiato, Cranberry Hibiscus* and *Orange Citron*—to the market. In the company's news release, Belinda Wong, Managing Director of Starbucks Coffee Singapore, states that these new, innovative mooncakes will make a delicious complement to their customers' favorite coffee, as well as great gift for friends and family in the Chinese Mid-Autumn Festival. To her, Starbucks mooncakes is a business innovation created by combining a sip of the American Starbucks Coffee culture with a bite of the Chinese custom of celebrating the Mid-Autumn Festival with a traditional sweet delight.

Evocation of Exclusionary Reactions

A major theme in this issue concerns the contextual and psychological factors that activate exclusionary and integrative reactions to foreign culture. In this issue,

Torelli, Chiu, Tam, Au, and Keh (2011) proposed that simultaneous activation of two cultures (e.g., Starbucks Coffee in China's Imperial Palace Museum) makes culture a central organizing category for processing information (see also Chiu et al., 2009). As a result, the perceivers become sensitive to the cultural significance of the stimuli (e.g., the presence of a Starbucks Coffee Shop) in the environment. Torelli et al. also showed that simultaneous activation of two cultures could increase defensive, exclusionary reactions when the perceiver experiences globalization as a threat to their heritage culture (see also Chen & Chiu, 2010; Cheng, Leung, & Wu, 2011).

Nonetheless, it is possible to cool down these exclusionary reactions. In this issue, Morris, Mok, and Mok (2011) showed that although individuals tend to close their mind to new ideas following exposure to foreign culture mixing with one's heritage culture, this reaction is less pronounced among those with strong foreign cultural identification, possibly because these individuals do not experience culture mixing as an impending cultural threat. Relatedly, in this issue, Tong, Hui, Kwan, and Peng (2011) collected data from both Singapore (Study 1) and the United States (Study 2) to examine exclusionary reactions to foreign culture in the context of cross-border acquisitions. Their results show that when a company that is widely known to be a symbol of the local culture (e.g., Ya Kun in Singapore or General Motors in the United States) faces an acquisition attempt by a foreign enterprise, citizens in the local economy may perceive the attempted acquisition to be a threat to their local culture. These citizens may then exhibit culturally motivated exclusionary reactions to the acquisition, particularly when these citizens identify strongly with local culture and perceive the culture of the acquirer to be dissimilar to local culture. Nonetheless, local citizens can be led to consider the cross-border acquisition as a profit-driven business transaction. Under the influence of an economic transaction mindset, people will evaluate the acquisition primarily on the basis of its potential economic gains or losses.

Focusing on the psychological adaptation of individuals Not in Employment, Education, or Training (NEETS)—a marginal subculture in Japan that has emerged in response to globalization, Norasakkunkit and Uchida (2011) discussed in this issue a maladaptive response to globalization. They observed that a sizable number of Japanese youth (estimated to be around one million) cannot adjust to the rapid changes in occupational life (characterized by increased competitiveness and decreased job security) that globalization has brought to Japan. Although these individuals do not suffer from any clinically diagnosable psychological disorder, they lack persistence in pursuing achievement goals and choose to move from the center to the periphery of society, displaying low identification with the core values of interdependence and self-improvement in Japanese society.

In short, exclusionary reactions to foreign cultures are particularly likely to emerge when cross-border interactions and transactions are perceived through a cultural lens and the vitality of the local culture is threatened. In addition, the increased lifestyle changes that accompany globalization might also lead to passive resistance to the new lifestyle and in some extreme cases withdrawal from society.

Activation of Integrative Reactions

Although intercultural contacts might increase the likelihood of exclusionary reactions to foreign culture and a globalized lifestyle, they also afford opportunities for intercultural understanding and learning (Leung et al., 2008). For instance, in this issue, Gries, Crowson and Cai (2011) contend that globalization compresses time and space through modern transportation and media technologies and increases opportunities for intercultural understanding. These investigators examined how interpersonal contacts with Chinese and exposure to media coverage about China differentially impact American attitudes and policy preferences toward a rapidly rising China. Their results showed that while both interpersonal contact and media exposure were associated with prejudice reduction, media exposure was associated with more negative attitudes toward the Chinese government. Interestingly, these effects were mediated by knowledge about China. As contact theory suggests, increased knowledge about China was associated with decreased prejudice, but increased knowledge about China was also associated with more negative attitudes toward the Chinese government. Knowledge, therefore, is not a panacea for the problems that beset United States–China relations.

Experiences with foreign cultures also afford opportunities for intercultural learning. With more multicultural experiences individuals are more creative (Leung et al., 2008; Maddux & Galinsky, 2009). Experimental evidence also shows that people become more creative after viewing symbols from their own culture *and* a foreign culture (mixed cultural priming). However, viewing symbols of one's own culture or a foreign culture alone (monocultural priming) has no creative benefits (Leung & Chiu, 2010). This result suggests that experiences with culturally mixed environment can enrich an otherwise mundane local environment, sparking creative combinations of ideas from diverse cultural sources.

Nonetheless, living in a culturally mixed environment can engender anxiety and discomfort. At the cognitive level, culturally mixed experiences expose individuals to seemingly incompatible ideas and invite investment of cognitive resources to reconcile and integrate the apparent contradictions. Accordingly, mixed cultural priming may have momentary negative impact on emotional experiences. However, investment in such cognitive effort may also enhance creative performance. Consistent with this idea, in this issue, Cheng et al. (2011) reported that mixed cultural priming can temporarily reduce pleasant affect or induce unpleasant affect, and that these emotional changes are accompanied by increased creative performance.

The need for cultural competence is particularly pronounced in high stake trans-cultural encounters, such as cross-border military assignments. In this issue, Rockstuhl, Seiler, Ang, Dyne, and Anne (2011) analyzed the core competencies that predict accomplishment of domestic military assignments and cross-border military assignments among a sample of Swiss military officers. These investigators found that cultural intelligence, which refers to an individual's capability to function effectively in culturally mixed situations, is an important predictor of leader effectiveness in cross-border military assignments.

In summary, cultural mixing in a global society confers intercultural learning opportunities that invite integrative response, while at the same time presents potential identity threats that evoke exclusionary reactions. A major challenge in the social psychology of globalization is to explain and predict when people would display exclusionary or integrative responses to the cultural effects of globalization. Previous research has provided some answers to this question. For example, the need for firm answers has been shown to increase the tendency to rely on one's heritage cultural perspective (and to exclude other cultural perspectives) as behavior guides (Chao, Zhang, & Chiu, 2010; Chiu, Morris, Hong, & Menon, 2000; Fu et al., 2007). Such culturocentric tendency fuels exclusionary reactions and inhibits integrative reactions. There is also evidence that cultural adaptation and open-mindedness facilitate intercultural learning in intercultural contacts (Leung et al., 2008; Maddux & Galinsky, 2009). The articles in this issue add to these growing insights and suggest that experience of existential anxiety (Torelli et al., 2011, this issue) and identification with heritage culture (Tong et al., 2011; this issue) can increase the likelihood of exclusionary reactions, whereas need for cognition (Torelli et al., 2011; this issue) and foreign cultural identification (Morris, 2011; this issue) can attenuate exclusionary reactions.

Conclusions

People's diverse reactions to the cultural impacts of globalization have given rise to the birth of a new "civil-society politics" pounding on the doors of major world forums demanding attention from both the public and the academia. In public discourse, opinions on the cultural effects of globalization are divided. Some writers have focused on the bright side of globalization; they discussed how globalization can enhance creativity and promote a global mindset or new ethics (e.g., cosmopolitanism). Meanwhile, others have written on the dark side of globalization, focusing on negative reactions ranging from fear of cultural erosion to culturocentric xenophobia and terrorism.

We believe that arguments from both sides are valid. On the one hand, as globalization proceeds, individuals are exposed to many novel ideas from other cultures. Thus, globalization can be a profoundly enriching process if people are open to new experiences and willing to learn from other cultures

(Appiah, 2006). On the other hand, increased cultural contacts can evoke fear of cultural contamination and erosion. If individuals manage their cultural fears by resorting to exclusionary practices, intercultural contacts can lead to clashes of civilizations, resulting in violent conflicts between cultures, wars, and terrorism.

Thus, how individuals manage their reactions to the cultural impacts of globalization is a topic that requires urgent research attention. It is important to identify the controlling stimuli of exclusionary responses, to know their downstream cognitive and motivational consequences, and to understand how the individual's self-regulatory competence moderates these responses. Furthermore, exclusionary responses seem to be highly contagious. In the Starbucks coffee shop incident, a provocative message in the Internet can incite widespread protestation against the coffee chain within a short period of time. It is important to know how exclusionary responses become contagious in a human group, and what can be done to stop the spread of the infection.

It is equally important to identify the controlling factors of integrative responses. Although globalization can be an enriching process, mere exposure to foreign cultures does not always lead to creative benefits. Thus, research should inform policy makers what is needed to make multicultural experience an empowering and constructive self-transformational experience.

Despite this, scholarly works on the social psychology of people's reactions to cultural exposure are scarce. We hope that the collection of articles in this issue will convince the readers that globalization is a timely and viable area of investigation in psychology. The research reported in this issue represents scholarships from different disciplines (social psychology, clinical psychology, cultural psychology, management studies, marketing, political science). We believe that a trans-disciplinary perspective is required to deepen the inquiry into the psychology of globalization. For example, to understand how the self-regulatory system works in multicultural contexts, we need inputs from personality psychology, cultural psychology and social cognitive neuroscience. To situate cultural contacts in their historical contexts and the power relations between the cultures in contact, we need contributions from humanists, sociologists and political scientists. We are optimistic that concerted effort from a multidisciplinary research team will deliver holistic answers to our global problems.

References

Aaker, J. L., Benet-Martinez, V., & Garolera, J. (2001). Consumption symbols as carriers of culture: A study of Japanese and Spanish brand personality constructs. *Journal of Personality and Social Psychology, 81*, 492–508. doi:10.1037//0022-3514.81.3.492

Alter, A. L., & Kwan, V. S. Y. (2009). Cultural sharing in a global village: Evidence for extracultural cognition in European Americans. *Journal of Personality and Social Psychology, 96*, 742–760. doi: 10.1037/a0014036

Appiah, K. A. (2006). *Cosmopolitanism: Ethics in a world of strangers*. New York: W. W. Norton and Co.

Arnett, J. J. (2002). The psychology of globalization. *American Psychologist, 57*, 744–783. doi: 10.1037//0003-066X.57.10.774

Bandura, A. (2001). The changing face of psychology at the dawning of a globalization era. *Canadian Psychology, 42*, 12–24.

Barber, B. R. (1996). *Jihad vs. McWorld*. New York: Ballantine Books.

Carnegie Endowment for International Peace. (2007). *Culture and globalization*. Retrieved from http://www.globalization101.org/issue/culture/

Castells, M. (1998). *The end of millennium*. Oxford: Blackwell.

Chao, M. M., Zhang, Z.-X., & Chiu, C.-y. (2010). Adherence to perceived norms across cultural boundaries: The role of need for cognitive closure and ingroup identification. *Group Processes and Intergroup Relations, 13*, 69–89. doi: 10.1177/1368430209343115

Chen, X., & Chiu, C.-y. (2010). Rural-urban differences in generation of Chinese and Western exemplary persons: The case of China. *Asian Journal of Social Psychology, 13*, 9–18. doi: 10.1111/j.1467-839X.2010.01296.x.

Cheng, C.-Y., Leung, A. K.-y., & Wu, T.-Y. (2011). Going beyond the multicultural experience-creativity link: The mediating role of emotions. *Journal of Social Issues, 67*, 806–824. doi: 10.1111/j.1540-4560.2011.01729.x

Cheng, S. Y.-y., Chao, M. M., Kwong, J., Peng, S., Chen, X., Kashima, Y., & Chiu, C-y. (2010). The good old days and a better tomorrow: Historical representations and future imaginations of China during the 2008 Olympic Games. *Asian Journal of Social Psychology, 13*, 118–127. doi: 10.1111/j.1467-839X.2010.01307.x.

Cheng, S. Y. Y., Rosner, J., Chao, M., Chiu, C.-Y., Hong, Y.-y., Chen, X., . . . Peng, S. (2011). One world, one dream? Intergroup consequences of the 2008 Beijing Olympics. *International Journal of Intercultural Relations, 35*, 296–306.

Cheung, T. S., Chan, H. M., Chan, K. M., King, A. Y. C., Chiu, C.-y., & Yang, C. F. (2006). How Confucian are contemporary Chinese? Construction of an ideal type and its application to three Chinese communities. *European Journal of East Asian Studies, 5*, 157–180.

Chiu, C.-y., & Cheng, S. Y.-y. (2007). Toward a social psychology of culture and globalization: Some social cognitive consequences of activating two cultures simultaneously. *Social and Personality Psychology Compass, 1*, 84–100.

Chiu, C.-y., & Cheng, S. Y.-Y. (2010). Cultural psychology of globalization. In R. Schwarzer & P. A. French (Eds.), *Personality, human development, and culture: International perspectives on psychological science* (Vol. 2, pp. 199–212). New York: Psychology Press.

Chiu, C.-Y., & Hong, Y.-Y. (2006). *Social psychology of culture*. New York: Psychology Press.

Chiu, C.-y., & Hong, Y. (2005). Cultural competence: Dynamic processes. In A. Elliot & C. S. Dweck (Eds.), *Handbook of motivation and competence* (pp. 489–505). New York: Guilford.

Chiu, C.-y., Mallorie, L., Keh, H.-T., & Law, W. (2009). Perceptions of culture in multicultural space: Joint presentation of images from two cultures increases ingroup attribution of culture-typical characteristics. *Journal of Cross-Cultural Psychology, 40*, 282–300. doi: 10.1177/0022022108328912

Chiu, C.-y., Morris, M., Hong, Y., & Menon, T. (2000). Motivated cultural cognition: The impact of implicit cultural theories on dispositional attribution varies as a function of need for closure. *Journal of Personality and Social Psychology, 78*, 247–259. doi: 10.1037//0022-3514.78.2.247

de Oliveria, E. A., Braun, J. L., Carlson, T. L., & de Oliveria, S. G. (2009). Students' attitudes toward foreign-born and domestic instructors. *Journal of Diversity in Higher Education, 2*, 113–125.

Fu, H.-y., & Chiu, C.-y. (2007). Local culture's responses to globalization: Exemplary persons and their attendant values. *Journal of Cross-Cultural Psychology, 38*, 636–653. doi: 10.1177/0022022107305244

Fu, H.-y., Morris, M. W., Lee, S.-l., Chao, M.-c., Chiu, C.-y., & Hong, Y.-y. (2007). Epistemic motives and cultural conformity: Need for closure, culture, and context as determinants of conflict judgments. *Journal of Personality and Social Psychology, 92*, 191–207. doi: 10.1037/0022-3514.92.2.191

Giddens, A. (1985). *The nation state and violence*. Cambridge: Polity Press.

Gries, P. H., Crowson, H. M., & Cai, H. (2011). When knowledge is a double edged sword: Contact, media exposure, and American China policy preferences. *Journal of Social Issues, 67*, 787–805. doi: 10.1111/j.1540-4560.2011.01728.x

Gries, P. H., Crowson, H. M., & Sandel, T. (2010). The Olympic effect on American attitudes towards China: Beyond personality, ideology, and media exposure. *Journal of Contemporary China, 19*, 213–231. doi: 10.1080/10670560903444181

Hermans, H. J. M., & Dimaggio, G. (2007). Self, identity, and globalization in times of uncertainty: A dialogical analysis. *Review of General Psychology, 11*, 31–61. doi: 10.1037/1089-2680.11.1.31

Huntington, S. P. (1996). *The clash of civilizations and the remaking of world order*. New York: Simon & Schuster.

Kashima, Y., Bain, P., Haslam, N., Peters, K., Laham, S., Whelan, J., ... Fernando, J. (2009). Folk theory of social change. *Asian Journal of Social Psychology, 12*, 227–246. doi: 10.1111/j.1467-839X.2009.01288.x

Kashima, Y., Shi, J., Tsuchiya, K., Kashima, E. S., Cheng, S. Y. Y., Chao, M. M., & Shin, S.-h. (2011). Globalization and folk theory of social change: How globalization relates to social perceptions about the past and future. *Journal of Social Issues, 67*, 696–715. doi: 10.1111/j.1540-4560.2011.01723.x

Leung, A. K.-y., & Chiu, C.-y. (2010). Multicultural experience, idea receptiveness, and creativity. *Journal of Cross-Cultural Psychology, 41*, 723–741. doi: 10.1177/0022022110361707

Leung, A. K-y., Maddux, W. W., Galinsky, A. D., & Chiu, C.-y. (2008). Multicultural experience enhances creativity: The when and how? *American Psychologist, 63*, 169–181. doi: 10.1037/0003-066X.63.3.169.

Li, Y.-m., Sakuma, I., Murata, K., Fujishima, Y., & Cheng, W.-m. (2010). From international sports to international competition: Longitudinal study of the Beijing Olympic Games. *Asian Journal of Social Psychology, 13*, 128–138. doi: 10.1111/j.1467-839X.2010.01308.x

Maddux, W.W., & Galinsky, A.D. (2009). Cultural borders and mental barriers: The relationship between living abroad and creativity. *Journal of Personality and Social Psychology, 96*, 1047–1061. doi: 10.1037/a0014861

Morris, M. W., Mok, A., & Mor, S. (2011). Cultural identity threat: The role of cultural identifications in moderating closure responses to foreign cultural inflow. *Journal of Social Issues, 67*, 760–773. doi: 10.1111/j.1540-4560.2011.01726.x

Norasakkunkit, V., & Uchida, Y. (2011). Psychological consequences of post-industrial anomie on self and motivation among Japanese youth. *Journal of Social Issues, 67*, 774–786. doi: 10.1111/j.1540-4560.2011.01727.x

Parameswaran, R. (2002). Local culture in global media: Excavating colonial and material discourses in National Geographic. *Communication Theory, 12*, 287–315.

Pickowicz, P. G. (1991). The theme of spiritual pollution in Chinese films of the 1930s. *Modern China, 17*, 38–75.

Pilkington, H., & Johnson, R. (2003). Relations of identity and power in global/local context. *Cultural Studies, 6*, 259–283.

Pinquart, M., & Silbereisen, R. K. (2008). Coping with increased uncertainty in the field of work and family life. *International Journal of Stress Management, 15*, 209–221.

Robertson, R, (1992). *Globalization: Social theory and global culture*. London: Sage.

Rockstuhl, T., Seiler, S., Ang, S., van Dyne, L., & Annen, L. (2011). Beyond IQ and EQ: The role cultural intelligence (CQ) on cross-border leadership in a globalized world. *Journal of Social Issues, 67*, 825–840.

Rui, C. (2007). *Why Starbucks needs to get out of the Forbidden City?* Retrieved from http://blog.sina.com.cn/u/4adabe27010008yg

Tong, Y.-y., Hui, P. P.-Z., Kwan, L., & Peng, S. (2011). National feelings or rational dealings? The role of procedural priming on the perceptions of cross-border acquisitions. *Journal of Social Issues, 67*, 743–759. doi: 10.1111/j.1540-4560.2011.01725.x

Torrelli, C. J., Chiu, C.-y., Tam, K.-p., Au, A. K.-C., & Keh, H. T. (2011). Exclusionary reactions to foreign culture: Effects of simultaneous exposure to culture in globalized space. *Journal of Social Issues, 67*, 716–742. doi: 10.1111/j.1540-4560.2011.01724.x

Van Strien, P. J. (1997). The American "colonization" of northwest European social psychology after
World War II. *Journal of the History of the Behavioral Sciences, 33*, 349–363.
Yang, D. Y.-J., Chi, C.-y., Chen, X., Cheng, S. Y. Y., Kwan, L., Tam, K.-P., & Yeh, K.-H. (2011). The
lay psychology of globalization and its social impact. *Journal of Social Issues, 67*, 677–695.
doi: 10.1111/j.1540-4560.2011.01722.x

CHI-YUE CHIU is the Executive Director of the Culture Science Institute and the
Research Director of the National Institute of Asian Consumer Insight at Nanyang
Technological University, Singapore. He received his PhD from Columbia University. His current research focuses on the social, cognitive, and motivational
processes that mediate the construction and evolution of cultural consensus.

PETER HAYS GRIES is the Harold J. & Ruth Newman Chair in US-China Issues
and Director of the Institute for U.S.–China Issues at the University of Oklahoma.
He is author of *China's New Nationalism: Pride, Politics, and Diplomacy* (University of California Press, 2004), and co-editor (with Stanley Rosen) of *State and
Society in 21st Century China: Crisis, Contention, and Legitimation* (Routledge
2004).

CARLOS J. TORELLI is Assistant Professor of Marketing at the Carlson School
of Management, University of Minnesota. He has a PhD in Business Administration from the University of Illinois at Urbana-Champaign. His research focuses
on cross-cultural consumer behavior, global branding, motivated information-processing, and persuasion.

SHIRLEY Y. Y. CHENG is an Assistant Professor of Marketing at the Hong Kong
Baptist University. She received her PhD in social psychology from the University
of Illinois at Urbana-Champaign, and her research focuses on the social psychology
of globalization, specifically on how consumers react to the cultural implications
of foreign brands.

Journal of Social Issues, Vol. 67, No. 4, 2011, pp. 677–695

Lay Psychology of Globalization and Its Social Impact

Daniel Y-J. Yang
University of Illinois at Urbana-Champaign

Chi-Yue Chiu*
Nanyang Technological University

Xia Chen
Shanghai Jiao Tong University

Shirley Y. Y. Cheng
Hong Kong Baptist University

Letty Y-Y. Kwan
Nanyang Technological University

Kim-Pong Tam
The Hong Kong University of Science and Technology

Kuang-Hui Yeh
National Taiwan University

As a first step to establish social psychology of globalization as a new area of investigation, we carried out two cross-regional studies to examine lay people's perception of globalization and its related concepts, as well as lay people's appraisal of the social impacts of globalization. The participants were undergraduates from regions with markedly different experiences with globalization (the United States, Mainland China, Taiwan, and Hong Kong). Despite regional

---

*Correspondence concerning this article should be addressed to Chi-Yue Chiu, S3–01C-81, Nanyang Business School, Nanyang Technological University, Nanyang Avenue, Singapore 639798 [e-mail: CYChiu@ntu.edu.sg].

The present article was supported by a research grant awarded to Chi-Yue Chiu by National Science Foundation Grant (NSF BCS 07–43119).

677

differences in experiences with globalization, cross-regional similarities were found in the way globalization-related issues were classified and how their social impacts were evaluated. Participants in all four regions (1) perceived globalization to be related to but not synonymous with modernization, Westernization, and Americanization; (2) used international trade versus technology, and globalization of consumption versus global consequences as the dimensions to categorize globalization-related issues; and (3) perceived globalization to have stronger positive effects on people's competence than on their warmth.

Globalization is a complex, multifacet concept, which lay people in the modern societies are exposed to every day. Social scientists (see Chiu, Gries, Torelli, & Cheng, 2011; Chiu & Hong, 2006) have debated what globalization is and what its consequences are. Nonetheless, there is general consensus among globalization scholars that the concept of globalization is multifaceted, dynamic, and highly complex (Appadurai, 1996; Croucher, 2004; Fiss & Hirsch, 2005; Kellner, 2002; Robertson & White, 2007). For example, Kellner (2002) holds that one should avoid viewing globalization as simply a product of technology and economics; rather, globalization should be viewed as a highly complex, contradictory, and thus ambiguous set of institutions and social relations, as well as one involving flows of goods, services, ideas, technologies, cultural forms, and people.

People develop lay categories and theories to make sense of their social experiences (Hong, Levy, & Chiu, 2001). Thus, a good starting point for understanding the social psychology of globalization is to understand the categories and theories lay people construct to understand their perceptions of globalization and globalization-related issues. There is, however, relatively little research on how people understand what globalization refers to and what its implications are. If social psychology of globalization is to be established as a new area of investigation, there is a need to understand lay perceptions of globalization and its social implications. The current research seeks to address this need by carrying out a cross-regional analysis of lay perceptions of globalization. Specifically, we seek to address a few important questions related to lay understanding of globalization and its social effects.

First, can lay people distinguish globalization from related concepts such as modernization, Westernization, and Americanization? On this issue, some writers observed that in public discourse, globalization is often mentioned together and potentially confounded with several other terms such as modernization, Westernization, and Americanization (Guillen, 2001; Robertson & Khondker, 1998; Taylor, 2000). Thus, there is a potential interpretational ambiguity over whether lay people are indeed thinking about globalization per se or not when they are responding to issues pertinent to globalization. Fu and Chiu (2007) however found that Hong Kong Chinese are able to differentiate modernity, which values objectivity, competence, and scientific knowledge, from Westernization, which refers to adoption of Western cosmological values such as human rights, democracy, and individuality. Nonetheless, it is still an open question whether lay people are aware of the distinction between globalization, which is concerned primarily with global flows of goods, services, ideas, technologies, cultural forms, and people, and its attendant effects on social relations. We explored this issue in Study 1.

A related issue concerns what issues are perceived to be most strongly associated with globalization. If lay people, like social scientists, construe globalization as a process anchored in global flows of economic activities, technologies, people, and ideas, the issues that lay people perceive to be most strongly associated with globalization should be those related to global connectedness in economic activities (e.g., international trade, globalization of consumption), geographic mobility (e.g., migration, international travels) and human connectivity (e.g., global connections through advanced communication technology and new media). We tested this possibility in Study 2.

A recurrent issue in the public discourse on globalization concerns the consequences of globalization (Woodward, Skrbis, & Bean, 2008). Some writers argue that globalization facilitates movement of people and ideas, weakens provincialism, and catalyzes creativity (Cheng, Leung, & Wu, 2011; Leung & Chiu, 2010). Others posit that globalization draws attention to cultural divides, fuels parochial exclusionism (Torrelli, Chiu, Tam, Au, & Keh, 2011) and causes or accelerates the spread of global calamities (e.g., HIV/AIDS, global warming, SARS).

Therefore, a third objective of the current research is to explore how people perceive the impact of globalization-related issues. There is some evidence (Cheng et al., 2010a; Kashima et al., 2009, 2011) that across cultures, people tend to see economic development to have positive effects on people's competence and negative effects on people's warmth. That is, people in economically advanced societies are more efficient in attaining their goals but economic development also tends to break up communities, creating colder and more dehumanized social milieus. However, it is unclear whether people expect globalization to have the same effects on people's competence and warmth. We examined this issue in Study 2.

Finally, different countries or regions have different experiences with globalization. Do people from different regions have similar or different perceptions of globalization and its social implications? Take the United States and Greater China as examples. The United States and Greater China (which comprises Mainland China, Hong Kong, Taiwan, and other regions in the Chinese diasporas) have played very different roles in globalization, with the United States being a major exporter of globalization and Greater China a major recipient of global influence. Furthermore, despite their shared cultural heritage, different regions in Greater China also differ considerably in their globalization experiences. For example, Hong Kong has been one of the most globalized cities in Asia for decades. In contrast, China was an internationally isolated Communist nation before it started its economic reforms 30 years ago. In the last two decades, China has surfaced as one of the major beneficiary of globalization, playing the role of the World's factory (Cheng et al., 2010a). Taiwan, which has positioned itself as a guardian of traditional Chinese culture, constantly faces conflicting expectations to globalize and to preserve the Chinese tradition (Lu & Yang, 2006). An important question is how different globalization experiences shape the perceptions of globalization and its consequences. The present research seeks to answer this question by examining cross-regional similarities and differences in the issues lay people tend to associate globalization with, and in the way people categorize globalization-related issues and evaluate their social implications. For the reasons described above, we compared the perceptions of people from the United States and three regions in Greater China (Mainland China, Hong Kong, and Taiwan).

Due to the lack of pertinent past research, we do not have specific hypothesis on whether people from different regions would categorize globalization-related issues in the same way. If lay people have nuanced understandings of the concept of globalization, they should be able to distinguish the concept of globalization from its related concepts (modernization, Westernization, and Americanization). On the one hand, people may acknowledge that some issues that are strongly associated with globalization are also associated with modernization, Westernization, or Americanization. On the other hand, people may also realize that not all globalization-related issues are associated with the other three concepts, and vice versa. In addition, issues that are perceived to be most strongly associated with globalization should express such defining issues of globalization as international trade, globalization of consumption, technology, human mobility, and global consequences of global flows of economic goods, technologies, and people.

Furthermore, as mentioned above, people across cultures view economic development as a process that empowers the individual and weakens human communities (Cheng et al., 2010a; Kashima et al., 2009, 2011). Therefore, we expect cross-regional similarities in the "global" evaluations of globalization on the dimensions of competence and warmth, expecting more favorable evaluations of the effects of globalization on competence than on warmth, although we do not rule out the possibility that region-specific experiences with globalization could cause nuanced variations in evaluations of the effects of "specific" globalization-related issues.

Given the exploratory nature of the current study, we adopted a bottom-up approach to understand lay conceptions of globalization. The Levin Institute of the State University of New York maintains the website of Globalization 101, which is dedicated to providing comprehensive reviews of information on 15 globalization-related issues: trade, technology, investment, health, culture, environment, migration, IMF and World Bank, development, women, international law, energy, human rights, education, and media. We extracted all globalization-related topics that are included in the comprehensive reviews of the globalization literature carried out by the Levin Institute and used these topics as items to explore lay people's understanding of globalization. To enhance the representativeness of the items, we also invited our research participants to supply additional items that they deemed to be strongly associated with globalization. In Study 1, participants rated the globalization-related issues generated through the process described above on their strength of association with globalization, modernization, Americanization, and Westernization. By examining the intercorrelations of the four sets of ratings across the globalization-related issues in each sample, we examined whether people from the four regions can differentiate globalization from the other three concepts. In Study 1, we also identified the 26 issues that were perceived by participants from the four regions to be most strongly associated with globalization. We used these 26 issues as stimuli in Study 2, which is a multidimensional scaling study designed to identify the ways individuals categorize globalization-related issues and the latent dimensions used in categorization.

In addition, in Study 2, we also asked the participants to evaluate the impact of each of the 26 globalization-related issues on people's competence and warmth. Competence and warmth have been found to be two major dimensions in the perceptions of individuals and social groups (Cuddy, Fiske, & Glick, 2009), organizations and companies (Aaker, Vohs, & Mogilner, 2010), as well as modernization-related societal changes (Cheng et al., 2010a; Kashima et al., 2009, 2011). Thus, in the current research, we also focused on participants' perceptions of the effects of globalization-related issues on people's competence and warmth.

In short, to establish social psychology of globalization as a new field of inquiry, it is important to first understand how people who have experienced and been influenced by globalization in different ways understand the concept of globalization and its effects. The present research represents the first attempt to examine cross-regional similarities and variations in the perceptions of globalization and its social impacts.

Study 1

The objectives of the current study are to identify a set of topics, issues or concepts that are perceived to be closely related to globalization and to examine the lay perceptions of the association between globalization and three related concepts (modernization, Westernization, and Americanization) in the United States and Greater China.

Method

Participants

The participants were undergraduate students in the United States (University of Illinois, $N = 87$, 66% female), Mainland China (Peking University, Beijing,

$N = 107$, 62% female), Hong Kong (The Hong Kong University of Science and Technology, $N = 38$, 50% female), and Taiwan (National Taiwan University, $N = 39$, 56% female).

Materials and Procedure

To generate a representative list of globalization-related issues, we reviewed all the essays in the Globalization 101 website (http://www.globalization101.org/), an authoritative website managed by the Levin Institute that tracks academic and popular discussions of globalization-related issues. A total of 53 issues, concepts, or topics were discussed in these essays, covering a broad range of domains (e.g., economy, health, technology, culture, and the environment): airplane travel, American Express, Ang Lee, Apple computer, Asus computer, Barbies, Bollywood, Coke, computer, craigslist, deforestation, Disneyland, eBay, Facebook, free trade agreement, feng shui, global warming, HIV/AIDS, Hollywood, human trafficking, hybrid cars, immigration, in-flight magazines, Internet, Jackie Chan, made in China, martial arts, McDonald's, Nike, Nintendo Wii, Obama, Olympics, passport, Polar bear, silk, standard of beauty, Starbucks, sweatshop factory, sweet and sour chicken, Taco, terrorism, the World Bank, Tokyo, Toyota, UBS, United Nations, VISA card, Vogue magazine, Wall Street, Walmart, WTO, Yao Ming, and YouTube.

Next, we presented this list to the participants. Because the list was generated from reviewing an American website, we also invited participants from Mainland, Taiwan, and Hong Kong to generate additional items that were deemed to be related to globalization. The Chinese Mainlanders added 22 items to the list (BBC, blog, Citibank, Christianity, learning English, pollution, environmental protection, Foreign Language Teaching and Research Press, Haier, hip hop, IBM, Lenovo, market economy, Mercedes-Benz, New Oriental School, NGO, Phoenix TV, rock and roll, Standard Chartered Bank, study abroad, Times, and World Expo), the Taiwanese 17 items (bond, Carrefour, cell phone, Chanel, financial crisis, flu, futures market, G8 Summit, gold, Google, Louis Vuitton, Microsoft, multinational corporation, oil, SARS, stock market, and Yahoo), and the Hong Kongers 28 items (biodiversity, capitalism, colonialism, democracy, food crisis, foreign domestic helper, foreign exchange, general education, genetic engineering, global village, GPS, green shopping bag, Greenpeace, international school, HSBC, income inequality, MSN, Nokia, PayPal, pirated DVD, satellite TV, swine flu, tariffs, U.S. dollar, U.S. Government, WHO, Wikipedia, and World Cup). For each item (including those generated by the participants), the participants rated how strongly the item was associated with: (1) globalization; (2) modernization; (3) Westernization; and (4) Americanization. The participants indicated their ratings on 7-point scales from 1 (*not at all*) to 7 (*very much*). To avoid imposing our definitions of globalization, modernization, Westernization, and Americanization

Table 1. Correlations between Globalization, Americanization, Westernization, and Modernization in the United States and Greater China

	Globalization	Americanization	Westernization	Modernization
United States				
Globalization				
Americanization	.54			
Westernization	.61	.96		
Modernization	.59	.73	.78	
Mainland China				
Globalization		.60	.67	.72
Americanization	.65		.76	.43
Westernization	.74	.89		.47
Modernization	.75	.50	.60	
Taiwan				
Globalization		.56	.60	.68
Americanization	.59		.88	.58
Westernization	.68	.93		.65
Modernization	.68	.52	.62	
Hong Kong				
Globalization		.46	.29	.66
Americanization	.42		.80	.45
Westernization	.51	.91		.39
Modernization	.72	.49	.57	

Note. Correlations below the main diagonal are correlations computed from the common items only. Correlations above the main diagonal are correlations computed from the common items and the region-specific, self-generated items. All correlations were significant. $ps < .01$.

on the participants, we did not explain to the participants what these concepts refer to and encouraged the participants to base their ratings on their own understandings of these concepts. The items were presented to each participant in a random order.

Results and Discussion

We used item as the unit of analysis in our analysis. For each sample and for each item, we took the mean rating of the item's association with globalization and its related concepts across participants. Through this procedure, for each region, we created a dataset that consisted of mean ratings on globalization, modernization, Westernization, and Americanization for each item. Table 1 presents the correlations between globalization and its related concepts across items in the four samples. The patterns of correlations were the same regardless of whether we included the items generated by the participants from Mainland China, Taiwan, and Hong Kong. Therefore, we focus on interpreting the results that included the common items generated from the review of the Globalization 101 website.

In all four regions, items that were perceived to be strongly (weakly) associated with Westernization were also perceived to be strongly (weakly) associated with Americanization ($.89 \leq rs \leq .96$). This is not surprising given the strong influence of the United States in the West.

The perceived associations of globalization with modernization were strong ($.59 \leq rs \leq .75$). Participants in Greater China perceived a slightly stronger association between globalization and modernization ($.68 \leq rs \leq .75$) than did the American participants ($r = .59$), probably because the Greater China regions experienced modernization and globalization at about the same time, whereas the United States was already a modern economy before it experienced the acceleration of globalization. Nonetheless, the correlation between globalization and modernization was far from being perfect. Some items that were rated as strongly associated with globalization across all regions were not rated as strongly associated with modernization. For example, Coke, the Olympics, and immigration had high globalization association ratings across regions (mean globalization association ratings across four regions ≥ 5.38) but were rated as only moderately associated with modernization (mean modernization association ratings across four regions ≤ 4.26). Likewise, some items that were rated as strongly associated with modernization across all regions were not rated as strongly associated with globalization. For example, Nintendo Wii and hybrid cars had high modernization association ratings across regions (mean modernization association ratings across four regions ≥ 5.55) but were rated as only moderately associated with globalization (mean globalization association ratings across four regions ≤ 4.22). In summary, although the participants acknowledged that globalization and modernization are related, the participants were able to distinguish globalization from modernization.

The perceived associations between globalization and Westernization/Americanization ranged from moderate to high in the four regions ($.42 \leq rs \leq .74$). These associations were weaker for participants in Hong Kong ($.42 \leq rs \leq .51$) and stronger for those in Mainland China ($.65 \leq rs \leq .74$), probably because in Hong Kong, globalization is accompanied of influences from both the East (Japan, South Korea) and the West, whereas globalization in China is driven primarily by increased interdependency with the West. Again, the correlations between globalization and Westernization/Americanization were not perfect. There are items that had strong globalization associations but only moderate Westernization and Americanization associations. Two such examples are passport and global warming (mean globalization association ratings across four regions ≥ 5.33; mean Westernization/Americanization association ratings across four regions ≤ 4.52). Likewise, there are items that had strong Westernization/Americanization associations but only moderate globalization associations. Some examples are Obama and Barbies (mean Westernization/Americanization association ratings across four regions $\geq$ 5.23; mean globalization association ratings across four regions $\leq$ 4.57).

In summary, the participants from all four regions perceived moderate to strong associations of globalization with modernization, Westernization, and Americanization. There are some small variations in the strength of these associations across regions; and these variations may reflect the different experiences with globalization in the four regions. Nonetheless, although the participants did not distinguish between Westernization and Americanization, they perceived globalization to be different from modernization, Westernization, and Americanization.

To determine which set of items were perceived to have the strongest associations with globalization across participants from the four regions, for each of the 53 globalization-related items generated from the review of Globalization 101, we took the mean of the mean ratings on its association with globalization across the four samples. The 26 items (out of 53, 49.1%) that had the highest ratings on perceived association with globalization from high to low were the Internet (6.80), computer (6.28), WTO (6.03), the United Nations (5.95), McDonald's (5.87), free trade agreement (5.87), VISA card (5.83), airplane travel (5.76), Olympics (5.60), the World Bank (5.60), global warming (5.58), immigration (5.49), Facebook (5.40), Hollywood (5.38), Nike (5.38), Coke (5.38), YouTube (5.36), passport (5.33), Wall Street (5.20), Starbucks (5.16), eBay (5.00), Apple computer (4.90), Made in China (4.89), Disneyland (4.71), Toyota (4.70), and HIV/AIDS (4.63). The mean rating of association with globalization for these 26 items ranged from 4.63 to 6.80 ($M = 5.47$ on a 7-point scale, $SD = 0.51$). Most of the items can be grouped into one of the following five categories: (1) information technology that promotes global connectivity (the Internet, computer, Facebook, YouTube, Apple Computer, eBay); (2) global consumer brands (McDonald's, Hollywood, Nike, Coke, Starbucks, Toyota, Hollywood, Disneyland); (3) global trade and international regulatory institutions (WTO, the World Bank, Made in China, Wall Street, free trade, VISA card); (4) geographic mobility (air travel, immigration, passport); and (5) global calamities (global warming, HIV/AIDS). The themes of these categories correspond closely to the defining issues of globalization. In summary, the participants from all four regions appear to have nuanced understanding of the concept of globalization.

Study 2

In the current study, we performed multidimensional scaling analysis on the 26 items that had the strongest association with globalization across the four samples in Study 1 to understand how lay people categorize and evaluate major globalization-related issues. Again, we included participants from the United States and Greater China to examine the regional similarities and differences in the perceptions of globalization and its social impacts.

Method

Participants

Participants in the main study were 108 undergraduates from the United States (60% female, mean age = 19.34, University of Illinois), 101 undergraduates from Mainland China (57% female, mean age = 23.30, Peking University), 104 undergraduates from Hong Kong (37% female, mean age = 20.76, The Hong Kong University of Science and Technology), and 101 undergraduates from Taiwan (58% female, mean age = 21.32, National Taiwan University).

Materials and Procedure

The study consisted of a sorting task and a rating task. In the sorting task, to understand how participants categorized the 26 issues, we had participants sort the issues into categories. The participants decided for themselves the number of categories they wanted to create and how many and which items would be assigned to each category. Before carrying out the sorting task, the participants were told that the items were issues associated with globalization. The participants were asked to reflect on each issue's associations with globalization and classify the issues in such a way that would capture the similarities and differences in these issues' globalization associations. After the participants had sorted the issues into the self-created categories, the participants provided a label for each category.

Following the sorting task, the participants were presented with the 26 issues again one at a time in a random order and rated how much each issue has changed the levels of competence and interpersonal warmth in their community on two 7-point scales (1 = *much less competence*, 7 = *much more competence*; 1 = *much less warmth*, 7 = *much more warmth*).

Results and Discussion

Dimensions and Clusters of Issues

To prepare the data for multidimensional scaling, we created a 26 × 26 distance matrix for each sample. Specifically, for each sample, each cell in the distance matrix corresponded to the number of participants who had sorted the pertinent pair of issues into different categories. For example, if N participants sorted McDonald's and global warming into different categories, the distance between McDonald's and global warming in the distance matrix would be N.

Next, we performed an individual difference multidimensional scaling analysis (INDSCAL) on the four distance matrices to determine how the 26 globalization-related issues were mentally represented. The fit statistics indicate

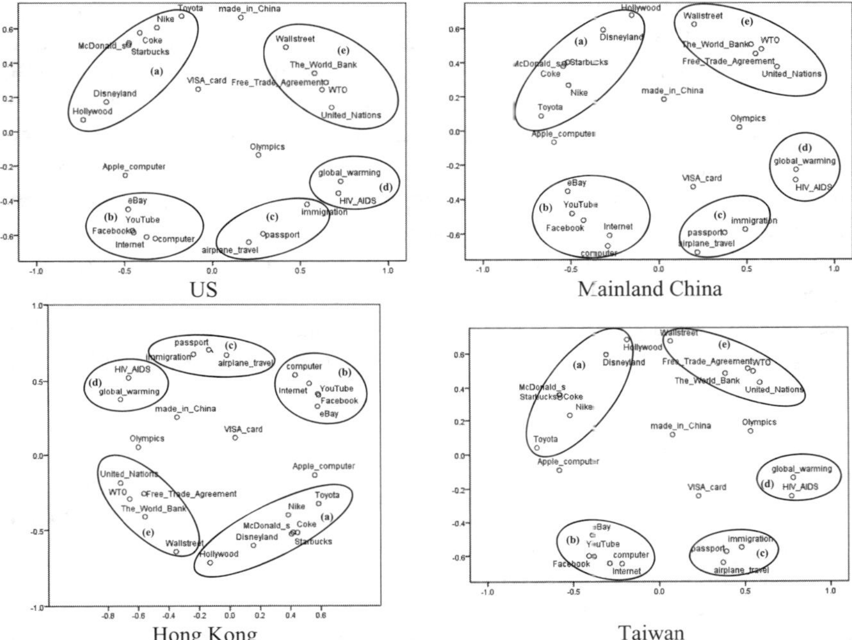

Fig. 1. Cognitive representations of the similarities and dissimilarities of the 26 globalization-related objects in four regions. Most objects fall into one of the five clusters: (1) global consumer brands; (2) information technology; (3) human mobility; (4) global calamities and (5) international trade and regulatory bodies.

that a two-dimensional solution provided a good fit to the data (variances accounted for were 59.90%, 63.98%, 61.61%, 59.31% for America, Mainland China, Hong Kong, and Taiwan, respectively).

As shown in Figure 1, the configurations of the 26 issues in the two-dimensional solution were similar across the four regions, reflecting a high level of regional similarity in the cognitive representation of the globalization-related issues. In each regional sample, five distinct but interrelated clusters of globalization-related issues can be identified on a two-dimensional plane: (1) global consumer brands (e.g., McDonald's, Starbucks); (2) information technology that promotes global connectivity (e.g., Facebook, YouTube, Internet); (3) geographic mobility (passport, air travel, immigration); (4) global calamities (global warming, HIV/AIDS); and (e) international trade and regulatory bodies (Wall Street, the World Bank). The themes of these categories correspond closely to the defining issues of globalization, again suggesting that participants from all four regions have nuanced understanding of what the defining issues of globalization are.

When interpreting the dimensions the participants used to categorize the globalization-related issues, we noticed that dimension 1 pitted global consumer brands against global calamities and geographic mobility. This dimension can be interpreted as one that pits the corporate agents of globalization (global consumer brands) against the effects of global business expansion on the individual and the environment (geographic mobility, global calamities). The second dimension pitted international trade and its associated international institutions against information technology. This dimension can be interpreted as one that pits the economic aspects against the technology aspects of globalization. This result underscores the salience of marketplace dynamics in lay understandings of globalization as some writers have noted (e.g., Flanagan, Frost, & Kugler, 2001; see also Croucher, 2004). This result also indicates that information technology is also a salient aspect of globalization in lay people's perceptions.

Perceived Social Impact

In Figure 2, we show the mean evaluations of the 26 issues on the dimensions of competence and warmth for the four regions. In all four regions, most globalization-related issues were located above the midpoint (4.0) of the competence and morality scales, indicating that the participants in all four regions perceived that most globalization-related issues have increased people's competence and warmth. "Olympics" was perceived to have the greatest positive effects on both competence and warmth. Two obvious exceptions are global warming and HIV/AIDS, which were perceived to have decreased people's competence and warmth in all four regions. Interestingly, participants from Taiwan and the United States also evaluated Made in China negatively on both competence and warmth, probably because made in China products have crowded out American and Taiwanese products in international markets. American participants also evaluated McDonald's negatively on both competence and warmth, probably because of the many anti-McDonald's campaigns in the United States that have portrayed McDonald's as a global restaurant chain that popularizes unhealthy food.

In addition, in all four regions, most issues were placed below the main diagonal, unit line in the figure, indicating that the participants perceived most globalization-related objects to have more positive impact on people's competence than on their warmth. Indeed, in all the four regions, using objects as the unit of analysis, the mean rating of competence was significantly higher than that of warmth: (1) in America, $M = 4.55$ versus 4.20, $t(25) = 2.41$, $p < .05$; (2) in Mainland China, $M = 5.22$ versus 4.69, $t = 4.08$, $p < .001$; (3) in Hong Kong, $M = 5.19$ versus 4.40, $t = 6.01$, $p < .0001$; and (d) in Taiwan, $M = 5.13$ versus 4.48, $t = 5.18$, $p < .0001$. Moreover, this difference between competence and warmth ratings was not moderated by the regions, $F(3, 100) = 1.90$, $p = .14$. Wall Street represents an extreme example of this pattern of perception; Wall Street was

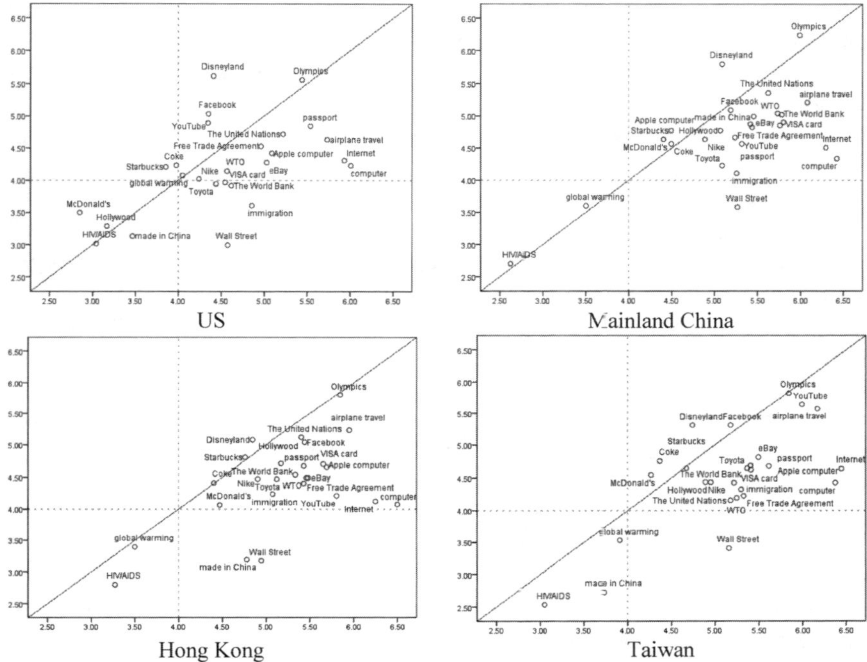

Fig. 2. Perceived psychological impact of globalization of the 26 globalization-related objects. The x-axis refers to the object's impact on people's competence and the y-axis the object's impact on people's warmth. Objects falling below (above) the main diagonal are perceived to have greater (smaller) impact on people's competence than on their warmth.

perceived to have positive impact on people's competence and negative impact on people's warmth in all four regions. This finding is consistent with the past finding that people perceived economic development to have more positive impact on the people's competence than on the warmth or morality (Cheng et al., 2010a; Kashima et al., 2009, 2011).

Despite these similarities, there are several noticeable regional differences. First, "immigration" was negatively evaluated on the dimension of warmth in America, but not in Mainland China, Hong Kong, and Taiwan, reflecting the fact that Mainland China, Hong Kong, and Taiwan are emigrant regions where more people are motivated to leave their regions for opportunities in the West. In contrast, the United States is an immigrant country that receives and faces competition from foreign immigrants. Second, participants from Taiwan evaluated the United Nations more negatively than did participants from Mainland China, Hong Kong, and the United States, reflecting the Taiwan's frustrations in its past attempts to join the United Nations. Finally, participants from the Greater China regions (Mainland

China, Hong Kong, and Taiwan) perceived most global consumer brands to have positive impacts on people's competence ($M = 4.87$, $SD = 0.38$) and warmth ($M = 4.68$, $SD = 0.35$). In comparison, American participants' perceptions of the global consumer brands were more variable. For instance, compared to the Chinese, Americans had more negative evaluations of McDonald's, Hollywood, Starbucks, Coke, Toyota, and Nike. This may reflect a more critical attitude toward global consumer brands among Americans than the Chinese.

In summary, with the exception of issues related to global calamities, people from both the United States and Greater China have favorable attitudes towards globalization-related issues. There is consensus among Americans and the Chinese that globalization-related issues have positive impacts on both people's competence and warmth, particularly on competence. Nonetheless, Americans have more critical attitudes toward global consumer brands than do the Chinese. Each region's unique experiences with specific globalization-related issues also contribute to regional variations in the evaluations of these issues.

General Discussion

People in the United States and the three regions in Greater China have very different experiences with globalization. Despite these differences, we discerned many similarities in the lay perceptions of globalization and its social impacts across the four regions. For example, people in all four regions do not differentiate between Westernization and Americanization. From lay people's perspective, issues that are associated with Westernization are also associated with Americanization, and vice versa.

Some writers (Guillen, 2001; Robertson & Khondker, 1998; Taylor, 2000) contend that people often confuse globalization with modernization and Westernization/Americanization. We found that across the four regions, there are moderate to strong correlations between globalization on one hand, and modernization and Westernization/Americanization on the other. Nonetheless, these correlations are not perfect. In line with Robertson and Khondker's (1998) observation, lay people perceive globalization to be related to but not synonymous with modernization and Westernization/Americanization.

The issues that are commonly perceived to be strongly associated with globalization fall into one of the five categories: (1) global consumer brands; (2) information technology that promotes global connectivity; (3) geographic mobility (passport, air travel, immigration); (4) global calamities; and (5) international trade and regulatory bodies. Lay perceivers understand globalization to be a multifaceted concept that is anchored in international trade and technology. Lay understandings of globalization also encompass awareness of the positive consequences (e.g., increased geographical mobility) of globalization as well as its negative consequences (e.g., global calamities). Indeed, international trade versus technology, and globalization of consumption versus its global consequences seem to be the dimensions that organize lay people's categorization of globalization-related issues.

With exception of the issues related to global calamities, people in all four regions have favorable evaluations of most globalization-related issues, feeling that these issues have increased people's competence and warmth. Consistent with past findings (Cheng et al., 2010a; Kashima, 2009, 2011), people in all four regions perceive globalization-related issues to have stronger positive effects on people's competence than on their warmth.

Despite these overall similarities, there are relatively minor regional differences in both the meanings of globalization and evaluation of the social impact of globalization-related issues. For example, globalization is more strongly correlated with modernization in Greater China than in the United States, and Americans are more critical toward global consumer brands. As noted, these differences may reflect differences between the United States and Greater China in their historical experiences with globalization. We also found cross-regional differences in the evaluation of specific globalization-related issues (e.g., Taiwanese have more negative perceptions of the United Nations and Americans have more negative perceptions of McDonald's). These regional variations are probably related to the pertinent region's unique experiences with particular issues.

Limitations and Future Directions

One limitation of the current investigation is that we analyzed only those issues that are perceived to be strongly associated with globalization. This may have restricted the range of the globalization ratings. Hence, we might have underestimated the size of correlations between globalization and its related concepts. However, this may not be a serious problem. We included a total of 120 globalization-related items in Study 1, more than half of which (67) were generated by the participants. The mean globalization association rating (collapsed across regions) of the 120 items was 4.98 on a 7-point scale ($SD = 0.75$). These ratings covered a wide range from 3.05 to 6.80. Nonetheless, we acknowledge the need for replication studies that would cover an even broader range of issues.

Another limitation concerns the samples in the current investigation, which consisted of undergraduate students only. Furthermore, the United States sample consisted of university students from Urbana-Champaign, Illinois, which is not a major global city in the United States. Whether participants from other populations and from other major cities in the United States (e.g., New York, Los Angeles) possess equally nuanced understandings of globalization or similar perceptions of globalization-related issues merits further investigations.

Furthermore, the current investigation focuses on lay people's general attitudes toward globalization-related issues. Research has shown that people's reactions to globalization-related issue are context-dependent (Cheng et al., 2010b; Tong, Hui, Kwan, & Peng, 2011; Torrelli et al., 2011). That is, contextual factors can change the perceiver's attitude toward a specific globalization-related issue. Thus, there is a need to understand how general attitudes and contextual variables jointly determine people's reaction to a certain globalization-related issue in specific contexts. In future research, the general attitude could be used as a baseline to gauge the effect of contextual factors on people's evaluations of globalization-related issues. As shown in Figure 2, evaluations vary across different clusters of globalization-related issues. For example, evaluations of global warming are negative, whereas evaluations of the Olympics are positive. It is possible that different types of globalization-related events have different thresholds for evoking exclusionary and integrative reactions toward globalization (Chiu et al., 2011). For example, the threshold of exclusionary reactions may be higher and the threshold of integrative reactions may be lower for the Olympics than for global warming. In addition, positivity and negativity associated with a certain globalization-related issue may spread to other globalization-related issues. For instance, the perceiver may evaluate McDonald's more negatively after being reminded of global warming than after thinking about the Olympics.

Our results also show that people from different regions have different perceptions of global consumer brands. For example, Americans have more negative attitudes toward McDonald's than the Chinese. There are many examples of people reacting negatively toward the presence of a global company in local heritage sites, including the French's objection to the plans to open a McDonald's at the Louvre Museum in 2009, and the Chinese's objection to the presence of a Starbucks Coffee at the Imperial Palace Museum in 2007. Such exclusionary reactions have started to attract empirical attention from behavioral scientists (Chiu & Cheng, 2007; Chiu, Wan, Cheng, Kim, & Yang, 2010). It is more possible that the presence of a global consumer brand in a world heritage site would evoke stronger exclusionary reactions from Americans than from the Chinese. This possibility deserves future research attention.

Conclusion

Lay theories are important sense-making tools people create to understand their social experiences (Hong et al., 2001). These tools guide people's judgment and reactions to social situations. Our analysis extends the lay theory perspective to social behaviors to the domain of globalization. Given the growing interest in lay people's reactions to globalization, it is important to understand how lay people understand the concept of globalization and appraise its social impacts. We hope that our analysis would inspire future systematic inquiry into the lay psychology of globalization and its social impacts.

References

Aaker, J. L., Vohs, K. D., & Mogilner, C. (2010). Non-profits are seen as warm and for-profits as competent: Firm stereotypes matter. *Journal of Consumer Research, 37*, 224–237. doi: 10.1086/651566.

Appadurai, A. (1996). *Modernity at large: Cultural dimensions of globalization.* Minneapolis: University of Minnesota Press. doi: 10.1353/jwh.2000.0021.

Cheng, C-Y., Leung, A. K-Y., & Wu, T-Y. (2011). Going beyond the multicultural experience-creativity link: The mediating role of emotions. *Journal of Social Issues, 67*, 806–824.doi: 10.1111/j.1540-4560.2011.01729.x.

Cheng, S. Y. Y., Chao, M. M., Kwong, J., Peng, S., Chen, X., Kashima, Y., et al. (2010a). The good old days and a better tomorrow: Historical representations and future imaginations of China during the 2008 Olympic games. *Asian Journal of Social Psychology, 13*, 118–127. doi: 10.1111/j.1467-839X.2010.01307.x.

Cheng, S. Y. Y., Rosner, J. L., Chao, M. M., Peng, S., Chen, X., Li, Y., Kwong, J. Y. Y., et al. (2010b). One world, One dream? Intergroup consequences of the 2008 Beijing Olympics. *International Journal of Intercultural Relations, 35*, 296–306. doi: 10.1016/j.ijintrel.2010.07.005

Chiu, C-Y., & Cheng, S. Y-Y. (2007). Toward a social psychology of culture and globalization: Some social cognitive consequences of activating two cultures simultaneously. *Social and Personality Psychology Compass, 1*, 84–100. doi: 10.1111/j.1751–9004.2007.00017.x.

Chiu, C-y., & Hong, Y-Y. (2006). *Social psychology of culture.* New York: Psychology Press.

Chiu, C-Y., Gries, P., Torelli, C. J., & Cheng, S. Y. Y. (2011). Toward a social psychology of globalization. *Journal of Social Issues, 67*, 663–676. doi: 10.1111/j.1540-4560.2011.01721.x.

Chiu, C-y., Wan, C., Cheng, Y-Y., Kim, Y-H., & Yang, Y-J. (2010). Cultural perspectives on self-enhancement and self-protection. In M. Alicke & C. Sedikides (Eds.), *The handbook of self-enhancement and self-protection.* New York: Guilford.

Croucher, S. L. (2004). *Globalization and belonging: The politics of identity in a changing world.* New York: Rowman & Littlefield.

Cuddy, A. J. C., Fiske, S. T., & Glick, P. (2007). The BIAS Map: Behaviors from intergroup affect and stereotypes. *Journal of Personality and Social Psychology, 92*, 631–648. doi: 10.1037/0022–3514.92.4.631.

Fiss, P. C., & Hirsch, P. M. (2005). The discourse of globalization: Framing and sensemaking of an emergent concept. *American Sociological Review, 7*, 29–52. doi: 10.1177/000312240507000103.

Flanagan, S., Frost, E. L., & Kugler, R. L. (2001). *Challenges of the global century: Report of the project on globalization and national security.* Washington, DC: National Defense University Press.

Fu, H-Y., & Chiu, C-Y. (2007). Local culture's responses to globalization: Exemplary persons and their attendant values. *Journal of Cross-Cultural Psychology, 38*, 636–653. doi: 10.1177/0022022107305244.

Guillen, M. F. (2001). Is globalization civilizing, destructive or feeble? A critique of five key debates in the social science literature. *Annual Review of Sociology, 27*, 235–260. doi: 10.1146/annurev.soc.27.1.235.

Hong, Y-Y., Levy, S. R., & Chiu, C-Y. (2001). The contribution of the lay theories approach to the study of groups. *Personality and Social Psychology Review, 5*, 98–106. doi: 10.1207/S15327957PSPR0502_1.

Kashima, Y., Bain, P., Haslam, N., Peters, K., Laham, S., Whelan, J., et al. (2009). Folk theory of social change. *Asian Journal of Social Psychology, 12*, 227–246. doi: 10.1111/j.1467–839X.2009.01288.x.

Kashima, Y., Shi, J., Tsuchiya, K., Cheng, S. Y. Y., Chao, M. M-C., Kashima, E., et al. (2011). Globalization and theory of social change: How globalization relates to social perceptions about the past and future. *Journal of Social Issues, 67*, 696–715. doi: 10.1111/j.1540-4560.2011.01729.x.

Kellner, D. (2002). Theorizing globalization. *Sociological Theory*, 2, 285–305. doi: 10.1111/0735–2751.00165.

Leung, A. K-Y., & Chiu, C-Y. (2010). Multicultural experience, idea receptiveness, and creativity. *Journal of Cross-Cultural Psychology*, 41, 723–741. doi: 10.1177/0022022110361707.

Lu, L., & Yang, K.-S. (2006). Emergence and composition of the traditional-modern bicultural self of people in contemporary Taiwanese societies. *Asian Journal of Social Psychology*, 9, 167–175. doi: 10.1111/j.1467–839X.2006.00195.x.

Robertson, R., & Khondker, H. H. (1998). Discourses of globalization: Preliminary considerations. *International Sociology*, 13, 25–40. doi: 10.1177/026858098013001004.

Robertson, R., & White, K. E. (2007). What is globalization? In G. Ritzer (Ed.), *The Blackwell companion to globalization* (pp. 54–66). Malden, MA: Blackwell.

Taylor, P. J. (2000). Izations of the world: Americanization, modernization and globalization. In C. Hay & D. Marsh (Eds.), *Demystifying globalization* (pp. 49–67). Basingstoke: Macmillan.

Tong, Y-Y., Hui, P. P-Z., Kwan, L., & Peng, S. (2011). National feelings or rational dealings? The role of procedural priming on the perceptions of cross-border acquisitions. *Journal of Social Issues*, 67, 743–759. doi: 10.1111/j.1540-4560.2011.01725.x.

Torrelli, C. J., Chiu, C-Y., Tam, K-P., Au, A. K-C., & Keh, H. T. (2011). Exclusionary reactions to foreign culture: Effects of simultaneous exposure to culture in globalized space. *Journal of Social Issues*, 67, 716–742. doi: 10.1111/j.1540-4560.2011.01724.x.

Woodward, I., Skrbis, Z., & Bean, C. (2008). Attitudes towards globalization and cosmopolitanism: Cultural diversity, personal consumption, and the national economy. *British Journal of Sociology*, 59, 27–226. doi: 10.1111/j.1468–4446.2008.00190.x

DANIEL Y-J. YANG received his PhD in social psychology from the University of Illinois at Urbana-Champaign (UIUC). His current research concerns psychological reactions to symbolic contamination of heritage culture, stereotype processes, and the social neuroscience of culture.

CHI-YUE CHIU received his PhD from Columbia University and is the Executive Director of the Culture Science Institute and Research Director of the National Institute on Consumer Insight at Nanyang Technological University in Singapore.

XIA CHEN received her PhD in social psychology from Peking University and is an Assistant Professor at the Institute of Arts and Humanities, Shanghai Jiao Tong University. Her research focuses on the social, cultural, and psychological effects of globalization in China.

SHIRLEY Y. Y. CHENG received her PhD in social psychology from UIUC, and is an Assistant Professor of Marketing at the Hong Kong Baptist University. Her research focuses on the social psychology of globalization.

LETTY Y-Y. KWAN received her PhD in social psychology from UIUC. She researches on the social functions of culture, interpersonal trust, leadership, and creative processes.

KIM-PONG TAM received his PhD from the University of Hong Kong and is currently an Assistant Professor of Social Science at the Hong Kong University of Science and Technology. He researches on people's perceptions of cultures, the psychological implications of such perceptions, forensic attitudes and judgments, happiness, and human-nature relationship.

KUANG-HUI YEH is a Research Fellow at the Institute of Ethnology in Academia Sinica and Professor of Psychology at National Taiwan University. His research interests focus on Chinese family interactions and their influence on the individual's adjustment.

Journal of Social Issues, Vol. 67, No. 4, 2011, pp. 696–715

Globalization and Folk Theory of Social Change: How Globalization Relates to Societal Perceptions about the Past and Future

Yoshihisa Kashima∗
The University of Melbourne

Junqi Shi
Peking University

Koji Tsuchiya
Nagoya University, Japan

Emiko S. Kashima
La Trobe University

Shirley Y. Y. Cheng
Hong Kong Baptist University

Melody Manchi Chao
The Hong Kong University of Science and Technology

Shang-hui Shin
The University of Melbourne

Folk theory of social change (FTSC) is a generic knowledge structure that frames societal perceptions. According to FTSC, society develops from a traditional

───────────

∗Correspondence concerning this article should be addressed to Yoshihisa Kashima, Psychological Sciences and Melbourne Sustainable Society Institute, The University of Melbourne, Parkville, Vic 3010, Australia [e-mail: ykashima@unimelb.edu.au].

Data collection for Study 2 in People's Republic of China was supported by a grant to Junqi Shi from the National Natural Science Foundation of China (No. 71021001). Preparation of the article was facilitated by a grant to Y. Kashima from the Australian Research Council (DP1095323).

community where people are trustworthy though unsophisticated to a more so-phisticated, but less warm-hearted modern society. People make future forecast about society within this generic structure while flexibly incorporating particular information about the past history and the present social trend. We report evidence for the proposition that globalization provides particular information that people incorporate in forming their future societal perceptions. We take an intranational perspective by examining people's beliefs about globalization (Study 1) and a cross-national perspective by comparing future societal perceptions in People's Republic of China, Japan, and Australia (Study 2). We suggest that future societal perceptions may play a constitutive role in the future of humanity, and FTSC and folk beliefs about globalization are a significant part of this process.

Where did our society come from, what is it like at present, and where is it going in the future? These are some of the critical questions about "societal perceptions," or perceptions about society. They are important not only for historians, social scientists, and social critics, but also for ordinary people who are experiencing the fast and furious pace of social change in the world of globalization. Understood roughly as an increasing trend of greater connectivity among disparate regions of the globe (e.g., Baylis & Smith, 2006), globalization has presented unprecedented opportunities and challenges to humanity. Humans are on average much wealthier than before with the world economy expanding multifold over the past decades; at the same time, perilous correlates of globalization abound, including the global financial crisis, rapid circulation of new diseases, and increasing greenhouse gas emissions and anthropogenic climate change. As people witness visible signs of globalization in their local environment (e.g., international franchise such as McDonald's and Starbucks) together with the obvious changes in technology, living standard, and general availability of international news and information, they are likely to marvel at the amount of change that they have gone through, and wonder how far they are going in the future

People's imaginations about their society in the future—future societal perceptions—are not social critics' idle speculation, but they are likely to play a significant role in public opinion and political discourse about the future of society. Kashima et al. (2009) found in Australia that future societal perceptions are related to the public preference about social policies. Those who believe their society is likely to become colder and callous in the future are more likely to prefer social policies geared toward community building rather than economic growth, especially if they think their societal characteristics can be changed by policy interventions. More generally, people's future societal perceptions may play an important role in their political, economic, and environmental preferences and decision making in the public arena.

In this article, we examine how globalization relates to future societal perceptions. In particular, we suggest that people construct their imaginations about their society's future by using their folk theory of social change (FTSC), a naïve theory-like generic knowledge structure about how society changes, while flexibly incorporating particular information about the past and present of their society. Our contention is that globalization plays an important role in the construction of future societal perceptions by providing a significant backdrop for people's particular experiences about the past history and the present trend.

What is a Future Societal Perception and How is it Formed?

Societal perceptions are a type of group perceptions or impressions, which social psychologists have considered since Asch (1952), through Allport's (1954) cognitive conceptualization of stereotypes and prejudice, to more recent developments in contemporary social psychology of group perception (for reviews, see Hamilton, 2007; Kashima, Woolcock, & Kashima, 2000; Yzerbyt, Judd, & Corneille, 2004). However, relatively little is known about *future societal perceptions*, namely, people's perceptions about their own society's future (cf. Diekman & Eagly, 2000).

A useful perspective can be provided by Kashima et al.'s (2009) work on FTSC, a naïve theory about the historical trend of their society from the past to the present, and into the future. As Levy, Chiu, and Hong (2006) noted, social psychology has a history of inquiry into people's "lay" or "folk" theories about a variety of phenomena. FTSC is an instance of such lay theories—a theory-like generic knowledge structure about society and its change over time. People typically believe that a society undergoes a natural course of evolution from a traditional community to a modern society. In many ways, FTSC is akin to the classic theorizing in sociology as Kashima et al. (2009) noted. Starting with Tönnies' (1955) theory of social evolution from Gemeinschaft to Gesellschaft, Durkheim's (1964) version from mechanical to organic solidarity, and other theories of modern sociology, the traditional and modern forms of sociality are seen as ideal types of social organization, and it is assumed that there is a single pathway for a traditional community to "develop" into a modern society. Based on A. Fiske's (1992) relational models theory and recent research on group perception (e.g., Eagly & Kite, 1987; Fiske, Cuddy, Glick, & Xu, 2002; Judd, James-Hawkins, Yzerbyt, & Kashima, 2005), Kashima et al. suggested that a traditional community is seen to be primarily characterized by communal sharing relations (i.e., sharing of resources regardless of status or power; Fiske, 1992) and warm, but not so competent; however, it is believed to evolve into a less warm though more competent modern society, in which market pricing relations (i.e., exchanges of resources in a market place; Fiske, 1992) are more prevalent. Research in Australia has provided general support for this characterization of FTSC, and also showed that people tend to extrapolate from this, and project the same trend into the future.

Although the past research delineates the contour of FTSC as a *generic* conceptual framework, and provides preliminary evidence that it frames people's imaginations about their future society, FTSC is unlikely to give a complete answer to the question about future societal perception. This is because people take into consideration their *particular* past and present experience in imagining their future. To put it differently, their future societal perceptions are likely informed by what they believe has happened in their society in the past, and what they know about the goings on in their contemporary society. Some recent findings (Cheng et al., 2010) are instructive in this juncture: Chinese people's societal perceptions became more optimistic during the successful campaign in the Beijing Olympic Games. This line of reasoning is also consistent with the recent theorization about concept and concept use. According to this literature, a domain of knowledge is often organized by a generic, theory-like knowledge structure (e.g., Murphy & Medin, 1985), but particular (or exemplar) information is flexibly used to adjust the domain of knowledge (Murphy, 2002). In this regard, the experience of globalization is one type of such particular information, which people are likely to take into consideration when they imagine the future of their society.

Then, how may globalization affect future societal perception? Kashima et al.'s (2009) research provides some clue. Their work suggests that one of the most central aspects of FTSC is a society's *perceived societal development*. It represents a cluster of ideas about how scientifically, technologically, and industrially "advanced" a society is seen to be, in conjunction with the society's economic prosperity and affluence. The dimension of perceived societal development presupposes a unilinear model of social change, and it can be criticized from a number of perspectives. That is, the very notion of "development" tends to valorize modernity; it often equates the well-being of a society with affluence and material wealth; and it tends to obscure the possibility of multiple pathways to societal change, that is, different societies may change and "develop" in ways that diverges from the singular pursuit of material wealth. It is also noted that Western stereotypes of the "Orient" often presupposes such a unilinear model of social evolution (Said, 1979).

Indeed, these criticisms apply to Australian FTSC. Kashima et al. noted that lay perceptions of societal development largely reflect the *material wealth* of a country (e.g., GDP per capita), and found that Australians' stereotypes about a variety of nations are critically related to the countries' perceived societal development as implied by the FTSC (also see Phalet & Poppe, 1997; Poppe & Linssen, 1999)—more "developed" countries were seen to be more competent, but less warm. Nonetheless, perceived societal development appears to be one of the main dimensions along which lay people construe their society and its change, and it seems to give a structure to their societal perceptions. Kashima et al. suggested that this dimension is associated with a loss of communal sharing and an increasing dominance of market pricing relationships. To put it differently, more scientifically developed, technologically advanced societies are seen to be wealthier, and more sophisticated, intelligent, and generally more competent, but less considerate, trustworthy, and generally less communal.

As we will argue below, globalization may be seen to be associated with a country's material wealth and societal development, and therefore, people may forecast their society's future development differently depending on their country's experience with globalization. Likewise, other societal perceptions (e.g., competence and warmth) may also covary with globalization accordingly. In the present article, we provide evidence that globalization—or more precisely beliefs about globalization—is associated with future societal perceptions through its effects on people's perception of societal development. We do so by highlighting societal perceptions in People's Republic of China (PRC) because it provides an intriguing case study about the historical experience of globalization in contrast to Australia, on which the past research on FTSC has primarily focused.

Globalization, Market Economy, and FTSC

Although globalization is often seen as a recent phenomenon in human history, globalization as we currently experience around the world can be conceptualized as a more contemporary segment of a broader historical trend of increasing connectivity among hitherto largely disconnected human groupings in the world (e.g., Bayly, 2004). Indeed, some theorists of globalization have pointed out the historical continuity of the contemporary globalization with the *belle époque* of international interdependence from 1890 to 1914 leading up to the First World War (see Held & McGrew, 2002). It was the era in which material, financial, human, and cultural resources circulated around the world thanks to the world order mainly sustained by the European colonial rule. Throughout the Inter-war Era, there was a great deal of international economic connectivity as epitomized by the global financial crisis of 1929, which was a prelude to the Second World War in which European, North American, and Japanese national interests collided on the global political and economic stage. When the nations were not at war with each other, though, the market economy was expanding, originating in Europe and North America, but eventually engulfing much of the world (see Baylis & Smith, 2006).

Thus, the expanding global market economy can be regarded as one of the significant aspects of "globalization" broadly conceived as above. In this light, it is not too surprising that FTSC in Australia is characterized by a change from a traditional community marked by communal sharing (and therefore warm) to a modern lifestyle dominated by market pricing (and therefore less warm) relationships. Australia has a history generally in line with the Western European experience of industrialization and the expansion of the market economy maintained initially by the European colonial rule (i.e., the UK), later as an independent nation state, and most recently as an active participant in global financial institutions (e.g., OECD, IMF, World Bank). Australians' FTSC is largely a reflection of this history. In contrast, PRC is a non-Western European political economy with a quite different history. If Australia has been in the thick of the European-led globalizing market economy from its inception in 1901, Mainland China, where PRC is located, was largely closed to it since PRC's establishment in 1949 until recently.

More specifically, PRC is different from Australia in its relation to global market economy in two critical respects. First, it was not a market economy, at least in theory, until Deng Xiaoping's reforms in the late 1980s, which adopted a generally market-based economy while maintaining its Maoist political doctrine. Even in the absence of a market economy (and at least in theory much less dominated by market pricing relationships), would people in PRC hold a generic conceptual framework compatible with the FTSC found in Australia? Second, PRC entered in the *global* market economy only recently. Although it is difficult to say whether participation in a global market economy *causes* economic growth and societal development, it is true to say that in the case of PRC, an entrance into the global market economy *coincided* with the visible signs of its recent economic growth. In light of this historical experience, people in PRC may have distinct beliefs about globalization, societal development, and therefore societal perceptions of the future.

The Present Investigation

We explore the globalization–societal perception nexus in two studies. First, we establish that people's beliefs about globalization are strongly associated with societal perceptions in Study 1. In Study 2, we adopt a cross-national perspective by comparing PRC, Japan, and Australia. To begin, PRC and Japan make a useful contrast. Although they are both non-European countries, they have had quite different historical trajectories in relation to the global market economy since the beginning of the 20th century. On the one hand, Japan participated in the globalizing market economy after its defeat in the Second World War, became one of the most prosperous countries toward the end of the 20th century, but recently experienced a relative slide in its economic status in global economy. On the other hand, PRC insulated Mainland China from the global market economy for the latter half of the 20th century, but since its adoption of an open market policy, it has experienced an explosive growth, recently overtaking Japan's status as the second largest economy in the world. Do these economic trajectories make a difference to their future societal perceptions? If perceived material wealth is seen to be a significant driver of a nation's societal development as Kashima et al.'s (2009) research suggests, and if this same FTSC is held in non-Western countries such as PRC and Japan, PRC may show a much stronger increasing trend in perceived economic development and future societal perceptions than Japan. To these East Asian countries, Australia provides a replication of Kashima et al. (2009) and a point of comparison as a generally Western European-based country.

We will examine one additional question regarding societal perceptions of morality. Recent research on group perception suggests that the content of societal perceptions may not be characterized by two dimensions of competence and warmth, but that the dimension of morality needs to be distinguished from warmth, especially in considering in-group virtues (Leach, Ellemers, & Barreto, 2007). In other words, people may distinguish morally significant social characteristics such as trustworthiness and sincerity from sheer likeability and niceness, and it may be the dimension of morality that plays a more central role in evaluating their in-group. This is because whether others are sincere and trustworthy (as opposed to deceitful) matters a great deal in engaging in transactions—economic or otherwise. Morally relevant traits are informative in evaluating one's partners' intentions to cooperate or compete in transaction. Given that people's future well-being is likely to depend on whether they can count on in-group others' cooperation, there is a good reason to be concerned about their future societal morality. We will examine this basic issue in these studies as well.

STUDY 1

To establish the globalization-societal perception link, this study measured people's beliefs about globalization, and examined its relations with their societal perceptions in PRC. In addition, we explored the question about the psychological mechanisms underlying people's societal perceptions, especially the role of *perceived societal development*—how "advanced and developed" their society is seen to be. Note that this is a lay concept of how people see their society; it is not about how social scientists evaluate their society. This involves two specific objectives. One is to replicate Kashima et al.'s (2009) earlier study and examine whether perceived societal development is a significant element in people's FTSC not only in Australia, but also in PRC and Japan. If so, perceived societal development should be associated with other societal perceptions on competence, warmth, and morality.

Method

Participants

Six hundred and seventy-one respondents (349 men and 322 women; mean age = 23.55 years, $SD = 3.26$) completed a survey in Mainland China during the Beijing Olympic Games between August 5 and 25, 2008. Of those, 62.9% lived in Beijing, 12.7% in Shanghai, and 22.5% in other major cities in China. The remaining 2% lived in a small town (1.9%) or a village (0.1%). To recruit research participants, in July 2008, email invitations were sent out to students in several universities in Mainland China, inviting them to participate in a "marketing survey." They were told that those who completed the survey were entered into a lottery to win Olympics souvenirs, and interested students replied via e-mail to a research assistant, who assigned the participants randomly to a day between 5 to 25 August. A portion of the data from the survey is reported here; Different aspects of the data were reported in Cheng et al. (2010).

Instrument

Beliefs about positive effects of globalization on societal development were measured by five items: "Globalization can benefit both developing and developed nations," "As long as they make due note of changing conditions and plan appropriately to counter the effects of local job loss, developed nations can benefit from globalization," "Globalization enables efficient use of resources and enables all nations to benefit in the long run," "Globalization can provide alternative employment opportunities for people in both developing and developed countries," and "Globalization enables people to cross national boundaries and learn from each other's technological advances." A principal component analysis suggested there was one factor, and the reliability of these items was adequate at $\alpha = .77$. They were averaged to index globalization belief.

Societal perceptions were measured by asking people to evaluate what they thought their society was in 1988 (20 years ago) and in 2018 (10 years in the future) relative to now (2008) in terms of morality (honesty, sincerity, and trustworthiness), warmth (likeability, warmth, and friendliness), and competence (competent, intelligent, skillful) on a 7-point scale ($-3 = $ *much worse than now*; $0 = $ *almost the same as now*; $+3 = $ *much better than now*). Given the participants' age, they would have personally experienced the past 20 years of change; it was surmised that 10 years was a reasonable point in the future to make any projection. In addition, following Kashima et al. (2009), perceptions of societal development was measured by asking them to indicate the extent to which they saw their society as industrialized, technologically advanced, scientific, and wealthy in the past and future again using the same 7-point scale. These items showed a coherent single factor structure. Relevant judgments were averaged to compute past morality, past warmth, past competence, and past development, as well as future morality, future warmth, future competence, and future development (all α ranged from .84 to .98).

Results and Discussion

For each societal perception, a general linear model analysis was conducted with past and future societal perceptions as repeated measures (time as a within-participants factor), and gender and age as between-participants factors. Replicating the Australian results, perceived societal development and competence increased $F(1,665) = 20.28$, $\eta_p^2 = .03$, $p < .01$, and $F(1,665) = 8.96$,

$\eta_p^2 = .01$, $p < .01$, respectively, but perceived morality declined from the past to the present, $F(1,665) = 3.96$, $\eta_p^2 = .01$, $p < .05$. However, perceived warmth showed no difference, $F(1,665) = 1.85$, $\eta_p^2 = .00$, $p > .10$.

Next, the same analysis was repeated with globalization belief as an additional between-participants factor. On perceived societal development, an interaction between globalization belief and time was the only significant effect, $F(1,664) = 36.17$, $\eta_p^2 = .05$, $p < .001$. When people thought globalization develops their society, societal development was seen to be much steeper than when they did not think globalization develops their society. Globalization belief deflated the perception of past development, $B = -0.27$, $t = -2.22$, $p < .05$, but inflated the perceived future development, $B = 0.51$, $t = 9.79$, $p < .001$.

Competence showed a similar pattern. An interaction between globalization belief and time became significant, $F(1,664) = 40.60$, $\eta_p^2 = .06$, $p < .001$. Globalization belief depressed perceived past competence, $B = -0.31$, $t = -3.43$, $p < .01$, but inflated perceived future competence, $B = 0.33$, $t = 5.51$, $p < .001$.

On warmth and morality perceptions, the only significant effect was a main effect of globalization belief on both warmth and morality, $F(1,664) = 6.76$, $\eta_p^2 = .01$, $p = .01$, and $F(1,664) = 9.14$, $\eta_p^2 = .01$, $p < .01$, respectively. The higher globalization belief meant warmer and more moral perceptions of their society.

Partial correlations were computed between perceived societal development and each of the other societal perceptions while controlling for other societal perceptions. Societal development was related positively with competence, .65 and .60 (both $p < .01$), negatively with morality, $-.25$ and $-.01$ (but the latter was almost zero), but unrelated with warmth, $-.02$ and $-.10$, for the past and future society, respectively.

In summary, people in PRC had bright future societal perceptions (Cheng et al., 2010). They thought future society would be more "developed" or affluent, more competent, but somewhat less moral. Nonetheless, their perceptions of societal change were clearly linked with globalization beliefs. Those who thought globalization brings a more generally positive outlook thought their future society would be more "developed" and competent. Globalization plays a significant role in the construction of future images of society. This study also suggests that perceived societal development is a significant aspect of FTSC. It is interesting to note that national wealth is seen to go together with the cluster of ideas consisting of science, technology, and industrialization to form a dimension of perceived societal development, which is in turn associated positively with perceived competence for both the past and the future, but negatively with societal morality for the past. Societal warmth was consistently unrelated to it; the critical dimension associated with perceived societal development appears to be morality, rather than warmth. Kashima et al.'s (2009) measure of warmth perception in fact included items related to the morality dimension, and this is presumably the reason why they found a relation between perceived societal development and warmth.

STUDY 2

Taking a cross-national perspective, Study 2 examined people's past and future societal perceptions in PRC, Japan, and Australia to ascertain the impact of globalization on people's intuitive judgments about their society's future.

This study also highlighted the role of perceived societal development. Not only was the relation of perceived societal development to other societal perceptions examined in three countries, a more fundamental question, the question about its origin, was also examined. That is, where does it come from? Our assumption is that perceived *past* societal development is based on the actual *material* wealth albeit imperfectly. We check this assumption preliminarily by examining a relation between perceived past societal development and data-based estimates of the past material wealth in the form of GDP per capita. With regard to *future* societal development, we have suggested that it is likely to be an intuitive extrapolation of the past trend combined with societal perceptions about the present. To examine this question, we attempt to predict perceived future societal development by perceived past societal development and current societal perceptions. To capture people's perceptions of society's current activity, we measured people's perception of group vitality (Meegan, 2008)—perceptions of their group as having "vitality" or energy and motivation to develop and grow. If our reasoning is correct, perceived past societal development and societal vitality perception should be able to predict perceptions about future societal development. Furthermore, they may be able to account for some of the expected national differences in future societal perceptions, which we expect to find between PRC, Japan, and Australia.

Method

Participants and Procedure

Participants were undergraduate students from three countries: 100 Australians (University of Melbourne; 23 men, 77 women; mean age = 22.2 years; all Australian citizens with 55 European, 15 East Asian, 23 South East Asian, and three South Asian backgrounds; there were four participants who did not identify their ethnic background), 126 Chinese (Peking University; 45 men, 81 women; mean age = 22.0 years; all Han Chinese), and 94 Japanese (Nagoya University; 43 men, 51 women; mean age = 20.2 years; all Japanese). A questionnaire was administered in classrooms. These data were collected shortly after the global financial crisis in 2008.

Instrument

The questionnaire was first developed in English, and translated to Chinese and Japanese by bilinguals, and then back translated by different bilinguals to check their equivalence. The instrument first asked about participants' demographics including age and gender. It then asked participants to imagine how their society had changed over time and were likely to change in the future. Participants then rated their society in terms of 13 personality trait-like characteristics at four different time periods, 100 years ago, 20 years ago, 20 years from now and 100 years from now relative to the present, using an 11-point scale ($-5 = a$ *lot less than now*, $0 = about$ *the same as current*, and $+5 = a$ *lot more than now*). The trait terms pertained to competence (competent, disorganized, skilled, unintelligent), warmth (insensitive, likeable, unfriendly, warm), and morality (dishonest, honest, sincere, untrustworthy). The competence and warmth traits were based on Kashima et al. (2009). The morality items were based on Leach et al. (2007), supplemented with one additional item, dishonest. In addition, participants evaluated their society's development at each time period in terms of how industrialized, technologically advanced, wealthy, and scientific it was or will be ($-5 = a$ *lot less than now*, $0 = about$ *the same as current*, and $+5 = a$ *lot more than now*). Finally, participants were asked to indicate the extent of their agreement with statements concerning societal vitality (five items) on an 11-point scale ($-5 = disagree$ *strongly*, $0 = neither$ *agree nor disagree*, $+5 = agree$ *strongly*). Example items are, I feel my society is strong and active as a collective; I feel my society is extremely energetic and vital as a collective.

Results and Discussion

Preliminary Analyses

We constructed a measure of present societal perception, societal vitality ($\alpha = .79$); past and future societal perceptions, perceived societal development (industrialized, technologically advanced, wealthy, and scientific; $\alpha = .74-.83$), and competence, warmth, and morality perceptions at four different time points ($\alpha = .44-.60, .43-.52$, and $.74-.83$). Although reliability coefficients for competence and warmth perceptions were relatively low, as we will see below, the pattern of findings is consistent with the theory and the past studies and Study 1, where reliability was high. This gives sufficient confidence in the overall results.

Cross-National Comparisons

Reflecting the different historical experiences with the global market economy in PRC, Japan, and Australia, there were national differences in their perceptions of the society's current state, societal vitality. It was highest in China ($M = 1.73$, $SD = 1.50$), then in Australia ($M = 0.67$, $SD = 1.60$), and lowest in Japan ($M = -1.09$, $SD = 1.67$); A country main effect was significant in a general linear analysis with country and gender as factors and age as covariates, $F(2,313) = 64.31$,

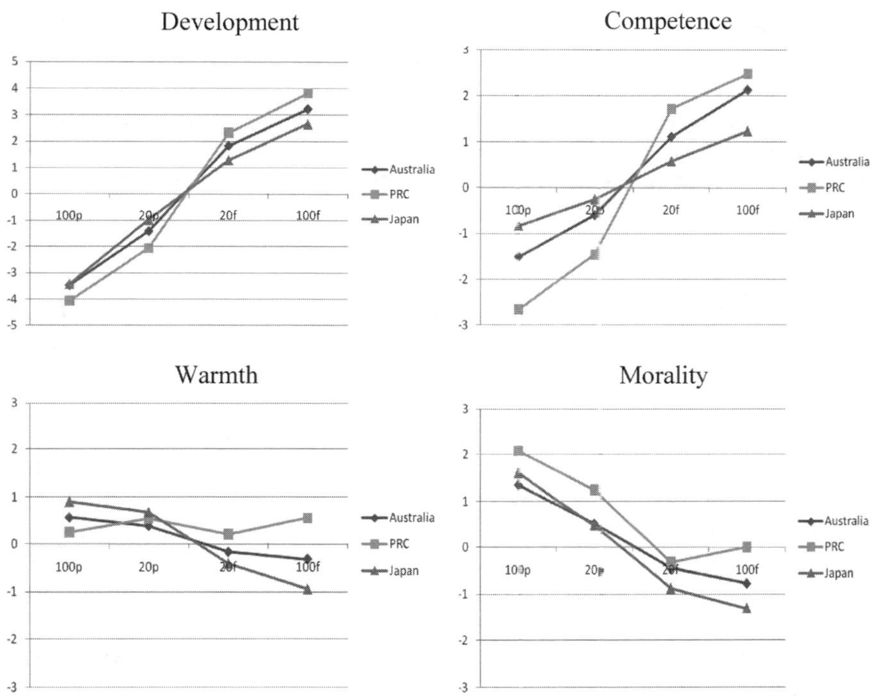

Fig. 1. Societal perceptions of development, competence, warmth, and morality in People's Republic of China, Japan, and Australia.

$\eta_p^2 = .29$, $p < .001$. By Tukey's method (critical $p = .05$), all countries were different from each other.

Perceived societal development was analyzed with a general linear model with the four time periods (time) as a within-participants factor and country and gender as factors, and age and societal vitality as covariates. We included societal vitality to explore if it can completely account for any national differences in societal perception. As we will see below, this was not the case; however, we report the results relevant to our hypotheses with this covariate below.

As expected, there was a main effect of time, $F(3, 374) = 52.39$, $\eta_p^2 = .30$, $p < .001$, which was qualified by country, $F(6, 748) = 6.24$, $\eta_p^2 = .05$, $p < .001$. Clearly, everyone thought development level to have increased from the past to the present and to continue increasing into the future (see Figure 1 for means). Societal vitality had a main effect, $F(1, 376) = 4.06$, $\eta_p^2 = .01$, $p = .011$, but this was qualified by time, $F(3, 374) = 3.34$, $\eta_p^2 = .03$, $p = .019$. Those who considered their society to have higher levels of vitality expected their society to rise to higher levels of development in the future, $B = 0.13$, $t = 3.18$, $p = .002$, and $B = 0.18$, $t = 3.59$, $p < .001$, for 20 and 100 years from now, respectively. By contrast, societal vitality did not correlate with either of the past levels of development, $B = -0.07$ and -0.06, for 100 and 20 years ago, respectively.

Other societal perceptions were examined within the same data analytical framework. As expected, there was a general increase in competence over time, $F(3, 374) = 11.87$, $\eta_p^2 = .09$, $p < .001$. However, the time effect was significantly qualified by country, $F(6, 748) = 7.78$, $\eta_p^2 = .06$, $p < .001$. Figure 1 shows that the increase in mean competence level was much steeper for China than for Australia or Japan.

For warmth, consistent with Study 1, there was no effect of time, $F(3, 372) = 1.67$, $\eta_p^2 = .01$, ns. Instead, a Time $\times$ Country interaction was significant, $F(6, 744) = 4.47$, $\eta_p^2 = .04$, $p < .001$, suggesting that a change in warmth differed across countries. Figure 1 shows that warmth declined in both Australia and Japan, replicating the earlier study. However, there was no discernible change in China. Generally, warmth levels remained positive throughout. This flat trend for China is consistent with Study 1.

For morality, there was a time main effect, country main effect and a Time $\times$ Country interaction, $F(3, 373) = 5.73$, $\eta_p^2 = .04$, $p = .001$, $F(2, 373) = 14.76$, $\eta_p^2 = .07$, $p < .001$, and $F(6, 746) = 4.30$, $\eta_p^2 = .03$, $p < .001$, respectively. Like in warmth, Australia and Japan showed the general declining pattern. Nonetheless, there was a subtle difference in the Chinese pattern. Although warmth was seen to be generally positive and stable over time in China, morality was seen to decline from now to the 20 years in the future (95% CI $[-.53, -.11]$); however, morality was predicted to pick up to the current level by 100 years in the future (95% CI $[-.16, .53]$).

Perceived Societal Development

In order to examine the psychological mechanisms underlying the construction of societal perceptions, we highlight the role of perceived societal development. First of all, people's perceptions of *past* societal development appear to be based on their general knowledge about their country's material wealth. The mean development judgments for 100 and 20 years ago for the three countries correlated with 1900 and 1973 (approximately 100 and 20 years before the time of data collection) estimated GDP per capita in the current US dollar terms for China, Japan, and Australia (http://www.nationmaster.com/; accessed on 1 December 2009) at .72.

We expected that to predict *future societal development*, people extrapolate from their country's past trend while taking into consideration the perception of their society at present, in particular, societal vitality. Multiple regression was used to predict future development in 20 years by perceived development in the past (20 years ago and 100 years ago). We also included dummy coded country variables, China (China as 1, and the other countries as 0) and Japan (Japan as 1, and the other countries as 0), as well as societal vitality as predictors. The model fit was reasonable, $R^2 = .25$, $F(5, 378) = 25.20$, $p < .001$. Those who thought their country was less developed in the past tended to see their future society to be more developed ($\beta = -0.26$ and -0.14, $t = -4.50$ and -2.26, for development 100 years and 20 years ago, respectively). Nonetheless, we also found that those who think their society has vitality tend to think their society would be more developed in 20 years ($\beta = 0.18$, $t = 3.13$, $p = .002$). Once these predictors were taken into consideration, there was no difference between China and the other two countries ($\beta = 0.01$, ns), but Japanese future forecast was somewhat bleaker than those from PRC and Australia ($\beta = -0.12$, $t = -2.05$, $p = .04$). Apparently, factors other than perceptions of the past societal development and the present societal vitality are contributing to societal perception about near future.

Future development in 100 years was also examined. Past development at two time points and future development in 20 years, dummy coded country variables, and societal vitality were used as predictors. Again, those who thought their society was less developed in the past tended to see their future society in 100 years to be more developed ($\beta = -0.17$ and -0.11, t $= -3.87$ and -2.33, for development 100 years and 20 years ago, respectively), but those who thought their society would be more developed in 20 years tended to forecast a more developed future in 100 years ($\beta = 0.58$, $t = 14.58$, $p < .001$). Again, societal vitality was a significant positive predictor: ($\beta = 0.09$, $t = 2.07$, $p < .05$). There was no significant country difference.

Perceived Development and Other Societal Perceptions

Kashima et al. (2009) found that the more developed a society is perceived to be, the more competent, but the less warm it is seen. However, Study 1 showed that morality, rather than warmth per se, was negatively associated with perceived societal development. We computed partial correlations of perceived development with each of the three societal perceptions while controlling for dummy coded variables of China and Japan, as well as the other societal perceptions, for each time period. Replicating Study 1, competence was positively (.40, .43, .49, .38, for 100 years ago, 20 years ago, 20 years in future, 100 years in future, respectively; all significant, $p < .01$), but morality was negatively ($-.15$, $-.18$, $-.15$, $-.09$, for 100 years ago, 20 years ago, 20 years in future, 100 years in future, respectively; all significant, $p < .01$, except for the last, which was significant at $p = .087$) associated with perceived development. There was no relation with warmth, however (.08, .05, .02, .05 for 100 years ago, 20 years ago, 20 years in future, 100 years in future, respectively).

General Discussion

FTSC is a widespread generic knowledge structure about society and its change over time. The same general trends were observed in all countries where past and future societal perceptions were examined so far. People in PRC as well as in Australia and Japan believe that society changes from a more moral, but less competent past to a less moral, but more competent future. Nonetheless, particular historical experiences of the past and present are also implicated in future imaginations about society. In particular, globalization is a factor that plays a significant role in the shaping of future societal perceptions. In Study 1, those who believed in globalization's positive effects on well-being forecast a more optimistic future trend than those who did not. In Study 2, Mainland China, which has been exposed to globalization more recently than Australia and Japan, showed a more optimistic outlook on their future society. In addition, more culturally specific beliefs about society and history may have shaped future societal perceptions of morality in PRC. Reflecting their strong economic growth associated with their experience with the global market economy, Mainland Chinese showed much more positive expectations about their future societal development than their counterparts. Japanese and Australian societal perceptions were very similar, again, reflecting their experience with global market economy in the recent past.

It is interesting to note that this pattern appears to be somewhat at odds with the past research on East–West cultural differences in prediction. Ji, Nisbett, and Su (2001) reported that Westerners tended to predict future trends by making linear projections, so that upward trends are typically predicted to continue unabated, or downward trends, to continue without turnaround. In contrast, Easterners, especially Chinese, tended to predict that neither upward nor downward trends would continue, but would eventually level off. However, the present findings suggest that Chinese participants predicted the steep upward trajectory of their societal change to continue, whereas Australians—Westerners—together with Japanese made a less optimistic prediction.

Nonetheless, it is difficult to say whether the current Chinese pattern is more or less linear than the Australian or Japanese pattern because the participants' perceived trajectories of the past differ across countries, and therefore their future predictions cannot be easily compared. It is also possible that more specific contemporary events in the broader context of globalization—the Beijing Olympic Games for Study 1 and the global financial crisis for Study 2—have contributed to the Chinese samples' generally optimistic outlook. Both events highlighted PRC's cultural and financial strengths relative to those of Australia and Japan. Indeed, past research has also shown that such contemporary events can affect lay perceptions (e.g., Hong, Chiu, Young, & Tong, 1999; Levy, Freitas, Mendoza-Denton, Kugelmaas, & Rosenthal, 2010).

Further, consistent with expectation, perceptions of the past societal development and the current societal vitality largely explained national differences in future societal development. More specifically, those who thought their country currently had strong vitality expected their future to be more developed, and those who thought their past was worse off predicted a more positive future. Our analyses suggest that these tendencies were present in all the countries we studied.

These findings basically suggest that, after controlling for people's perceptions about the past, their future forecast is much like a linear extrapolation from the past: The steeper is the increase from the past, the steeper will be an increase in the future.

As expected, their perceptions of past societal development were not completely fanciful, but anchored in their perceptions of the historical *economic* trajectory. Although it is too early to draw a general conclusion, people's societal perceptions of the past development may be a reasonable approximation to their general impressions of their historical change in affluence. Nonetheless, this raises obvious questions—how accurate are those general impressions, and how do people gain those impressions? Clearly, most of the participants in this study had no direct experience of their society 100 years before. Education and information from reliable sources would constitute one basis: it is easy to speculate that other sources such as historical novels and dramas, and perhaps personal narratives passed down from previous generations would be other sources. Examination of people's beliefs about history (see Liu & Hilton, 2005) seems to be an important topic for further research if we are to examine their future societal perceptions.

Of the more generic aspect of FTSC, one central element is societal development. It is seen to be associated with greater competence, but less morality. Intriguingly, it is the perception of morality that is implicated, rather than that of warmth, suggesting that competence and morality are seen to be in compensatory relationship (Judd et al., 2005). In the present context, one possible explanation for this is based on Fiske's (1992) relational models theory. Greater morality may be associated with communal sharing, but greater competence may be associated with market pricing. Given that communal sharing and market pricing are seen to be incompatible with each other, societal development associated with market pricing relationships brought about by the global market economy may be viewed antithetical to communal sharing, and therefore morality. Further research needs to be conducted to examine the cognitive basis of this phenomenon.

In this juncture, it is intriguing to consider further the national differences in perceived future societal perceptions of morality. Recall that people in PRC thought their society would be less moral in the near future (i.e., 20 years) than in the present, but would be as moral as now in the distant future (i.e., 100 years). This trend is markedly different from those in Japan and Australia, where future society was seen to be less and less moral. Why is this difference?

Although the present data cannot provide a clear answer, we speculate that Chinese people's recent experience is at work. On the one hand, the strong economic growth has coincided with a perceived rise of materialism and erosion of moral community, and this may have resulted in their prediction that morality declines in the near future (see Cheng et al., 2010). On the other hand, the Chinese Communist Party's campaign of "harmonious society" (和谐社会) portrays the future of China under its regime as a society where everyone lives harmoniously.

This rosy vision of a distant future is perhaps the government's policy response to the perceived decline in societal morality in recent times, and may have formed a basis of people's forecast in the distant future.

Nonetheless, it is possible that other more distant cultural elements are at work. First of all, the official government narrative may follow the doctrine of the proletariat utopia in the Marxist historical narrative that society will take an inevitable course of evolution to achieve an egalitarian society through socialist and communist revolutions. In fact, the adoption of this doctrine may be influenced by an even older view of society by an ancient Chinese political figure, Guanz (管子), who suggested倉廩実則知礼節衣食足則知栄辱. That is, "It is when people are prosperous that they behave morally and learn their pride and shame." In other words, when society becomes prosperous, people become more moral. Perhaps it is immaterial to argue which is more important; if the current government campaign and both the recent and past worldviews make a similar prediction about future, why should people not believe in the predicted future? In contrast, Japanese future societal perceptions are much less optimistic, presumably reflecting their recent economic downward slide in the global market economy. In imagining future society, people appear to use their impressions about the past societal development and their beliefs about the present society to forecast the fortunes of their future society. In Study 2, past societal development negatively predicted future societal development, suggesting that people more or less linearly extrapolated the trajectory of societal development from the past to the present into the future. Nonetheless, the past was not the only factor that they took into consideration. Their *current* societal beliefs were also significant predictors of their future societal imaginations. It was globalization beliefs—beliefs that globalization brings greater benefits in Study 1 and perceived societal vitality—beliefs that their society has energy and vitality—in Study 2 that influenced perceptions of future societal development. Future societal perceptions seem to be constructed by flexibly integrating particular information about the past and the present within the generic knowledge structure of FTSC.

Broadly speaking, the current research contributes to the growing literature on conceptual knowledge and its use. Just as generic knowledge structures such as folk physics (e.g., McCloskey & Kohl, 1983), folk biology (e.g., Medin & Atran, 2004), folk psychology (e.g., Malle, 1999), and even folk metaphysics (White, 2009) play a significant role in the human mental life, folk sociology (e.g., Hirschfeld, 2001; Kashima et al., 2009), of which FTSC is a part, constitutes an important part of social cognition. Perhaps because folk sociology seems like an obvious and unsurprising part of social knowledge that social psychologists have paid less attention to this domain of folk knowledge. Nonetheless, examination of folk sociology may bring out a surprising level of systematicity and regularity in people's inferences and judgments about societal perception. More importantly, folk understandings about society and culture may be not only a reflection of people's observations about their familiar social world of the past and present, but also may be *constitutive* of their future social world. Recall that Australians' social policy preferences were in part shaped by their future societal perceptions. Through the political process of democratic voting or other forms of expressions of public opinion even in nondemocratic countries, societal perceptions informed by folk sociology can shape the course of social change in the future. In the context of the present research and the special issue, it is worth reminding ourselves that people's globalization beliefs can contribute to the process of globalization itself, thus potentially shaping the future of humanity as a whole. Folk understandings about social and cultural processes are a critical topic for issue-relevant research in social psychology.

References

Allport, G. W. (1954). *The nature of prejudice*. Reading, MA: Addison-Wesley.

Asch, S. E. (1952). *Social psychology*. Englewood Cliffs, NJ: Prentice Hall.

Baylis, J., & Smith, S. (2006). *The globalization of world politics: An introduction to international relations* (3rd. ed.). Oxford, UK: Oxford University Press.

Bayly, C. A. (2004). *The birth of the modern world*. Oxford, UK: Blackwell.

Cheng, S. Y.-Y., Chao, M. M., Kwong, J., Peng, S., Chen, X., Kashima, Y., & Chiu, C.-Y. (2010). The good old days and a better tomorrow: Historical representations and future imaginations of China during the 2008 Olympic games. *Asian Journal of Social Psychology, 13*, 118–127. doi:10.1111/j.1467-839X.2010.01307.x

Diekman, A. B., & Eagly, A. H. (2000). Stereotypes as dynamic constructs: Women and men of the past, present and future. *Personality and Social Psychology Bulletin, 26*, 1171–1188. doi: 10.1177/0146167200262001

Durkheim, E. (1964). *The division of labor in society* (G. Simpson, Trans.). New York: Free Press.

Eagly, A. H., & Kite, M. (1987). Are stereotypes of nationalities applied to women and men? *Journal of Personality and Social Psychology, 53*, 451–462. doi: 10.1037/0022–3514.53.3.451

Fiske, A. P. (1992). The four elementary forms of sociality: Framework for a unified theory of social relations. *Psychological Review, 99*, 689–723. doi: 10.1037/0033–295X.99.4.689

Fiske, S. T., Cuddy, A. J. C., Glick, P., & Xu, J. (2002). A model of (often mixed) stereotype content: Competence and warmth respectively follow from perceived status and competition. *Journal of Personality and Social Psychology, 82*, 878–902. doi: 10.1037/0022–3514.82.6.878

Hamilton, D. L. (2007). Understanding the complexities of group perception: Broadening the domain. *European Journal of Social Psychology, 37*, 1077–1101. doi: 10.1002/ejsp.436

Held, D., & McGrew, A. (2002). *Globalization/anti-globalization*. Cambridge, UK: Polity.

Hirschfeld, L. A. (2001). On a folk theory of society: Children, evolution, and mental representations of social groups. *Personality and Social Psychology Review, 5*, 107–117. doi: 10.1207/S15327957PSPR0502_2

Hong, Y., Chiu, C., Young, G., & Tong, Y. (1999). Social comparison during the political transition: Interaction of entity versus incremental beliefs and social identities. *International Journal of Intercultural Relations, 23*, 257–279. doi: 10.1016/S0147–1767(98)00038–8

Ji, L.-P., Nisbett, R. E., & Su, Y. (2001). Culture, change, and prediction. *Psychological Science, 12*, 450–456. doi: 10.1111/1467–9280.00384

Judd, C. M., James-Hawkins, L., Yzerbyt, V., & Kashima, Y. (2005). Fundamental dimensions of social judgment: Understanding the relations between agency and communality. *Journal of Personality and Social Psychology, 89*, 899–913. doi: 10.1037/0022–3514.89.6.899

Kashima, Y., Bain, P., Haslam, N., Peters, K., Laham, S., Whelan, J., ... Fernando, J. (2009). Folk theory of social change. *Asian Journal of Social Psychology, 12*, 227–246. doi: 10.1111/j.1467–839X.2009.01288.x

Kashima, Y., Woolcock, J., & Kashima, S. E. (2000). Group impressions as dynamic configurations: The tensor product model of group impression formation and change. *Psychological Review, 107*, 914–942. doi: 10.1037/0033–295X.107.4.914

Leach, C. W., Ellemers, N., & Barreto, M. (2007). Group virtue: The importance of morality (vs. competence and sociability) in the positive evaluation of in-groups. *Journal of Personality and Social Psychology, 93*, 234–249. doi: 10.1037/0022–3514.93.2.234

Levy, S. R., Chiu, C. Y., & Hong, Y. Y. (2006). Lay theories and intergroup relations. *Group Processes and Intergroup Relations, 9*, 5–24. doi: 10.1177/1368430206059855

Levy, S. R., Freitas, A. I., Mendoza-Denton, R., Kugelmaas, H., & Rosenthal, L. (2010). When socio-political events strike cultural beliefs: Divergent impact of Hurricane Katrina on African Americans' and European Americans' endorsement of the Protestant work ethic. *Basic and Applied Social Psychology, 32*, 207–216. doi: 10.1080/01973533.2010.495673

Liu, J. H., & Hilton, D. J. (2005). How the past weighs on the present: Social representations of history and their role in identity politics. *British Journal of Social Psychology, 44*, 537–556. doi: 10.1348/014466605X27162

Malle, B. F. (1999). How people explain behavior: A new theoretical framework. *Personality and Social Psychology Review, 3*, 23–48. doi: 10.1207/s15327957pspr0301_2

McCloskey, M., & Kohl, D. (1983). Naïve physics: The curvilinear impetus principle and its role in interactions with moving objects. *Journal of Experimental Psychology; Learning, Memory and Cognition, 9*, 146–156. doi: 10.1037/0278–7393.9.1.146

Medin, D. L., & Atran, S. (2004). The native mind: Biological categorization and reasoning in development and across cultures. *Psychological Review, 111*, 960–983. doi: 10.1037/0033–295X.111.4.960

Meegan, C. (2008). *Perceiving group discrimination and its consequences for psychological well being: The impact of group identification and perceptions of group vitality.* Unpublished Doctoral Thesis. La Trobe University, Melbourne, Australia.

Murphy, G. L. (2002). *The big book of concepts.* Cambridge, MA: MIT Press.

Murphy, G. L., & Medin, D. L. (1985). The role of theories in conceptual coherence. *Psychological Review, 92*, 289–316. doi: 10.1037/0033–295X.92.3.289

Phalet, K., & Poppe, E. (1997). Competence and morality dimensions of national & ethnic stereotypes: a study in six eastern-European countries: A study in six eastern-European countries. *European Journal of Social Psychology, 27*, 703–723. doi: 10.1002/(SICI)1099–0992(199711/12)27:6<703::AID-EJSP841>3.0.CO;2-K

Poppe, E., & Linssen, H. (1999). In-group favouritism and the reflection of realistic dimensions of difference between national states in central and eastern European nationality stereotypes. *British Journal of Social Psychology, 38*, 85–102. doi: 10.1348/014466699164059d

Said, E. W. (1979). *Orientalism.* New York: Vintage Books.

Tönnies, F. (1955). *Community and association* (C. P. Loomis, Trans.). London: Routledge & Kegan Paul. [Original work published in 1887].

White, P. A. (2009). Property transmission: An explanatory account of the role of similarity information in causal inference. *Psychological Bulletin, 135*, 774–793. doi: 10.1037/a0016970

Yzerbyt, V., Judd, C. M., & Corneille, O. (2004). *The psychology of group perception: Perceived variability, entitativity, and essentialism.* New York: Psychology Press.

YOSHIHISA KASHIMA is Professor of Psychology, Psychological Sciences and the Melbourne Sustainable Society Institute, The University of Melbourne. His research is mainly concerned with cultural dynamics, namely, the stability and change of culture over time.

JUNQI SHI is Assistant Professor of Psychology, Peking University, whose research is mainly concerned with organizational behavior.

KOJI TSUCHIYA is a PhD candidate at Nagoya University, whose research is concerned with social dynamics of attitudes.

EMIKO S. KASHIMA is Senior Lecturer at School of Psychological Science, La Trobe University, interested in culture and threat reactions.

SHIRLEY Y. Y. CHENG is an Assistant Professor of Marketing, whose research is primarily on culture and marketing.

MELODY M. CHAO is an Assistant Professor of Management, who is interested in culture and social behavior.

SHANG-HUI SHIN is a PhD candidate at the University of Melbourne, whose research is concerned with people's perceptions of history.

Journal of Social Issues, Vol. 67, No. 4, 2011, pp. 716–742

Exclusionary Reactions to Foreign Cultures: Effects of Simultaneous Exposure to Cultures in Globalized Space

Carlos J. Torelli*
University of Minnesota

Chi-Yue Chiu
Nanyang Technological University

Kim-pong Tam
Hong Kong University of Science and Technology

Al K. C. Au
National University of Singapore

Hean Tat Keh
University of Queensland

In globalized economies, people often encounter symbols of dissimilar cultures simultaneously. Research on the psychological effects of simultaneous exposure to dissimilar cultures is therefore strategically located at the intersection of globalization, culture, and psychology. In seven experiments, we showed that exposure to a commercial product that embodies symbols of two dissimilar cultures can enhance perceptibility of cultural differences (Experiments 2, 5, and 6) and perceptions of cultural incompatibility (Experiment 1). Furthermore, following simultaneous exposure to two dissimilar cultures, individuals may display defensive responses to "cultural contamination" of an iconic cultural brand when mortality concerns are salient (Experiments 3, 4, and 7). Finally, although we obtained a robust

*Correspondence concerning this article should be addressed to Carlos J. Torelli, Marketing at the Carlson School of Management, University of Minnesota, 321 Nineteenth Avenue South, Suite 3-150, Minneapolis, MN 55455-0438 [e-mail: ctorelli@umn.edu]

This article was supported by a research grant awarded to Chi-yue Chiu by National Science Foundation Grant (NSF BCS 07–43119).

716

bicultural exposure effect across experiments, thoughtful elaboration about cultural complexities can attenuate this effect and its attendant defensive responses to "cultural contamination" (Experiments 5–7).

Globalization has resulted in experiential compression of time and space (Giddens, 1985). In globalized societies, symbols of different cultural traditions are often found in the same location or product (Starbucks in Beijing's Forbidden City; Batman toys with a "Made in China" label). Increased cultural contacts attending globalization has also increased the tension between accepting foreign cultural influence and preserving the heritage culture (Fu & Chiu, 2007). Such tension is evident in the marketplace, where contrastive cultural meanings and messages of global and local brands interact to jointly influence consumer perceptions (Robertson, 1995).

Recent research (Chiu, Mallorie, Keh, & Law, 2009) has shown that simultaneous exposure to two cultures in globalized space draws the perceivers' attention to the stereotypic qualities of the respective cultures, and hence enhances the perceived distance between the two cultures and the permanence of their boundaries. These perceptual phenomena are referred to as the *bicultural exposure effect*. The objectives of this research are three-fold. First, we seek to replicate and further clarify the nature of the bicultural exposure effect. Second, we examine the implications of this effect on exclusionary reactions to foreign culture, defined as emotional, reflexive responses evoked by perceived threats to the integrity and vitality of one's heritage culture (Chiu, Gries, Torelli, & Cheng, 2011). Finally, we attempt to identify the boundary of the bicultural exposure effect.

As an overview, we propose that simultaneous exposure to two dissimilar cultures or their symbols (hereafter referred to as *bicultural exposure*) will draw the perceivers' attention to the defining characteristics of the two cultures. In turn, this will enhance the perceived incompatibility of the two cultures. This perception, when coupled with a situation-induced cultural defense mindset (as when the individual is under the influence of mortality salience), can lead to defensive resistance of ideas from foreign cultures. Finally, the effect of bicultural exposure, despite its robustness, will be attenuated when the perceiver is motivated to engage in thoughtful elaboration about cultural complexities (either situation-induced or driven by chronic tendencies). In this article, we report evidence from seven experiments for this proposal.

Bicultural Exposure Effect

According to the dynamic constructivist theory of culture (Hong, Morris, Chiu, & Benet-Martinez, 2000), people with some direct or indirect experiences with a certain culture will develop a cognitive representation of the culture. Upon seeing an iconic symbol of the culture, people automatically retrieve from memory their cognitive representation of the culture.

When symbols of two cultures are present in the environment, which is often the case in globalized space, the cognitive representations of both cultures will be activated (Chiu et al., 2009). For example, Americans may experience bicultural activation when they see Mattell toys (e.g., Batman action figures) with a made-in-China label. When two cultural representations are activated simultaneously, the perceiver will attend to the defining characteristics that distinguish the two cultures, which in turn enlarges the perceived differences and incompatibility of the two cultures. These processes are less likely to occur when only one cultural representation is activated, even when that representation is one of a foreign culture.

Results from two experiments (Chiu et al., 2009) supported the hypothesized perceptual effects of bicultural exposure. For example, in one experiment (Chiu et al., 2009, Experiment 1), Beijing Chinese undergraduates were asked to evaluate a McDonald's hamburger advertisement that was placed either next to another McDonald's hamburger advertisement (i.e., single culture exposure condition) or next to a Chinese moon cake (a traditional Chinese confection) advertisement (i.e., bicultural exposure condition). Following the manipulation, the participants were presented with two commercial messages for *Timex*, one appealing to individualist values, and one to collectivist values. The participants rated how likely a Chinese student would choose the individualist and collectivist messages for designing a Chinese website for Timex. In previous research (Aaker & Schmitt, 2001), the individualist message was found to be more popular in individualist cultures (e.g., U.S. culture) than in collectivist cultures (e.g., Chinese culture), whereas the collectivist message was found to be more popular in collectivist cultures. Thus, a high estimation for the collectivist (vs. individualist) message would indicate a greater tendency to attribute a culture-typical quality to a Chinese. As expected, compared to those in the single culture exposure condition, those in the bicultural exposure condition believed that the Chinese student was more likely to choose the collectivist message. Similar results were obtained among European Americans (Chiu et al., 2009, Experiment 2).

However, questions concerning the bicultural exposure effect's generality, underlying mechanisms, behavioral consequences, and boundaries remain. To address the generality of the effect, we seek to replicate and extend Chiu et al.'s (2009) results. Specifically, we examine whether exposure to commercial products that embody symbols of two cultures, such as a British brand (with an English brand name) of Tequila (icon of Mexican culture), would also produce the bicultural exposure effect. Like other symbols, a consumer brand or product can be a cultural icon or a vehicle for cultural meaning (Ortner, 1973). Iconic brands and products are loaded with cultural meanings; they are strongly associated with the culture's values, needs, and aspirations (Torelli, Keh, & Chiu, 2010). For brands loaded with cultural meanings, incidental exposure to these brands may spontaneously evoke its attendant cultural meanings (e.g., Marlboro can activate the value of rugged individualism in U.S. culture). Exposure to an iconic brand made in a foreign country should then elicit the bicultural exposure effect on perceptions of cultural incompatibility. This was tested in experiment 1.

Second, we submit that the bicultural exposure effect is a perceptual effect: Seeing symbols of the ingroup culture and an outgroup culture simultaneously can evoke a perceptual contrast. Nonetheless, bicultural exposure may also evoke a self-categorization process that reinforces categorical perceptions of cultures (Hogg, 2004) and promotes intergroup comparison (Turner, Hogg, Oakes, Reicher, & Wetherell, 1987), one consequence of which is self-stereotyping—the tendency to attribute the ingroup's defining features to its members. To clarify the underlying mechanism of the bicultural exposure effect, we investigated the extent to which self-categorization processes are involved in the effect. If a self-categorization process drives the effects, individuals with high cultural identification (a chronic tendency to self-categorize as a member of the local culture) should be particularly prone to the dual cultural activation effect when exposed to juxtaposed local and foreign icons. However, the effect should dissipate when these individuals are exposed to juxtaposed icons of two outgroup cultures. If the bicultural exposure effect is found among individuals both high and low in cultural identification (Experiment 1), as well as when both stimuli cultures are outgroup cultures (Experiment 2), the effect should be primarily driven by a perceptual contrast, and self-categorization is not necessary for the occurrence of the bicultural exposure effect.

Exclusionary Reactions to Foreign Culture

Chiu (2007) proposed that attending to the differences between local and foreign cultures—a perceptual consequence of bicultural exposure—can under some circumstances alert individuals to the potential contamination effects of foreign cultures on the local culture, leading to exclusionary behaviors. The second objective of this research is to identify when bicultural exposure would lead to exclusionary reactions to foreign cultures.

Past research has shown that thoughts of one's own death may evoke a culture defense mindset. According to the Terror Management Theory (Greenberg, Solomon, & Pyszczynski, 1997), when reminded of their mortality, people would experience existential anxiety. To manage existential anxiety, people would adhere to and defend their cultural worldview. They do so because a cultural worldview confers a sense of symbolic immortality—when the self is seen as a part of an imperishable culture, the self seems immortal. For instance, when mortality is made salient, people tend to endorse punitive reactions toward those who violate conventional standards in the society (Rosenblatt, Greenberg, Solomon, Pyszczynski,

& Lyon, 1989), and encourage aggression against those who violate the cultural worldview (McGregor et al., 1998). The defensive reactions that mortality salience evokes also include intolerance of using cultural icons in an inappropriate way (e.g., using the crucifix as a hammer; Greenberg, Porteus, Simon, & Pyszczynski, 1995). Accordingly, we hypothesize that participants would be particularly intolerant of cultural contamination of their culture's iconic brand when they are under the *joint* influence of bicultural exposure and mortality salience. We tested this hypothesis in Experiments 3, 4, and 7.

Boundary Condition: Thoughtful Elaboration

The third objective is to identify the boundary of the bicultural exposure effect and its attending exclusionary reactions. Cultural priming effects are largely automatic processes that occur without conscious elaboration about cultural implications (Hong et al., 2000). As a result, culture's influence on judgments and behaviors is often stronger when people process information in a cursory, spontaneous manner, but dissipates when people engage in more deliberative thought processes (Briley & Aaker, 2006). By extension, engaging in thoughtful elaboration about cultural complexities can attenuate the bicultural exposure effect and hence its attendant exclusionary reactions. Elaborate thoughts on cultural similarities and differences could interfere with 'schematic' processing of cultures and diminish perceived incompatibilities between cultures. Need for cognition is an individual difference variable reflecting the extent to which people engage in and enjoy effortful cognitive activities (Cacioppo & Petty, 1982). Because individuals high in need for cognition engage in thoughtful elaborations, they are likely to think deeply about cultural similarities and differences and correct the spontaneous cultural inferences produced by the dual activation of cultures. Consistent with this idea, research shows that the correlation between automatic associations toward an ethnic minority and explicit judgment of the ethnic group decreases as need for cognition increases (Florack, Scarabis & Bless, 2001), suggesting that individuals high (vs. low) in need for cognition can more effectively correct their spontaneous impression of an ethnic group. Thus, we hypothesize that thoughtful elaboration about cultural complexities (either measured as a chronic individual difference or induced in the experimental setting) can attenuate the effect of bicultural exposure on perceptions of cultures and its attendant exclusionary reactions to foreign culture. We tested this hypothesis in Experiments 5, 6, and 7.

In summary, seven experiments were conducted to test the hypotheses advanced in this research. Experiment 1 sought to extend the bicultural exposure effect to the domain of commercial products that embody symbols of two cultures. Experiments 1 and 2 tested whether cultural identification would moderate the bicultural priming effect. Experiments 3 and 4 were carried out to investigate the hypothesized joint effect of bicultural exposure and mortality salience on American participants' exclusionary reactions to incorporating foreign symbols into an iconic (vs. non-iconic) brand. The last three experiments examined whether thoughtful elaboration about cultural complexities attenuate the bicultural exposure effect and its attendant exclusionary reactions.

Experiment 1

Experiment 1 tested the hypothesis that simultaneous exposure to symbols of American and Chinese cultures would increase attribution of stereotypic American values to other Americans and perceived incompatibility of American and Chinese cultures. As noted, previous research has found robust cognitive and cultural effects of bicultural priming in both American and Asian contexts (Chiu et al., 2009), suggesting that these effects are not culture-dependent. For the sake of convenience in data collection, we sampled American participants in most of the studies reported in this article. Nonetheless, in Experiment 5, to establish the generality of our results in Asian contexts, we tested our hypotheses in Hong Kong.

Method

In a study described as a survey of new products introduced by global companies, participants (125 European American introductory business students; 51.2% male; mean age = 20.69 years) were asked to review three new product names. We manipulated exposure to Chinese and/or American culture by manipulating the cultural associations of the products and country of origin. Half of the participants evaluated three products that were icons of U.S. culture: Running shoes, jeans, and breakfast cereal. The remaining participants reviewed three products that were not icons of U.S. culture: Table lamps, bread toasters, and umbrellas. We selected these products based on pretest results. In the pretest, 46 participants from the same participant pool ranked 12 products (the other six products were: film, cars, software, microwave ovens, washers, and sodas) according to the extent to which the products were icons of U.S. culture. Umbrellas, table lamps and toasters received the lowest ranks (mean ranks $\geq$ 9.15; $M = 9.75$, $SD = 1.32$). Jeans, breakfast cereal and running shoes received much higher ranks and matched the non-iconic products in prices (mean ranks $\leq$ 6.11, $M = 5.12$, $SD = 1.64$). The average rank of the three iconic products was higher than that of the three non-iconic ones, $t(45) = 15.06$, $p < .001$.

Half of the participants in each cultural iconicity condition were told that the products were China-made products ("products manufactured in China by Chinese corporations"). To make the cover story believable, and to increase the products' associations with Chinese culture, we used novel Chinese brand names for the products: CHENXIAO for breakfast cereal, QINJIN for running shoes,

XENSHI for jeans, BEIHUA for bread toaster, ZHONGYAN for table lamps, and WUFENG for umbrellas. For comparison purpose, the remaining participants were presented with U.S.-made products with novel English brand names (breakfast cereal: UNCLE BOB; running shoes: ASPIRE; jeans: NINE ZERO; table lamp: SCHONBEK; bread toaster: ROBIN; umbrella: MURRAY) that looked real but conveyed little meaning. Note that participants in the Chinese Brands/Iconic U.S. Products Condition were exposed to both Chinese culture (through country of origin) and American culture (through the product category), whereas participants in the remaining conditions were exposed to one culture only.

Following the manipulations, the participants rated each product on three dimensions (bad-good, unappealing-appealing, and unfavorable-favorable) on a scale from 1 (very bad/unappealing/unfavorable) to 9 (very good/appealing/favorable). An evaluation index was computed by averaging the responses to the three items for the three products ($\alpha = .90$).

Dependent measures.   Next, in an "unrelated" social perception study, participants completed a measure of cultural perception and a measure of perceived incompatibility of cultures previously used in the Chiu et al. (2009) studies. The cultural perception measure was designed to assess participants' expectation that other Americans possess value preferences characteristic of American culture. Participants learned that an American student was redesigning a web page for *Timex* and was considering two commercial messages for *Timex*, with one appealing to individualist values and the other to collectivist values. The messages were taken from Aaker and Schmitt (2001). The individualist message was as follows: "The Timex watch. It embodies so much. It's like a person. It has an impressive personality, very individualistic, and with a strong focus and concern for oneself—in a positive way." The collectivist message matched the individualist message in writing style and social desirability but focused on social connectedness: "The Timex watch. It embodies so much. It's like a person. It's an impressive social being, very connected to others, and with a strong focus and concern for others—in a positive way." Participants were asked to estimate, using an 11-point scale (from *very unlikely* to *very likely*), how likely the American student would use each message for *Timex*. The tendency to attribute culture-characteristic value preference to Americans would be reflected in the tendency to estimate strong preference for the individualist message and weak preference for the collectivist message.

Another dependent measure was designed to assess participants' perceived incompatibility of cultures. Based on past research in cross-cultural psychology (Chiu & Hong, 2006), we identified six values or beliefs that are widely held in East Asia (holism, collectivism, belief in fixed world, situationism, duties, and the importance of impression management) and four that are widely held in North America (individualism, individual agency, dispositionism, and individual rights).

Next, we formed 14 items by pairing culturally incompatible East Asian and North American values and beliefs. More specifically, each item required the participants to estimate the extent to which another American would endorse one of the six East Asian values or beliefs given that the same American also endorsed one of the four American values or beliefs, or vice versa. A sample item combining a belief in holism (East Asian) with one in individual rights (North American) was: "Assuming that he agreed strongly with the statement, 'It is not possible to understand the pieces without considering the whole picture,' how likely would he be to agree with the statement, 'I feel that I have the right to refuse to help my relative'?" All estimations were made on a percentage scale (0–100%). Arithmetic means of the 14 estimations of simultaneous endorsement of values/beliefs was computed to form a measure of perceived cultural incompatibility ($\alpha = .68$), with low scores indicating higher levels of perceived incompatibility of North American and East Asian cultures.

For the European American participants, U.S. culture is the ingroup culture and Chinese culture is an outgroup culture. To test whether self-categorization moderates the bicultural exposure effect, toward the end of the experiment, we measured the participants' level of American identification with the Patriotism/Nationalism Questionnaire (Kosterman & Feshbach, 1989). The questionnaire consists of 11 items (e.g., "The fact that I am an American is an important part of my identity"; $\alpha = .88$). Respondents rated how much they agreed or disagreed with each item on a 5-point scale (1 = Strongly disagree; 5 = Strongly agree).

Results and Discussion

As expected, reviewing products that embodied symbols of U.S. culture (iconic products of the United States) and Chinese culture (the products' origin in China) increased the perceived incompatibility of American and Chinese cultures and strengthened the expectancy that Americans do not prefer collectivist values. First, a Product Iconicity X Brand Culture analysis of variance (ANOVA) was performed on the likelihood of adopting the collectivist message, controlling for product evaluation. The result revealed a significant interaction, $F(1,117) = 6.55, p = .01, \eta^2_p = .053$. Participants expected other Americans to be less likely to adopt a collectivist message after evaluating Chinese brands of iconic U.S. products (after being exposed to two cultures simultaneously; $M = 4.32, SD = 2.27$) than after evaluating U.S. brands of iconic U.S. products (after being exposed to the U.S. culture only; $M = 5.78, SD = 2.43$), $F(1,59) = 5.61, p < .05, \eta^2_p = .087$. The simple main effect of brand culture was not significant for non-iconic products ($M_{China} = 5.50, SD = 2.65; M_{US} = 5.09, SD = 2.19$), $F(1,62) = 0.43$, ns. The product iconicity and brand culture manipulations did not influence the estimated likelihood of adopting the individualist message; all Fs in the Product

Iconicity X Country of Origin ANOVA < 1, ns. In short, following exposure to cues of U.S. and Chinese cultures, the European American participants expected an American not to choose the collectivist message.

In addition, on the measure of perceived cultural incompatibility, the Product Iconicity X Brand Culture interaction was significant, $F(1,121) = 4.32, p < .05$, $\eta^2_p = .035$. Participants expected another American not to simultaneously hold both American and Chinese beliefs or values; the overall mean was below 50% ($M = 38.5$), $t(124) = 11.91$, $p < .001$. This expectancy was lower after the participants had reviewed Chinese brands of iconic U.S. products ($M = 32.76$, $SD = 9.82$) than after they did U.S. brands of iconic U.S. products ($M = 40.41$, $SD = 10.75$), $F(1,59) = 8.01$, $p < .01$, $\eta^2_p = .120$. The simple main effect of brand culture was not significant for non-iconic products ($M_{China} = 40.63$, $SD = 9.58$; $M_{US} = 40.25$, $SD = 10.47$), $F(1,62) = 0.12$, ns.

Finally, American Identification did not moderate these results. When we performed a Product Iconicity X Brand Culture X American Identification (mean-centered) General Linear Model (GLM) on the likelihood of adopting the collectivist message and the probability of holding both American and Chinese beliefs or values, all effects involving American identification were nonsignificant, highest $F = 2.48$, ns. There was also no significant effects of Product Iconicity and Brand Culture on the identification measure, highest $F = 2.24$, ns.

In summary, consistent with past findings (Chiu et al., 2009), simultaneous exposure to symbols of the U.S. culture (iconic products of the United States) and Chinese culture (Chinese brands) in commercial products increased American participants' tendency to attribute culture-typical characteristics to other Americans and the perceived incompatibility of American and Chinese cultures. Furthermore, contrary to the self-categorization theory, these effects do not depend on the perceivers' level of cultural identification, suggesting that self-categorization is not necessary for the occurrence of the bicultural exposure effect.

Experiment 2

Experiment 2 was designed to provide further evidence for and to clarify the nature of the effect of bicultural exposure on perception of cultural distance. To further demonstrate that the bicultural exposure effect is not identity-dependent, we had European American participants review British brands of iconic Mexican products and responded to a measure of perceived cultural distance. To the participants, both British and Mexican cultures are outgroup cultures. Accordingly, self-categorization should not influence perception of cultural distance here.

This new bicultural exposure manipulation also addressed another interpretive issue in Experiment 1. In Experiment 1, we manipulated bicultural exposure by having American participants review Chinese brands of iconic American products. This manipulation could have evoked a realist threat (the competition of Chinese brands with American products), which could in turn increase perceived cultural distance. This account did not explain why the perceptual effect was absent when American participants reviewed Chinese brands of non-iconic American products. Nonetheless, in this experiment, because both British and Mexican cultures are outgroup cultures, reviewing British brands of iconic Mexican products should not present a realist threat to the American participants. Replication of Experiment 1 results would suggest that realist threat is not a primary driver of the bicultural exposure effect.

Finally, to test whether the bicultural exposure effect generalizes beyond perceptions of the two cultures implicated in the product evaluation task, aside from the perceived distance between British and Mexican cultures, we also measured the perceived distance between Puerto Rican and Canadian cultures following the manipulation.

Method

Participants (42 European American business students; 40% male; mean age = 21.3 years) were presented with a new product evaluation task, in which they evaluated British products likely to be introduced in the Mexican market. Half of the participants, randomly selected, evaluated two British brands (with novel British names: 'Williams' and 'Jones') of products that were icons of Mexican culture (Tequila and Taco's corn tortilla; Bicultural Exposure Condition). The remaining participants evaluated two products (with the same British names) that were not Mexican icons (backpack and bread toaster; Single Culture Exposure Condition). Participants evaluated the products on the same scale ($\alpha = .91$) used in Experiment 1.

Following the manipulation, the dependent measure was introduced in an "un-related" study about "intercultural relationships." To provide convergent evidence for the bicultural exposure effect, we used a different measure of perceived cultural distance. Specifically, we had the participants draw on a half-a-letter-sized sheet in any way they deemed appropriate a bubble to represent each of the following cultures: Mexican, Puerto Rican, Canadian and British cultures. We measured the distance, in millimeters, between each pair of cultures. To obscure the purpose of the measure, we did not ask the participants to draw the four bubbles to represent the extent of intercultural similarity or difference. Finally, the participants rated their familiarity with the four cultures using a 7-point scale (1 = Not familiar at all; 7 = Extremely familiar).

Pretest participants ($N = 22$) rated their familiarity with Mexican, Puerto Rican, Canadian and British cultures (on a 7-point scale, with 1 = Not familiar at all, and 7 = Extremely familiar) and the degree of similarity between each pair of cultures (on a 7-point scale, with 1 = Very dissimilar, and 7 = Very similar). Participants were moderately familiar with the four cultures (mean familiarity ratings $= 4.53$ to 5.21). Participants perceived British and Canadian cultures to be very similar to each other ($M = 6.10$, $SD = 1.50$), as they did Mexican and Puerto-Rican cultures ($M = 5.80$, $SD = 1.80$). However, the participants perceived British and Canadian cultures to be very different from Mexican and Puerto-Rican cultures ($M_{B-PR} = 2.50$, $SD = 0.86$; $M_{B-M} = 2.60$, $SD = 1.00$; $M_{C-PR} = 2.60$, $SD = 1.00$; $M_{C-M} = 3.00$, $SD = 1.00$). On average, the similar pairs were perceived to be more similar to each other than the dissimilar ones ($M_{\text{similar}} = 5.90$, $SD = 1.30$ and $M_{\text{dissimilar}} = 2.70$, $SD = 0.80$), $t(21) = 11.77$, $p < .001$.

Pretest participants also rated the products used in the manipulation in terms of their cultural iconicity for Mexican culture on a 7-point scale ($1 = $ not associated with Mexican culture in any way; definitely not an icon of Mexican culture, and $7 = $ very strongly associated with Mexican culture; definitely an icon of Mexican culture). The mean level of cultural iconicity was higher for Tequila and Taco's corn tortillas than for backpacks and bread toasters ($M_{\text{Icons}} = 6.50$, $SD = 1.50$ and $M_{\text{Non-Icons}} = 2.40$, $SD = 0.90$), $t(21) = 11.01$, $p < .001$. A second pretest ($N = 52$) showed that none of the products were culturally significant to Americans (means cultural iconicity rating $= 2.20$ to 2.90 on a 7-point scale). Finally, in the main study, during debriefing, we checked and found that none of the participants connected the "intercultural relationship" study with the manipulation task.

Results and Discussion

We took the mean of the perceived distances between the two similar culture pairs to form a measure of perceived distance between similar cultures, and the mean of the perceived distances between the four dissimilar culture pairs to form a measure of perceived distance between dissimilar cultures. A Cultural Exposure X Cultural Similarity (within-subject factor) ANOVA revealed a significant main effect of cultural similarity, $F(1,40) = 150.11$, $p < .0001$, $\eta^2_p = .79$: Participants drew the bubbles representing dissimilar cultures ($M = 267.62$, $SD = 108.63$) farther apart than they did the bubbles representing similar cultures ($M = 81.79$, $SD = 51.58$). More importantly, the Cultural Exposure X Cultural Similarity interaction was significant, $F(1,40) = 6.33$, $p < .025$, $\eta^2_p = .137$. This interaction remained significant after controlling for participants' familiarity with the cultures and their average evaluation of the products, $F(1,38) = 5.31$, $p < .05$, $\eta^2_p = .123$. Participants in the Bicultural Exposure Condition ($M = 318.30$, $SD = 115.65$) drew the bubbles representing dissimilar cultures farther apart than did the participants in the Single Culture Exposure Condition ($M = 221.55$, $SD = 79.19$), $F(1,40) = 10.17$, $p < .005$, $\eta^2_p = .203$. The manipulation did not affect the distances between the bubbles representing similar cultures (for bicultural exposure, $M = 92.10$, $SD = 64.52$; for single culture exposure, $M = 72.41$, $SD = 35.13$ respectively, $p > .2$), indicating that the cultural exposure manipulation did not produce a generalized tendency to place the bubbles apart.

Additional analysis revealed that the bicultural exposure effect was equally strong in the participants' perception of the distance between British and Mexican cultures (the two cultures involved in the product evaluation task) and that between Canadian and Puerto-Rican cultures (the two cultures not involved in the product evaluation task). Specifically, when we performed a Cultural Exposure X Culture Pair (British-Mexican or Canadian-Puerto-Rican; within-subject factor) ANOVA on perceived distances, the main effect of cultural exposure was significant, $F(1,40) = 7.78$, $p < .01$, $\eta^2_p = .163$, but the interaction was not, $F(1,40) < 1$, ns.

In summary, consistent with Experiment 1 results, bicultural exposure enlarged the perceived distances between dissimilar cultures. The finding that simultaneous exposure to two outgroup cultures (British and Mexican) enlarged perceived cultural difference suggests that bicultural exposure effect can occur without involving self-categorization. Because the new bicultural exposure manipulation did not pose a realist threat to the participants, replication of the bicultural exposure effect in this study suggests that realist threat is not the primary driver of the bicultural exposure effect, although self-categorization and realist threat may be implicated in other phenomena related to people's reactions to globalization.

Experiment 3

Having documented the bicultural exposure effect and clarified its nature, we now turn to its psychological consequences. In Experiment 3, we examined the effect of simultaneous exposure to ingroup and outgroup cultures on Americans' exclusionary reactions to foreign cultural influence. As mentioned, previous research has shown that making mortality concerns salient would increase people's adherence of their cultural worldview and lower their tolerance of contamination of their cultural icons (McGregor et al., 1998). In this study, we tested the hypothesis that simultaneous exposure to ingroup and outgroup cultural symbols would increase the salience of cultural contrast and hence exacerbate the mortality salience effect.

Method

Manipulations.   As a cover story, the participants (83 European American business students, 50% male; mean age = 20.9 years) were informed that they would complete several unrelated surveys during a 30-minute session. In the first survey, they were asked to complete a questionnaire that contained the mortality salience manipulation. Following standard procedures in inducing mortality salience (Arndt, Greenberg, Solomon, Pyszczynski, & Simon, 1997), participants in the mortality salient condition were instructed to answer two open-ended questions: "Please, briefly describe the emotions that the thought of your own death arouses in you" and "Jot down, as specifically as you can, what you think will happen to you physically as you die and once you are physically dead." Participants in the control condition answered parallel questions concerning the experience of dental pain. Next, all participants completed the Positive and Negative Affect Schedule (PANAS; Watson & Clark, 1992), which consists of a positive affect scale (10 items, e.g., interested, proud; $\alpha = .89$) and a negative affect scale (10 items, e.g., distressed, nervous; $\alpha = .83$). Participants rated each item on a scale from 1 to 5 (1 = very slightly or not at all; 5 = extremely) based on the strength of emotion they experienced at the time of the study.

Next, participants were presented with the new product survey used in Experiment 1. They were randomly assigned to evaluate three Chinese brands of products that were icons of U.S. culture (Bicultural Exposure Condition) or three Chinese brands of products that were not U.S. icons (Single Cultural Exposure Condition), using the same scale used in Experiment 1 ($\alpha = .96$). The products and brand names were the same as those used in the respective conditions in Experiment 1.

Dependent measure. Following the manipulations, the participants were presented with an "unrelated" study about "perception of marketing managers," where the dependent measure was introduced. To measure the participants' evaluative reactions to cultural contamination of an American iconic brand, we had the participants respond to the following business case: The Marketing VP of Nike Inc. in the Middle East had developed an "out-of-the-box" marketing plan to "strengthen Nike brand's connection to Arab values." The plan included the following actions: (1) Launch a new line of products under a new brand name using Arabic characters without the *"Swoosh"* mark from the product, (2) Replace the "Nike" brand name that lacks a semantic meaning in Arabic with the Arabic word for "Sportsmanship," (3) launch the new campaign in an alliance with local brand names that would further boost the connection between the new brand and traditional values of the Arab world, (4) use well-known local soccer players (soccer is a popular sport in the Middle East) as endorsers of the new line of products, (5) develop advertisements in which the endorsers wear traditional Islamic attire and a pair of "sportsmanship" running shoes, and (6) adopt the slogan "dress modestly, the Islamic spirit" (in Arabic). Participants were asked to evaluate the marketing plan by answering the following questions: (1) What would the impact of the news about the plan on Nike's stock price in the New York Stock Exchange be? (1 = very negatively; 9 = very positively), (2) How much would the plan increase/decrease Nike's percentage market share in the U.S. after the news about the plan are made public? ("-10% or more" to "+10% or more"; this item was re-scaled to a scale that ranged from 1 to 9), and (3) they were also asked to indicate their intentions to buy Nike's products after hearing about the news (1 = very low intention; 9 = very high intention). An index of participants' attitude toward the marketing plan was computed by averaging the responses to these three items ($\alpha = .72$).

Results and Discussion

We performed a Mortality Salience X Cultural Exposure ANOVA on positive and negative affect and found no significant effects on either measure; all Fs $< .55$, ns, indicating that the manipulations did not affect the participants' affect. As expected, a Mortality Salience X Cultural Exposure ANOVA performed on the evaluative reaction to the marketing plan revealed a significant interaction, $F(1,79) = 3.94$, $p < .05$, $\eta^2_p = .048$. This interaction remained significant after controlling for positive affect, negative affect and evaluation of the Chinese products, $F(1,76) = 4.61$, $p < .05$, $\eta^2_p = .057$. In the Bicultural Exposure condition, the simple main effect of mortality salience was significant, $F(1,40) = 5.69$, $p < .025$, $\eta^2_p = .125$; the participants evaluated the marketing plan less favorably in the Mortality Salient Condition ($M = 4.34$, $SD = .71$) than in the Control Condition ($M = 5.02$, $SD = 1.08$). In contrast, in the Single Culture Exposure Condition, the simple main effect of mortality salience was not significant, $F(1,39) = .16$, ns, $M_{\text{MortalitySalient}} = 4.92$ and $M_{\text{Control}} = 4.81$. Furthermore, evaluation of the marketing plan was also lower in the Bicultural Exposure-Mortality Salient Condition than in the other three conditions ($ps \leq .06$).

In short, consistent with our hypothesis, the participants displayed a significant worldview defense effect (evaluated cultural contamination of iconic brands of the United States unfavorably when they were under the influence of mortality salience) only after simultaneous exposure to ingroup and foreign cultures, which had rendered cultural contrast salient in the condition. Because the dependent measure was European Americans' evaluative reaction to an iconic American brand's attempt to increase its market competitiveness in a foreign market, realist threat to the U.S. market competitiveness cannot account for the bicultural exposure effect.

Interestingly, mortality salience did not lead to an unfavorable evaluation of the plan in the single culture exposure condition. This result seems to contradict past finding that mortality salience itself is enough to increase people's reluctance to use cultural icons in an inappropriate way (Greenberg et al., 1995). However, the dependent measure used in this study differs from those used in the past research. Past studies have examined reactions to clearly inappropriate use of cultural icons (e.g., using a crucifix as a hammer, see Greenberg et al., 1995). In this study, the marketing plan can be seen as an act of cultural contamination or as a marketing-savvy effort to increase the brand's appeal among foreign consumers. Past findings have shown that ambiguous marketing scenarios are typically not interpreted as threats to one's worldview (Nelson, Moore, Olivetti, & Scott, 1997). Instead, participants in the single culture exposure condition might have interpreted the marketing plan from a marketing perspective as opposed to a "cultural" perspective (see Tong, Pam, Kwan, & Peng, 2011), and hence did not react defensively to the plan following the mortality salience manipulation.

Although the pretest result in Experiment 1 indicated that running shoes are considered an iconic product in the United States, it can be argued that the reactions we observed in Experiment 3 are not specific to iconic U.S. products. Awareness of cultural contrast and mortality salience may lead to a blanket rejection of any attempts to incorporate foreign cultural elements in global marketing. To address this alternative interpretation, we conducted the next experiment to show that the effects we obtained in Experiment 3 resulted from participants' concern about the contamination effect of global marketing on American culture vis-à-vis iconic American brands.

Experiment 4

Method

The procedures were similar to those in Experiment 3, with the following exceptions. First, all participants (63 European American business students; 71.9% male; mean age $= 20.7$ years) rated the Chinese brands of products that are U.S. icons in the first part of the experiment. That is, all participants were put under the influence of bicultural exposure. Second, participants in the High Target Brand Iconicity Condition were presented with the Nike marketing plan in Experiment 3, whereas those in the Low Target Brand Iconicity Condition were presented with a marketing plan of Proctor-Silex (an American brand of bread toaster). The Proctor-Silex marketing plan was similar to the Nike plan, except for the following changes: (1) no mention about the "Swoosh," which is a Nike-specific feature, (2) the new brand name was changed from "Sportsmanship" to "Crusty" (in Arabic), (3) the endorsers in the advertisements sat in traditional Islamic kitchens and had breakfast using a "Crusty" bread toaster, and (4) the slogan used in the advertisement was changed from "Dress modestly, the Islamic spirit" to "Eat with family, the Islamic spirit" (in Arabic). A separate group of participants ($N = 22$) rated Nike and Proctor-Silex in terms of how much the brands were icons of American culture on a 7-point scale (see Experiment 2 pretest). Nike was rated as an icon of American culture ($M = 6.09$) and Proctor-Silex was not ($M = 1.91$), $t(21) = 14.34$, $p < .001$.

To extend the generality of our findings to actual behaviors, we used a new dependent measure. Instead of evaluating the plan, participants were asked to write a message supporting the new marketing plan, highlighting in the message all the potential benefits from the plan as if they were to convince the local allies in the Middle East. Two raters, who were blind to the participants' experimental condition, independently rated the essays in terms of its level of enthusiasm

(1 = very unenthusiastic, 7 = very enthusiastic). The two raters' ratings were highly correlated ($r = .91$) and were averaged to form the dependent measure.

Results and Discussion

We performed separate Mortality Salience X Target Brand Iconicity ANOVAs on positive affect ($\alpha = .85$), negative affect ($\alpha = .81$), and the number of words in the message. All Fs ≤ 1.18, ns. Next, we performed a Mortality Salience X Target Brand Iconicity ANOVA on the essays' level of enthusiasm and obtained a significant main effect of target brand iconicity, $F(1,63) = 5.22$, $p < .05$, $\eta^2_p = .076$; participants wrote more enthusiastic essays about the marketing plan of Proctor-Silex ($M = 4.58$, $SD = 1.31$) than that of Nike ($M = 3.72$, $SD = 1.79$). More importantly, the predicted interaction was significant, $F(1,63) = 4.58$, $p < .05$, $\eta^2_p = .068$. This interaction remained significant after controlling for positive affect, negative affect, and number of words in the essay, $F(1,60) = 6.82$, $p < .001$, $\eta^2_p = .186$. Consistent with our hypothesis, the essays supporting Nike's marketing plan were less enthusiastic in the Mortality Salient Condition ($M = 3.09$, $SD = 1.58$) than those in the Control Condition ($M = 4.35$, $SD = 1.80$), $F(1,32) = 4.73$, $p < .05$, $\eta^2_p = .129$. Also as predicted, the essays supporting Proctor-Silex's plan were similarly enthusiastic in Mortality Salient Condition ($M = 4.74$, $SD = 1.45$) and in the Control Condition ($M = 4.41$, $SD = 1.17$), $F(1,31) = 0.51$, ns. Furthermore, the level of enthusiasm in the Iconic Brand-Mortality Salient Condition was significantly lower than that in the remaining three experimental conditions ($ps < .05$).

Experiment 4 replicated the results of Experiment 3. After having evaluated foreign brands of iconic American products (and hence became more cognizant of cultural contrast), the participants displayed the mortality salience effect—when mortality was salient (vs. not salient), they were more concerned about the potential contamination of American culture vis-à-vis Nike (an iconic U.S. brand), and were less enthusiastic in supporting Nike's plan to incorporate foreign cultural elements to enhance its global competitiveness. However, when the target brand was not an iconic U.S. brand (Proctor-Silex), the mortality salience effect was not found.

Experiment 5

The primary objective of this study is to test the hypothesis that individuals high in need for cognition will think deeply about cultural similarities and differences, and correct the spontaneous cultural inferences produced by the bicultural exposure. A secondary objective is to further establish the generality of the bicultural exposure effect. Thus far, we have focused on the effects of bicultural exposure among European Americans. In Experiment 5, we recruited Hong Kong Chinese individuals as research participants and examined how simultaneous exposure to American and Chinese cultures would influence their perceptions of American and Chinese cultures. We hypothesized that bicultural exposure would increase the perceived differences between the two cultures, such that the participants would expect Chinese to hold stronger Chinese beliefs and Americans to hold stronger American beliefs.

Method

The participants were 117 Hong Kong Chinese undergraduates (28.2% male; mean age = 21.14 years) who received US$6.5 for their participation. We used the materials in the Chiu et al. (2009) to manipulate bicultural exposure. The participants were randomly assigned to one of the three experimental conditions. Participants in the American Culture Exposure Condition reviewed two print advertisements of McDonald's Hamburger and those in the Chinese Culture Exposure Condition reviewed two print advertisements of Chinese moon cake. Finally, participants in the Bicultural Exposure Condition viewed a McDonald's Hamburger advertisement and a moon cake advertisement. The participants indicated their evaluation of the advertisements on a scale from 0 (extremely dislikable) to 10 (extremely likable).

Next, the participants were given an "unrelated" social perception study. They were presented with descriptions of lay dispositionism and lay situationism taken from Norenzayan, Choi, and Nisbett (2002). The lay dispositionism item argues that personality determines and reliably predicts behaviors. Moreover, behaviors are remarkably stable across time and consistent across situations. In contrast, the lay situationism item argues that the situation determines behaviors and is a powerful predictor of behaviors, and that behaviors of the same person can vary drastically across situations. For each item, the participants estimated the extent to which European Americans in general and Hong Kong Chinese in general would agree with it. Previous research has shown that compared to each other, Asians believed more strongly in situationism and European Americans believed more strongly in dispositionism (Norenzayan et al., 2002). The participants recorded their estimations on a 9-point scale (1 = strongly disagree; 9 = strongly agree). The order of the American and Chinese estimations was counterbalanced. Because the goal of this study was not to replicate Norenzayan et al.'s (2002) cross-cultural results, we did not include measures of personal beliefs in dispositionism and situationism. Our key prediction here is that bicultural exposure (compared to single culture exposure) would increase the perceived difference between American and Chinese cultures, as evidenced by the beliefs attributed to members of each culture.

Toward the end of the study, the participants completed the 18-item Need for Cognition Scale (Cacioppo, Petty, & Kao, 1984; α = .87 in this study), which measures the extent to which individuals enjoy and engage in effortful cognitive activities. Sample items of the scale are: "I find satisfaction in deliberating hard and for long hours," and "I only think as hard as I have to" (reverse scored). Participants indicated their extent of agreement with each item on a 5-point scale ($1 =$ extremely unlike me; $5 =$ extremely like me). The culture exposure manipulation did not influence the need for cognition score, $F(2,114) = 1.54$, ns.

Results and Discussion

We performed a Culture Exposure (American, Chinese, or Bicultural) X Belief (Dispositonism or situationism; within-subject factor) X Target (Americans or Chinese; within-subject factor) X Question Order ANOVA on the participants' estimated responses to the belief items. The predicted Culture Exposure X Belief X Target interaction was significant, $F(2,111) = 3.25$, $p < .05$, $\eta^2_p = .055$. Question order did not qualify these interactions, $Fs < 1.28$, ns. After controlling for evaluation of the advertisement, the Culture Activation X Belief X Target interaction remained significant, $F(2,109) = 3.21$, $p < .05$, $\eta^2_p = .055$.

To understand the nature of the Culture Activation X Belief X Target interaction, we performed a Belief X Target within-subject ANOVA separately for each cultural exposure condition. As predicted, the Belief X Target interaction was significant in the Bicultural Exposure Condition, $F(1,38) = 12.78$, $p < .001$, $\eta^2_p = .252$. Under the influence of bicultural exposure, participants perceived stronger agreement with dispositionism among Americans than Chinese [$M_{\text{Americans}} = 6.03$, $M_{\text{Chinese}} = 4.92$; $t(38) = 2.99$, $p < .01$], stronger agreement with situationism among Chinese than Americans [$M_{\text{Americans}} = 5.31$, $M_{\text{Chinese}} = 6.10$; $t(38) = 2.27$, $p < .05$], stronger agreement with dispositionism (vs. situationism) among Americans [$t(38) = 1.92$, $p = .06$], and the opposite pattern among Chinese [$t(38) = 2.90$, $p < .01$].

In the Chinese Culture Exposure Condition, the only significant effect was the main effect of belief, $F(1,38) = 5.07$, $p < .03$, $\eta^2_p = .118$. The participants expected stronger endorsement of dispositionism than situationism for both Americans [$M_{\text{dispositionism}} = 6.05$, $SD = 1.79$; $M_{\text{situationism}} = 5.26$, $SD = 1.57$] and Chinese [$M_{\text{dispositionism}} = 6.08$, $SD = 1.56$; $M_{\text{situationism}} = 5.74$, $SD = 1.62$]. In the American Culture Exposure Condition, no effects in Belief X Target ANOVA were significant, $Fs < 1.50$, ns.

Next, we examined whether need for cognition attenuated the perceptual effects of dual cultural activation. We performed a Culture Exposure X Belief X Target X Need for Cognition (continuous predictor, mean-centered) General Linear Model (GLM) on the estimated responses to the belief items. The four-way interaction was significant, $F(2,111) = 3.88$, $p < .05$, $\eta^2_p = .065$. This interaction remained significant after controlling for evaluation of the advertisement, $F(2,110) = 3.87$, $p < .05$, $\eta^2_p = .066$.

To understand the nature of this interaction, we performed a separate Belief X Target X Need for Cognition GLM on the estimated responses to the belief items for each cultural exposure condition. The Belief X Target X Need for Cognition interaction was significant in the Bicultural Exposure Condition, $F(1,37) = 7.18$, $p = .01$, $\eta^2_p = .161$, but not in the other two cultural exposure conditions, $Fs < 1.39$, ns. Simple slope analysis was performed to understand the nature of the Belief X Target X Need for Cognition interaction in the Bicultural Exposure Condition. The Belief X Target interaction was significant when Need for Cognition was low (one standard deviation below the mean), $F(1,37) = 21.10$, $p < .001$, $\eta^2_p = .363$, but not when it was high (one standard deviation above the mean), $F(1,37) = 1.04$, ns. This result indicates that Need for Cognition attenuated the bicultural exposure effect on perceived cultural contrast, possibly because participants high in Need for Cognition had elaborated on cultural similarities and differences. In the next study, we tested this possibility more directly by manipulating the degree of elaboration on cultural complexities.

Experiment 6

Method

The procedures were similar to those in Experiment 2, with the following exceptions. First, all participants (49 European American business students; 40% male; mean age $= 21.1$ years) rated the British brands of iconic Mexican products in the first part of the experiment. This procedure put all participants under the influence of bicultural exposure. Second, the elaboration manipulation, developed on the basis of the need for cognition construct (Cacioppo & Petty, 1982), was introduced after the product evaluation task to engage half of the participants in the type of thoughtful elaboration driven by the need for cognition. All participants performed the same drawing task in Experiment 2. Whereas those in the Elaboration Condition completed the task while prompted to think carefully about the complexity of intercultural relationships, those in the Control Condition performed the drawing task without this instruction.

Results and Discussion

A Cognitive Elaboration (Elaboration or Control) X Cultural Similarity (similar or dissimilar cultures; within-subject factor) ANOVA performed on the two cultural distance measures revealed a significant main effect of cultural similarity, $F(1,38) = 134.73$, $p < .001$, $\eta^2_p = .78$. Participants drew the bubbles representing dissimilar cultures ($M = 275.28$, $SD = 105.13$) farther apart than they did the bubbles representing similar cultures ($M = 84.88$, $SD = 50.91$). More importantly, the Cognitive Elaboration X Cultural Similarity interaction was significant, $F(1,38) = 4.55$, $p < .05$, $\eta^2_p = .107$. This interaction remained significant after controlling for participants' familiarity with the cultures and their average evaluation of the products, $F(1,36) = 4.96, p < .05, \eta^2_p = .121$. Participants drew the bubbles representing dissimilar cultures farther apart in the Control Condition ($M = 319.75, SD = 107.05$) than they did when prompted to elaborate on cultural complexities ($M = 230.80, SD = 84.04$), $F(1,38) = 8.54, p < .01, \eta^2_p = .184$. There were no differences in the distance between the bubbles representing similar cultures in the two elaboration conditions (for the Elaboration Condition: $M = 75.40$, $SD = 33.93$; for the Control Condition: $M = 94.35, SD = 63.09, p > .2$).

Results from this experiment again showed that exposure of products that embody symbols of two outgroup cultures enlarged perceived distances of dissimilar cultures. The results also confirmed the hypothesis that engaging in thoughtful elaboration on cultural complexities attenuates the bicultural exposure effect on perceived cultural contrast. In the next experiment, we tested whether need for cognition also moderates the consequence of the joint effect of bicultural exposure and mortality salience on subsequent judgments.

Experiment 7

Method

One hundred and twelve European-American business students (44.6% males; mean age = 20.9 years) participated in the experiment for course credit. The procedures were similar to those in Experiment 4, with the following exceptions. First, to ensure that realist threat is not the primary driver of the bicultural exposure effect, we used a bicultural exposure procedure that did not present a realist threat to the American participants. Specifically, we put all participants under the influence of bicultural exposure by means of presenting them with an "artsy collage" depicting symbols of the United States and China side-by-side. The participants were asked to write down anything that came to mind while seeing the collage. Second, we further standardized the stimulus materials in the two brand iconicity conditions by changing the slogans of both the Nike and Proctor-Silex marketing plans to: "Do it your way, the Islamic spirit" (both plans had the same slogan). This change ensured that the participants would respond to the same slogan in both conditions. Third, instead of writing an essay supporting the plan, participants evaluated the marketing plan on the same items used in Experiment 3 ($\alpha = .78$). Finally, at the end of the questionnaire, participants completed the 18-item need for cognition scale ($\alpha = .84$).

Results and Discussion

We performed separate Mortality Salience X Brand Iconicity ANOVAs on positive affect ($\alpha = .73$) and negative affect ($\alpha = .76$). All $Fs \leq .97$, ns.

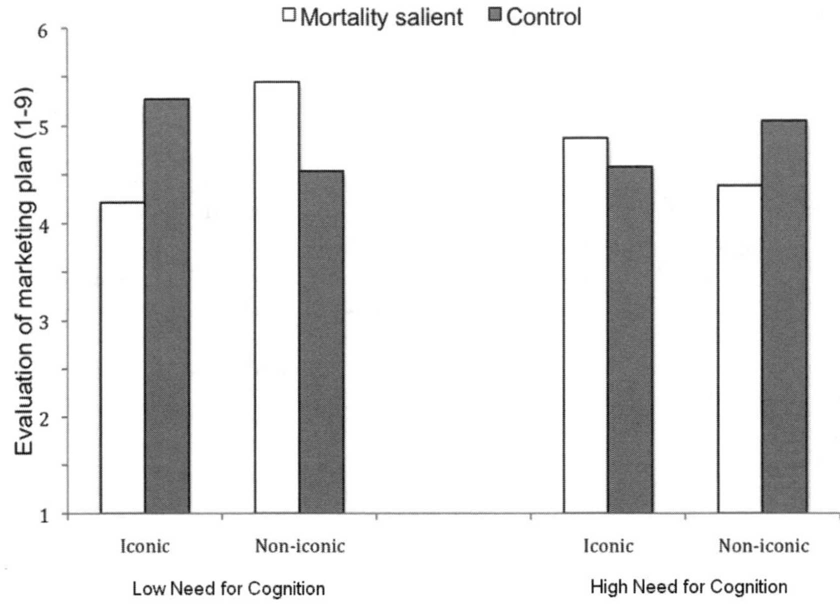

Fig. 1. Evaluation of marketing plan as a function of brand iconicity, mortality salience, and need for cognition (Experiment 7).

To test our hypothesis, we performed a Mortality Salience X Brand Iconicity X the average Need for Cognition score (mean-centered) GLM on the evaluation of the marketing plan. The predicted Mortality Salience X Brand Iconicity X Need for Cognition interaction was significant, $\beta = .86$, $t(104) = 2.85$, $p < .005$.

As depicted in Figure 1, when Need for Cognition was low (one standard deviation below the mean), participants in the Mortality Salient Condition ($M = 4.21$) evaluated Nike's marketing plan more negatively than those in the Control Condition ($M = 5.27$), $t(104) = 2.26$, $p < .05$. In contrast, when Need for Cognition was high (one standard deviation above the mean), participants evaluated Nike's plan similarly in the Mortality Salient condition ($M = 4.86$) and the Control condition ($M = 4.57$), $p > .5$. For Proctor-Silex's marketing plan, participants evaluated the plan similarly in the Mortality Salient condition and Control condition regardless of whether Need for Cognition was low ($M = 5.44$ and 4.53, respectively, $p > .1$) or high ($M = 4.38$ and 5.04, respectively, $p > .2$).

In summary, Experiment 7 results showed that need for cognition, a chronic tendency to engage in thoughtful elaboration, can attenuate the joint effects of bicultural exposure and mortality salience. Following bicultural exposure, only participants low in need for cognition displayed the mortality salience effect; these participants reacted defensively to the potential contamination of American culture vis-à-vis Nike (an iconic U.S. brand) when mortality was salient than when it was not. However, when the target brand was not an iconic U.S. brand (Proctor-Silex), the mortality salience effect was not found regardless of participants' need for cognition scores.

General Discussion

Globalization is a complex process with many different facets. It also has far-reaching impacts on both nations and individuals. This research focuses on one small aspect of globalization: Simultaneous exposure to symbols of multiple cultures in a globalized economy. Because the globalizing space in many parts of the world is richly ornamented with symbols of multiple cultures, research on the social cognitive effects of multicultural exposure is strategically located at the intersection of globalization, culture, and psychology—an unexplored frontier in current social psychological investigations. In seven experiments, we showed that when a commercial product embodies symbols of two dissimilar cultures (as in the case of a Chinese brand of an iconic U.S. product or a British brand of a Mexican product), the product becomes a stimulus that can activate representations of both cultures simultaneously. Consistent with previous theoretical and empirical analyses of the effect of bicultural exposure (Chiu & Cheng, 2007; Chiu et al., 2009), we found that exposure to such products renders culture a salient organizing construct for perceiving culturally pertinent information. Such exposure also increases the perceiver's tendency to attribute characteristic values and beliefs of the activated cultures to members of the respective culture and hence increases perceptions of cultural differences (Experiments 2, 5, and 6) and cultural incompatibility (Experiment 1).

Because initial evidence for the bicultural exposure effect came from studies comparing the perceptual effects of simultaneously presenting symbols of ingroup and outgroup cultures to the perceivers, it was unclear whether the effect always involves self-categorization. Evidence from Experiments 1, 2, and 6 showed that self-categorization is not necessary for the bicultural exposure effect to take place. First, having weak cultural identification does not weaken the bicultural exposure effect (Experiment 1). Second, exposure to two outgroup cultures also increases perceived cultural difference (Experiments 2 and 6).

Because bicultural exposure increases the perceived incompatibility of cultures, the perceiver under the influence of bicultural exposure is vulnerable to its psychological consequences. In Experiments 3 and 4, we found that only after bicultural exposure, participants were more likely to display defensive responses to "cultural contamination" of an iconic U.S. brand when they felt the need to manage their existential fear than when they did not. Finally, although we found a bicultural exposure effect across experiments, thoughtful elaboration about cultural complexities (due to chronic tendencies, Experiments 5 and 7, or situation-induced,

Experiment 6) ameliorates this effect on perceptions of cultures as well as its joint effect with mortality salience on reaction to cultural contamination.

Our results also show that exposure to foreign culture alone does not have the same effect as bicultural exposure. When the American participants in Experiments 1 and 3 were exposed to Chinese culture only, or when the Chinese participants in Experiment 5 were exposed to U.S. culture only, they did not exhibit the perceptual and defensive responses as the participants in the bicultural exposure condition did. In short, simultaneous exposure to two cultures seems to be an important aspect of globalization that has far reaching cultural and psychological consequences.

Implications for the Cultural Impacts of Globalization

With the rapid progress of globalization, the possible consequences of cultural contacts have become a major issue in the heated debates in many public forums and the academia. Thus far, social psychologists have remained relatively silent on this issue (Chiu & Cheng, 2007). The research reported in this article is among the first few research endeavors in social psychology to systematically address this issue. By focusing on the social cognitive consequences of multicultural exposure, this research has shed some light on when exposure to foreign culture can incite exclusionary responses. As such, this research provides a new behavioral science perspective on the current debates that have arisen over the psychological impacts of intercultural contacts in the context of globalization.

Furthermore, previous research on the psychological effects of cultural exposure has relied heavily on qualitative research methods. This research suggests that it is possible to develop experimental paradigms to study the experiences of foreign cultural exposure in a laboratory setting. These paradigms will allow researchers to make precise observations on how exposure to two cultures simultaneously may affect an individual's psychological processes in controlled experiments. The psychological principles derived from such observations will explain and predict variations in people's psychological reactions to foreign cultures.

Our results have important policy implications on international relations and international business. For instance, in international business, our results draw attention to the importance of managing cultural symbolisms in cross-border business transactions, including introduction of new brands of culturally symbolic products, and merge and acquisition of culturally symbolic brands (Tong et al., 2011). Business practitioners can avoid evoking strong exclusionary reactions to foreign or global business in cross-border transactions by deepening understanding of cultural complexities rather than focusing local consumers on simplistic, essential differences between cultures. Our findings also draw attention to the effect of globalization via bicultural priming on increased political volatility. For example, our results can explain the surprising win by an anti-immigration party of its first parliamentary seat in Swedish election, after running political messages juxtaposing symbols of Muslim and Swedish cultures (i.e., women in black burqas along a frail blond pensioner).

Future Directions and Conclusion

Globalization increases the frequency of cultural contacts that can lead to integrative or exclusionary responses to foreign culture (Chiu et al., 2011). Thus, how individuals manage their reactions to the cultural impacts of globalization is a research topic that requires urgent research attention. It is important to identify the controlling stimuli and personality determinants of the exclusionary responses, as well as their downstream cognitive and motivational consequences. Our results suggest that the motivation to engage in thoughtful elaboration about cultural complexities can "cool down" exclusionary responses triggered by bicultural exposure. Although the need for cognition may be related to nationalism or political conservatism, Experiment 1 results show that American cultural identification measured with an established nationalism/patriotism scale, did not moderate the bicultural priming effect. Thus, it is unlikely that the cooling effect of need for cognition in Experiments 5–7 is ideologically driven. Nonetheless, we do not exclude the possibility that some ideological factors could moderate exclusionary responses through their associations with cognitive complexity (see Jost, Glaser, Kruglanski, & Sulloway, 2003). This possibility merits future research.

The over sampling of American college students is a limitation in this research. The robust bicultural priming effects obtained among Hong Kong Chinese in Experiment 5 and in past research (Chiu et al., 2009), including field studies conducted in the context of the 2008 Beijing Olympics (Cheng et al., 2011), indicates that our results may not be culture-dependent. In addition, field research that assessed the psychological effects of frequency of bicultural priming by comparing perceptions of foreign cultures of community samples in cosmopolitan cities and suburban environments (Chen & Chiu, 2010) have provided further evidence for the generality of our results beyond college samples.

Cultural contacts can also elicit integrative reactions to foreign culture by bolstering cognitive complexity. For example, through exposure to multiple cultures, individuals may develop complex understandings of cultural differences (Benet-Martinez, Lee, & Leu, 2006), and hence be less likely to exhibit the exclusionary responses triggered by bicultural priming. In addition, multicultural exposure may lead individuals to view the newly arrived foreign cultures as intellectual resources that complement their heritage culture for achieving valued goals. These individuals are willing to appropriate ideas from foreign cultures to generate creative solutions to a problem (Leung & Chiu, 2010). Nonetheless, mere exposure to foreign cultures does not always lead to creative benefits

(Leung & Chiu, 2010). Future research is needed to understand when multicultural experience will lead to empowering and constructive self-transformational experience.

References

Aaker, J. L., & Schmitt, B. (2001). Culture-dependent assimilation and differentiation of the self: Preferences for consumption symbols in the United States and China. *Journal of Cross-Cultural Psychology, 32*, 561–576. doi: 10.1177/0022022101032005003.

Arndt, J., Greenberg, J., Solomon, S., Pyszczynski, T., & Simon L. (1997), Suppression, accessibility of death-related thoughts, and cultural worldview defense: Exploring the psychodynamics of terror management. *Journal of Personality and Social Psychology, 73*, 5–18. doi: 10.1037/0022–3514.73.1.5.

Benet-Martinez, V., Lee, F., & Leu, J. (2006). Biculturalism and cognitive complexity: Expertise in cultural representations. *Journal of Cross-Cultural Psychology, 37*, 386–407. doi: 10.1177/0022022106288476.

Briley, D. A., & Aaker, J. L. (2006). When does culture matter? Effects of personal knowledge on the correction of culture-based judgments. *Journal of Marketing Research, 43*, 395–408. doi: 10.1509/jmkr.43.3.395.

Cacioppo, T. J. & Petty, R. E. (1982). The need for cognition. *Journal of Personality and Social Psychology, 42*, 116–131. doi: 10.1037/0022–3514.42.1.116.

Cacioppo, J. T., Petty, R. E., & Kao, C. E. (1984). The efficient assessment of need for cognition. *Journal of Personality Assessment, 48*, 306–307. doi: 10.1207/s15327752jpa4803_13.

Chen, X., & Chiu, C-y. (2010). Rural-urban differences in generation of Chinese and Western exemplary persons: The case of China. *Asian Journal of Social Psychology, 13*, 9–18. doi: 10.1111/j.1467–839X.2010.01296.x.

Cheng, S. Y. Y., Rosner, J., Chao, M., Chiu, C-y., Hong, Y-y., Chen, X., Kwong, J. Y. Y., Li, Y., & Peng, S. (2011). One world, one dream? Intergroup consequences of the 2008 Beijing Olympics. *International Journal of Intercultural Relations, 35*, 296–306, doi: 10.1016/j.ijintrel.2010.07.005.

Chiu, C-y. (2007). Managing cultures in a multicultural world: A social cognitive perspective. *Journal of Psychology in Chinese Societies, 8*, 101–120.

Chiu, C-y., & Cheng, S. Y-y. (2007). Toward a social psychology of culture and globalization: Some social cognitive consequences of activating two cultures simultaneously. *Social and Personality Psychology Compass, 1*, 84–100. doi: 10.1111/j.1751–9004.2007.00017.x.

Chiu, C-y., Gries, P., Torelli, C. J., & Cheng, S. Y.-y. (2011). Toward a social psychology of globalization. *Journal of Social Issues, 67*, 663–676. doi: 10.1111/j.1540-4560.2011.01724.x.

Chiu, C-y., & Hong, Y-y. (2006). *Social psychology of culture*. New York: Psychology Press.

Chiu, C-y., Mallorie, L., Keh, H. T., & Law, W. (2009). Perceptions of culture in multicultural space: Joint presentation of images from two cultures increases in-group attribution of culture-typical characteristics. *Journal of Cross-Cultural Psychology, 40*, 282–300. doi: 10.1177/0022022108328912.

Florack, A., Scarabis, M., & Bless, H. (2001). When do associations matter? The use of automatic associations toward ethnic groups in person judgements. *Journal of Experimental Social Psychology, 37*, 518–524. doi: 10.1006/jesp.2001.1477.

Fu, H-y., & Chiu, C-y. (2007). Local culture's responses to globalization: Exemplary persons and their attendant values. *Journal of Cross-Cultural Psychology, 38*, 636–653. doi: 10.1177/0022022107305244.

Giddens, A. (1985). *The nation state and violence*. Cambridge: Polity Press.

Greenberg, J., Porteus, J., Simon, L., & Pyszczynski, T. (1995). Evidence of a terror management function of cultural icons: The effects of mortality salience on the inappropriate use of cherished cultural symbols. *Personality and Social Psychology Bulletin, 21*, 1221–1228. doi: 10.1177/01461672952111010.

Greenberg, J., Solomon, S., & Pyszczynski, T. (1997). Terror management theory of self-esteem and cultural worldviews: Empirical assessments and conceptual refinements. In M. P. Zanna (Ed.), *Advances in experimental social psychology* (Vol. 29. pp. 61–139). San Diego, CA: Academic Press. doi:10.1016/S0065–2601%2808%2960016—7.

Hogg, M. A. (2004). Social identity, self-categorization, and communication in small groups. In S. H. Ng, C. N. Candlin, & C-y. Chiu (Eds.), *Language matters: Communication, culture, and identity* (pp. 221–243). Hong Kong: City University of Hong Kong Press. doi: 10.1111/j.1468–2885.2006.00003.x.

Hong, Y-y., Morris, M. W., Chiu, C-y., & Benet-Martinez, V. (2000). Multicultural minds: A dynamic constructivist approach to culture and cognition. *American Psychologist, 55*, 709–720. doi: 10.1037/0003–066X.55.7.709.

Jost, J. T., Glaser, J., Kruglanski, A. W., & Sulloway, F. J. (2003). Political conservatism as motivated social cognition. *Psychological Bulletin, 129*, 339–375. doi: 10.1037/0033–2909.129.3.339.

Kosterman, R., & Feshbach, S. (1989). Toward a measure of patriotic and nationalistic attitudes. *Political Psychology, 10*, 257–274. doi: 10.2307/3791647.

Leung, A. K-y., & Chiu, C-y. (2010). Multicultural experience, idea receptiveness, and creativity. *Journal of Cross-Cultural Psychology, 41*(5–6), 723–741. doi: 10.1177/0022022110361707.

McGregor, H. A., Lieberman, J. D., Greenberg, J., Solomon, S., Arndt, J., Simon, L., & Pyszczynski, T. (1998). Terror management and aggression: Evidence that mortality salience motivates aggression against worldview-threatening others. *Journal of Personality and Social Psychology, 74*, 590–605. doi: 10.1037/0022–3514.74.3.590.

Nelson, L. J., Moore, D. L., Olivetti, J., & Scott, T. (1997), General and personal mortality salience and nationalistic bias, *Personality and Social Psychology Bulletin, 23*, 884–92. doi: 10.1177/0146167297238008.

Norenzayan, A., Choi, I., & Nisbett, R. E. (2002). Cultural similarities and differences in social inference: Evidence from behavioral predictions and lay theories of behavior. *Personality and Social Psychology Bulletin, 28*, 109–120. doi: 10.1177/0146167202281010.

Ortner, S., B. (1973). On key symbols. *American Anthropologist, 75*, 1338–1346.

Robertson, R. (1995). Globalization: Time-space and homogeneity-heterogeneity. In M. Featherson, S. Lash, & R. Robertson (Eds.), *Global modernities* (pp. 25–44). London: Sage.

Rosenblatt, A., Greenberg, J., Solomon, S., Pyszczynski, T., & Lyon, D. (1989). Evidence for terror management theory: I. The effects of mortality salience on reactions to those who violate or uphold cultural values. *Journal of Personality and Social Psychology, 57*, 681–90. doi: 10.1037/0022–3514.57.4.681.

Torelli, C. J., Keh, H. T., & Chiu, C.-Y. (2010). Cultural symbolism of brands. In B. Loken, R. Ahluwalia & M. J. Houston (Eds.), *Brands and brand management: Contemporary research perspectives* (pp. 113–132). New York: Routledge.

Tong, J. Y. Y., Pam, P. P-Z., Kwan, L., & Peng, S. (2011). National feelings or rational dealings? The moderating role of procedural priming on perceptions of cross-border acquisitions. *Journal of Social Issues, 67*, 743–759. doi: 10.1111/j.1540–4560.2011.01725.x.

Turner, J. C., Hogg, M. A., Oakes, P. J., Reicher, S. D., & Wetherell, M. (1987). *Rediscovering the social group: A self-categorization theory*. Oxford: Basil Blackwell.

Watson, D., & Clark, L. A. (1992). Affects separable and inseparable On the hierarchical arrangement of the negative affects. *Journal of Personality and Social Psychology, 62*, 489–505. doi: 10.1037/0022–3514.62.3.489

CARLOS J. TORELLI is Assistant Professor of Marketing at the Carlson School of Management, University of Minnesota. He has a PhD in Business Administration from the University of Illinois at Urbana-Champaign. His research focuses on cross-cultural consumer behavior, global branding, motivated information-processing, and persuasion.

CHI-YUE CHIU received his PhD from Columbia University and is the Executive Director of the Culture Science Institute and Research Director of the National Institute on Consumer Insight at Nanyang Technological University in Singapore.

KIM-PONG TAM received his PhD from the University of Hong Kong and is currently an Assistant Professor at the Division of Social Science, Hong Kong University of Science and Technology. He is interested in understanding how people perceive their own culture and other cultures and the psychological implications of such perceptions.

AL K. C. AU received his PhD from the University of Hong Kong and is an Assistant Professor at the Department of Psychology, National University of Singapore. His primary research interests are interpersonal processes including conflict, negotiation, and leader-member exchange in organizational and social contexts.

HEAN TAT KEH received his PhD in Marketing from the University of Washington. He is a Professor of Marketing at the UQ Business School, University of Queensland, Australia. His research interests include services marketing, brand management, strategic marketing, and cross-cultural research.

Journal of Social Issues, Vol. 67, No. 4, 2011, pp. 743–759

National Feelings or Rational Dealings? The Role of Procedural Priming on the Perceptions of Cross-Border Acquisitions

Yuk-yue Tong*

Singapore Management University

Pamsy Pun-Zee Hui

Chinese University of Hong Kong

Letty Kwan

University of Illinois at Urbana-Champaign

Siqing Peng

Peking University

Cross-border transactions are often perceived by the general public as national threats instead of rational business deals. We propose two interpretational mindsets that attenuate (transactional mindset) and agitate (categorization mindset) these culturally motivated responses. Three studies were conducted in Singapore and the United States with various cross-border acquisition scenarios. As predicted, transactional mindset, which centers around cost–benefit calculations, nudged participants to evaluate the foreign acquisition more rationally and evoked fewer social–cultural considerations than categorization mindset, which focuses on categorizing and comparison procedures, and when no mindset was primed. Furthermore, the effects of categorization mindset are particularly strong when one perceives the two transacting parties as dissimilar and when he/she identifies closely with the local culture. We conclude that while economic

*Correspondence concerning this article should be addressed to Yuk-yue Tong, School of Social Sciences, Singapore Management University, 90 Stamford Road, Singapore 178903 [e-mail: jtong@smu.edu].

This research was supported by a grant C242/MSS6E015 from Singapore Management University awarded to the first author. The authors are grateful to Ying-yi Hong and Daphna Oyserman for their helpful advice.

activities such as cross-border acquisitions can inadvertently evoke nationalistic reactions, it is possible to mitigate them or even encourage rational evaluations by influencing people's interpretational mindset.

Cross-border economic transactions are curiously contradictory. On one hand, they provide organizations and their stakeholders means to explore ideas and opportunities that are otherwise not present locally; on the other hand, they often evoke culturally motivated exclusionary reactions, stunting these very exchanges. Despite findings confirming myriad factors that can anchor decisions (for extensive reviews, see Shiller, 2005; Thaler & Sunstein, 2008), theories and research pertaining to economic transactions have clung onto the notion that economic actors are generally rational, dismissing social–cultural considerations and other so-called market anomalies as "curiosity items" of no real importance, being born out of methodological illusions (Fama, 1998; Krugman, 2009). As a result, research on international business has tended to build on the assumption that transactions between social groups are driven primarily by cool calculations. If a deal is mutually beneficial to both sides of the transaction, it will happen in a relatively frictionless manner, with hardly a role for stakeholders who are indirectly affected or seemingly unaffected by the deal (e.g., the general public).

Yet, time and again, the world witnesses initially innocuous and sensible international transactions quickly descending into episodes that evoke strong national feelings among individuals outside the exchanges, resulting in protectionist sentiments and reactions that bring unfavorable outcomes for all parties involved. The proposed acquisition of a privately owned Chinese juice-maker, Huiyuan by Coca-Cola of the United States, and the intended investment from Chinalco, an aluminum company in China in its Australian peer, Rio Tinto were two such cases (Powell, 2009). Both were considered mutually beneficial transactions for the organizations involved, but both evoked negative nationalistic sentiments among people who were not directly affected by the transactions, leading to prolonged and costly negotiations and devastating outcomes, such as a government blockage of the deal and plummeting share prices, as in the Huiyuan case. Hence, the social–cultural implications of economic transactions of ostensibly irrelevant stakeholders are anything but trivial. These culturally motivated exclusions of cross-border transactions between iconic organizations are a form of exclusionary reactions to the global culture (Chiu, Gries, Torelli, & Cheng, 2011), and we seek to identify psychological factors that can mitigate such reactions.

Cognitive processes, such as categorization (i.e., a "us versus them" intergroup comparisons), can heavily influence rational calculations when exchanges occur between social groups. Categorization tends to be triggered if the transacting parties are highly iconic representatives of their respective social groups, as Coca-Cola is of the United States (Torelli, Chiu, Tam, Au, & Keh, 2011). This is because these organizations are perceived as more than just pure economic actors.

Symbols, languages, narratives, and practices that are uniquely attributed to iconic organizations signify their values and ideologies, and reminds people of their impressions of the specific cultures from which these organizations originated (Chiu & Hong, 2006). Thus, seeing the golden arches may remind people of McDonald's corporate culture, as well as evoking their impressions of the American culture, be it accurate or stereotypical. When two organizations iconic to their respective social groups appear side-by-side in a transaction, it is likely that the impressions of the cultures from these two social groups are activated simultaneously and heightens the awareness of the difference between cultures (Chiu, Mallorie, Keh, & Law, 2009). In a situation where an iconic local organization is involved, stakeholders who are otherwise not directly involved in the transaction will feel that "one of their own" is dealing with a certain foreign entity. They will feel personal connection to the transaction and react according to their assessments of the well-being of "one of their own."

If such culturally motivated reactions of stakeholders can wreak havoc on sensible transactions, it will then be helpful to understand the conditions in which these reactions are mitigated or amplified. The basic premise for our studies is that the emotional reactions toward and the approval of cross-border acquisitions between iconic organizations often hinge on the two factors: The first factor is the mindset through which individuals perceive and interpret the information about the transaction (i.e., interpretational mindset). Individuals induced to focus on economic details (i.e., transactional mindset) will tend to accept deals that bring economic gains and disapprove deals that make little economic sense. Those induced to rely heavily on "us versus them" intergroup comparisons and social–cultural implications of the acquisitions (i.e., categorization mindset), however, tend to be highly agreeable to culturally compatible acquisitions but are likely to reject deals that appear to threaten the local cultures; The second factor is whether an individual has the heightened feeling that his/her cultural identity is threatened when perceiving an acquisition through a categorization mindset. We propose that under the categorization mindset, individuals are more likely to perceive their cultural identity threatened, and thus, react according to social–cultural considerations if they perceive cultural dissimilarity between the two organizations (i.e., the local culture is at risk of being contaminated) and if they identify closely to the local culture (i.e., it is "their" culture to defend). In the following sections we will further elaborate on the premise discussed.

Interpretational Mindset as Attention Guide

Interpretational mindset—the cognitive procedures through which individuals perceive and interpret information—is moldable via procedural priming (Navon, 1977; Smith, 1994). A cognitive procedure may be conceptualized as a set of cognitive operations that characterize the performance of a particular task

(Higgins, 1989). Frequent or recent use of certain cognitive procedures increases the propensity to use the same procedures on a subsequent task (Förster, Liberman, & Shapira, 2009; Kirmani, Lee, & Yoon, 2004). In other words, it represents the "how" of task performance in cognitive terms. For example, if induced to pay attention to positive (vs. negative) aspects of a list of choices, people tend to judge things more favorably (vs. unfavorably) in a subsequent unrelated situation (Shen & Wyer, 2008). Such a procedural priming process has been demonstrated in various settings (Liberman & Trope, 1998; Mussweiler, 2002; Mussweiler & Epstude, 2009; Navon, 1977; Vallacher & Wegner, 1989).

We posit that the perception and interpretation of a cross-border acquisition can be influenced much in the same way through procedural priming. Specifically, we attempted to induce participants to understand the same cross-border acquisition by directing their attention to different aspects of the transaction. Two distinct interpretational mindsets are identified: transactional mindset, which focuses on cost–benefit calculations, and categorization mindset, which is dominated by categorizing and comparing objects and people. In the three studies discussed later, participants received a transactional prime, a categorization prime, or no prime prior to the presentation of a cross-border acquisition case. The transactional prime comprises five items of cost–benefit calculations (e.g., whether it makes more economic sense to get a soda (i) at a supermarket nearby for $4.5 or (ii) at another supermarket for $4.5 but at a $0.75 bus trip away) that activated procedural knowledge to understand or analyze with economic considerations. The categorization prime comprises five items of stereotype-matching that activated stereotypes concerning occupation, food choice, and countries (e.g., Alvin wears t-shirts and jeans to work everyday. It is more likely that Alvin's occupation is (i) marketing executive, or (ii) software engineer). In the face of a cross-border acquisition, a transactional mindset gears the understanding and interpretation of the case away from categorization and toward economic considerations, leading to high approval of the transaction if it had economic merits. In contrast, a categorization mindset will amplify the categorization process triggered by the juxtaposition of two cultural icons, nudging participants to analyze the acquisition in terms of cultural matches and mismatches. As social–cultural considerations take the front seat, a transaction deemed threatening to one's culture might be rejected despite its economic merits.

Conditions that Heighten the Perceived Threats to Cultural Identity

Directing attention to social–cultural considerations by inducing a categorization mindset does not always trigger culturally motivated reactions. Culturally motivated reactions are likely to occur if the individual, after considering the social–cultural implications of the acquisition, perceives a threat to the integrity of his/her own cultural heritage. Such a perception is likely if: (1) the individual considers the foreign acquirers as culturally dissimilar to the local entity; and (2) he/she identifies closely with the local culture.

The sense that the integrity of one's cultural heritage is threatened by an acquisition tends to be heightened if the cultures represented by the transacting parties are perceived to be dissimilar. When the two transacting parties—the representatives of the two cultures—are considered similar, it is unlikely to evoke the feeling that one's culture is at risk of being contaminated, weakening the inclination to defend it despite tremendous amount of social–cultural considerations. Research has shown that in a condition where no more than one culture is clearly noticeable, as in the case of a table lamp—uncharacteristic of any culture—with a distinctively Chinese name, the juxtaposition of cultures and the subsequent reactions are unlikely (Torelli et al., 2011). In contrast, if one is exposed to entities that reflect two dissimilar cultures, as a bottle of Bordeaux wine with Chinese label does to French and Chinese cultures, concerns about the contamination of one's cultural heritage surface. One may begin to question, for instance, the authenticity of the bottle of wine, and the impact the Chinese label has on the purity of the French identity of Bordeaux wines in general.

One also tends to feel that the integrity of his/her cultural heritage is threatened by an acquisition if he/she identifies closely with one of the social groups involved in the deal. Individuals who identify closely with their social groups tend to regard ingroup members favorably and seek to distinguish themselves from outgroup members (Tajfel & Turner, 1979). Being closely identified with one's own social group and its culture makes categorization a natural process when the impression of one's own culture is juxtaposed against the impression of a foreign one. Moreover, it is unlikely for individuals to react defensively and impulsively against a transaction between two social groups if they are not personally attached to and invested in one of the social groups and its culture—especially if they are not an integral part of the transaction and will not be economically affected by it (Morris, Mok, & Mor, 2011).

We tested our hypotheses in Singapore and United States. Although both countries are globalized countries, the United States is a major exporter and Singapore a major importer of global business practices (Yang et al., 2011). That is, these two countries have gone through diverse experiences with globalization. If our hypotheses are confirmed in both countries, the results would suggest that the effect of cultural identity on interpretational mindset on reactions to cross-border acquisitions are independent of specific globalization experiences.

Study 1: McDonald's Acquiring Ya Kun in Singapore

We set out to test the abovementioned arguments in Study 1. Specifically, we hypothesize that when individuals encounter news of an iconic local organization being courted by a quintessential foreign organization, they tend to resort to social–cultural considerations if they maintain a categorization mindset instead of a transactional one. We expect the effects of categorization mindset to be present only among individuals who perceive the two organizations to be culturally dissimilar and identify themselves as locals. This is because the rest of the people do not perceive the local culture being threatened because the acquirer is not considered foreign enough, or do not perceive their own (i.e., nonlocal) cultural heritage threatened by the acquisition of a local organization.

Method

Two hundred and seven university undergraduates in Singapore (52.7% females, $M_{age} = 21.62$, 58% self-reported as Singaporeans and 42% as non-Singaporeans) participated in this study. The non-Singaporeans in the sample were foreign students who had stayed in Singapore between 2 and 6 years. Most of them came to study in Singapore and would return to their home country upon graduation. It is unlikely that they would develop a strong emotional link with local Singaporean companies. Hence, they made a good comparison group for evaluating the hypothesized effects of Singaporean (local) identity on culturally motivated reactions to the acquisition.

Participants were randomly assigned into the transactional mindset, categorization mindset, or no prime condition. Participants in the transactional and categorization mindset conditions were instructed to read and complete different sets of five questions. Those in the transactional mindset condition answered questions such as: (1) Mrs. Lim earns \$12/hour sewing at home. Today she will go to the wet market to buy fish. For each 5 minutes she bargains with the vendor, she can save \$1.25. Which is a better deal for her? (a) Bargain for 5 minutes, or (b) No bargain and work for extra 5 minutes; and (2) A latte at café costs \$3. Mei Ling is a regular customer who always orders latte. The café is now selling a coffee passport at \$14.9, with which Mei Ling can get six lattes. What should Mei Ling do to save money? (a) Buy the coffee passport, or (b) Not to buy the coffee passport. Those in the categorization mindset condition answered questions such as: (1) Alvin wears t-shirts and jeans to work everyday. What occupation do you think he is in? (a) Marketing executive, or (b) Software engineer; and (2) David is planning to take his girlfriend out for a nice, romantic Valentine's Day dinner. Ideally, the place should be quiet and the food should not be too messy to consume. He walks by an upscale hotel and saw two restaurants, one serving French cuisine, and the other, seafood. Which one should he pick? (a) French restaurant, or (b) Seafood restaurant. Those in the no prime condition were not given any question to answer.

Afterwards, all participants read a fictitious case titled "McDonald's in takeover talks with Ya Kun Kaya Toast," which described McDonald's, a dominant foreign company, initiating a hostile acquisition of Ya Kun Kaya Toast, an iconic, locally grown breakfast chain famous for toast and local-style coffee. The logos of the two organizations were on the top of the page to emphasize the identity of the two organizations. The scenario highlighted the possible economic benefits for both organizations as a result of the acquisition (e.g., Ya Kun gaining customer base and franchise capability, and McDonald's gaining sales and product offerings), as well as the cultural incompatibility between the two organizations (e.g., McDonald's highly American management style, and Ya Kun's Singaporean management culture). In other words, the scenario presented an ambiguous picture, with those focusing on economic benefits (cultural compatibility) evaluating the acquisition more (less) favorably.

After reading the scenario, participants answered questions with regards to their feelings and perceptions toward the acquisition. Participants rated on a 7-point scale whether they felt fear toward the acquisition (1 = *absolutely not*; 7 = *absolutely*). We were particularly interested in fear as a dependent measure because fear was elicited by the perceived threat from another individual (Frijda, Kuipers, & ter Schure, 1989) or outgroup (Stephan & Stephan, 2000). This emotion tended to occur toward groups viewed as competent but hostile (i.e., high in competence but low in warmth; Cuddy, Fiske, & Glick, 2007). In this study, McDonald's played the role of this hostile cultural outsider. We expected participants who perceived threats from its acquisition attempt to exhibit higher levels of fear than those who did not. Participants also rated how their impression toward Ya Kun would change if the acquisition occurred (1 = *much less favorable*; 7 = *much more favorable*). We computed the perceived similarity between the organizations by averaging the scores on perceived business compatibility and perceived cultural similarity between them ($r = .48$, $p < .001$, Cronbach's $\alpha = .64$).

A manipulation check was included at the end to see whether the mindset induced by procedural priming persisted throughout the study. The procedure followed closely to that of Torelli et al. (2011, Study 2). Participants were given three round stickers with the names "Lexus," "BMW," and "Nissan" to represent three commonly known automobile brands. Participants were instructed to freely arrange the stickers on a piece of paper to represent their perceived relationships among the brands. The clustering, measured by the distances among the labels, reflects the classification criteria—by perceived status (cost-oriented, with Lexus and BMW in a cluster) or by country of origin (culture-oriented, with Lexus and Nissan in a cluster). Participants with transactional (categorization) mindset should be more likely to organize the brands by status (country of origin).

Results and Discussion

For the manipulation check, the distances among stickers were measured and standardized for each participant. A transactional classification index was calculated by subtracting the standardized distance between Lexus and BMW

Table 1. Estimated Fear toward the Pending Acquisition and Change in Impression towards Ya Kun If Acquisition Took Place by Interpretational Mindset and Perceived Similarity between Organizations in Study 1

	Perceived similarity	Interpretational mindset		
		Transactional	Categorization	Control
Fear	Dissimilar (1 *SD* below the mean)	2.73	4.10	3.70
	Similar (1 *SD* above the mean)	3.51	2.84	3.26
Change in perception toward Ya Kun	Dissimilar (1 *SD* below the mean)	3.08	2.59	2.81
	Similar (1 *SD* above the mean)	3.40	4.02	4.22

from the standardized distance between Lexus and Nissan, with a higher value indicating clustering by status. Participants under transactional prime ($M = 1.07$) showed a greater tendency to cluster by status than those under categorization prime ($M = 0.37$), with those under no prime in between ($M = 0.65$; $F(2, 204) = 3.57, p < .05, \eta^2_p = .058$). This suggests that the procedural priming task was successful in guiding participants to different mindsets in understanding the same stimuli, and that the effects of the priming lasted throughout the whole study.

We performed regressions for the Singaporean and non-Singaporean samples separately, with interpretation mindset as two dummy variables (categorization mindset vs. transactional mindset; transactional mindset vs. control) and perceived similarity between the two organizations as a moderator. For Singaporeans, no main effect for interpretation mindset was found ($F(2, 117) = 0.89, ns$). Interpretational mindset and perceived similarity between organizations interacted to predict fear ($F(5, 114) = 2.60, p < .05, \eta^2_p = .10$) and change in impression toward Ya Kun after acquisition ($F(5, 114) = 8.88, p < .0001, \eta^2_p = .28$). Participants exhibited significantly more fear with categorization than transactional mindset if they perceived the two organizations to be more dissimilar ($B = 1.02$, $t(114) = -2.91, p < .005$, Table 1). To explore this interaction further, we performed regression for perceived similarity on fear separately for each interpretation mindset condition. Participants with categorization mindset were more fearful if they perceived the organizations to be less similar ($F(1, 36) = 9.50, p < .005$; $B = -0.63, t(36) = -3.08, p < .005$). No significant effect was found in the other conditions ($Bs < 0.22, ps > 0.20$).

As for their impression toward Ya Kun would change if the acquisition went through, participants with categorization mindset also reported significantly less favorable impression toward Ya Kun in case the acquisition took place than those with transactional mindset if they perceived the two organizations to be more dissimilar ($B = 0.56$, $t(114) = 2.19$, $p < .05$). Similarly, we explored whether perceived similarity between organizations had different effects for participants in different conditions. Participants with categorization mindset formed more favorable impression toward the postacquisition Ya Kun if they perceived the organizations to be more similar ($B = -0.71$, $t(36) = 4.34$, $p < .0001$). Participants in the control condition exhibited similar reactions ($B = -0.70$, $t(42) = 4.76$, $p < .0001$), but no effect was in the transactional prime condition ($B = 0.16$, $p > .41$). Finally, none of the abovementioned patterns was observed among non-Singaporean participants ($Bs < 0.74$, $ps > .29$).

In sum, the interaction effect of interpretational mindset and perceived similarity between the two organizations influenced the way the acquisition was perceived by Singaporeans. Those who viewed McDonald's and Ya Kun Kaya Toast as dissimilar reported more fear and less favorable attitude toward the acquisition if they also maintained a categorization mindset, and those who viewed the two organizations as similar reported the least unfavorable attitude toward the acquisition if they also maintained a transactional mindset. Non-Singaporeans, whose cultures were unlikely to be threatened by the acquisition, were not significantly influenced by interpretational mindset.

Study 2: Tata Motors Acquiring General Motors in the United States

Study 2 aimed to replicate the earlier findings with data from a different industry (automobile manufacturing) in a different country (United States). The study was conducted in the United States from late April to early May of 2009, when General Motors (GM) was at the brink of bankruptcy. Meanwhile, India had risen as a global economic power, and Tata Motors as a major player in the automobile manufacturing industry, developing the cheapest passenger car in the world and acquiring prestigious brands such as Jaguar and Land Rover. Yet, it remained relatively unknown in the United States. This provided a naturalistic platform for our study. This setting differed from Study 1 in two key aspects: (1) the local company (GM) being acquired in the current study was in a financial crisis while that of Study 1 (Ya Kun Kaya Toast) was financially healthy, putting the acquisition in the current study in a less hostile light and making the acquirer (Tata) a "white knight" instead of an aggressor; and (2) the foreign acquirer in the current study, Tata, though on the rise, was less well-known, less dominant, and probably less popular in the United States than McDonald's in Singapore. This created a scenario in which an iconic local organization is being "rescued" by a relatively unknown foreign entity. Despite these differences, we still expected a replication of the basic pattern in our findings—if people considered the two organizations dissimilar, those prodded to take the "us versus them" mentality were

Table 2. Estimated Fear toward the Pending Acquisition in Study 2

	Interpretational mindset		
	Transactional	Categorization	Control
Dissimilar (1 *SD* below the mean)	38.35	50.56	39.49
Similar (1 *SD* above the mean)	43.34	36.78	50.09

far from being enthused by the prospect of their own organizations being "rescued" by a foreign entity; instead, they would express fear toward the acquisition while hoping for less threatening resolutions.

Method

Participants were 121 undergraduates (42.5% females, $M_{age} = 19.41$) of a midwestern university in United States. The same procedural priming items as in Study 1 were used. Afterwards participants were asked to read and imagine vividly a scenario titled "India's Tata Motors in Takeover Talks with General Motors." The scenario described Tata's previous international acquisitions of other carmakers, the economic benefits for GM (e.g., financial support and survival) and for Tata (e.g., market GM cars in India and enter the American market); it also mentioned concerns for possible cultural clashes between the two companies. Participants then answered questions concerning their feelings and perceptions toward the acquisition, including the extent to which they felt fear toward the acquisition on a 100-point scale (0 = *absolutely not*; 100 = *absolutely*). They also rated the extent to which they perceived the cultures of GM and Tata to be similar (0 = *very dissimilar*; 100 = *very similar*).

Results and Discussion

As in Study 1, we performed regressions with interpretational mindset as two dummy variables and perceived similarity between organizations as a moderator. Although the general model for the interaction of interpretation mindset and perceived similarity was not significant ($F(5, 99) = 1.31$, *ns*), planned comparison results appeared to support our predictions. First, no main effect for interpretation mindset was found ($Bs < 3.95$, $ps > .51$). Participants with categorization than transactional mindset exhibited significantly more fear if they perceived the two organizations as more dissimilar ($B = -12.20$, $t(99) = -2.38$, $p < .05$, Table 2). We performed additional regressions with each interpretational mindset as a subsample to explore this interaction further. Participants with categorization mindset were marginally more likely to express fear if the perceived similarity between organizations was lower ($B = -6.89$, $t(39) = -2.00$, $p < .06$). No significant effect was found in the other conditions ($Bs < 5.30$, $ps > .19$). The results of Studies 1 and 2 corroborate each other. In the current study, participants with categorization (vs. transactional) mindset exhibited more fear only if they also considered GM and Tata dissimilar.

Study 3: McDonald's Acquiring Ya Kun in Singapore (Reversed Valence)

We propose the priming of interpretational mindset as a way of influencing people's understanding of an international transaction. Those primed with transactional mindset will comprehend the deal in terms of calculative economic factors. Thus far, we have portrayed acquisitions that appear to be culturally threatening but financially beneficial. As a result, we observed fewer emotional reactions and more favorable perceptions from participants under transactional prime. It is possible that these findings were results of the transactional prime muting emotional reactions and perceptions toward the acquisition rather than diverting participants' attention to different information. In other words, it is possible that participants with transactional mindset were simply rendered less emotional and more indifferent toward the acquisition. To rule out this alternative explanation, we conducted a study that resembled Study 1, but with the implications of the acquisition reversed. In this study, the acquisition of Ya Kun Kaya Toast by McDonald's was described as financially detrimental to both but with no cultural compatibility issue at all.

If transactional prime indeed served to divert attention toward cost–benefit calculations and not mute emotional reactions, participants under transactional prime would have their attention focused on potential economic losses of the acquisition and would feel worse about it than those under categorization prime. Instead of showing fewer negative emotions, the transaction-minded participants would display more negative emotions. This is particularly the case if these participants did not identify closely with Singapore, and thus, were less predisposed to pay attention to any of the positive-sounding social–cultural information in the first place. Presented with negative-sounding economic information about the pending acquisitions, these individuals were prone to express their disapproval.

Method

Ninety-nine university undergraduates (66% females, $M_{age} = 21.28$, 73% self-reported as Singaporeans and 27% as non-Singaporeans) in Singapore participated in this study. The same procedural priming items as in the previous studies were used. Afterwards participants were asked to read and imagine vividly a scenario titled "McDonald's in takeover talks with Ya Kun Kaya Toast." The scenario described how the acquisition would burden both organizations financially (e.g., growing debt burden, no net gain in customer base, and potential cannibalization

Table 3. Negative Emotions by Interpretational Mindset and Identification with Singapore in Study 3

	Interpretational mindset		
Identification with Singapore	Transactional	Categorization	Control
Not close (1 *SD* below the mean)	5.12	3.10	2.75
Close (1 *SD* below the mean)	3.34	3.12	4.17

of each other's businesses). Culturally, however, the two were said to be extremely compatible (e.g., similarly efficient business philosophies, management styles, and family-friendly images). Participants then answered questions about their feelings toward the acquisition, including the extent to which they felt angry, sad, upset, helpless, uncertain, and fearful (1 = *absolutely not*; 7 = *absolutely*). Due to uncertainty about the kind of emotions elicited by this reversed scenario, we included a broader range of emotions. A composite score was calculated by averaging the score for the individual negative emotions (Cronbach's α = .83). Participants were also asked to indicate the extent to which they identified with Singapore (1 = *very distantly*; 7 = *very closely*).

Results and Discussion

Regressions were performed with interpretational mindset as two dummy variables (as in Studies 1 and 2) and identification with Singapore as a moderator on positive and negative emotions. The results provide general support to our predictions. Table 3 presents the effects of interpretational mindset on negative emotions for participants with varying degrees of identification to Singapore. The main effect for interpretational mindset was not significant ($F(2, 70) = 1.88$, *ns*). The interaction of Singapore identification and interpretation mindset was significant, ($F(5, 67) = 5.56, p < .0001, \eta^2_p = .29$). Participants with transactional mindset reported more negative emotions than those in the control condition ($B = -1.28$, $t(67) = -4.45$, $p < .0001$) and categorization mindset condition ($B = -1.13, t(67) = -2.35, p < .05$) if they identified less closely with Singapore. We explored this interaction further by performing regressions on the relationships between Singapore identification and negative emotions with each interpretational mindset as a subsample. Participants with transactional mindset were more likely to express negative emotions if they identified less with Singapore ($B = -0.62$, $t(21) = -2.79$, $p < .05$). Participants in the control condition exhibited more negative emotions if they identified more with Singapore ($B = 0.66$, $t(22) = 3.56$, $p < .005$), but we did not find any significant effect in the categorical mindset condition ($B = 0.51, p > .23$).

General Discussion

We open this article with a conjecture that international exchanges are affairs that can be far less rational than most theories and research pertaining to economic transactions have typically suggested. Time and again, we have observed seemingly rational business deals being agreed upon by all transacting parties, only to be foiled by protectionist reactions from stakeholders who are ostensibly irrelevant to the deals (e.g., the general public). We contend that these reactions toward otherwise sensible cross-border transactions are systematic rather than market anomalies—and that they deserve more careful investigation. Symbols and people from different cultures are thrust to the forefront of everyone's mind in transactions between organizations that are iconic representatives of their cultures. This juxtaposition of impressions of two cultures heightens people's awareness of the differences between them, making people sensitive to the implications that exchanges with foreigners have on the integrity of their own culture. If they perceive these exchanges as threats to the integrity of their own culture, they will resort to defensive reactions.

But not all international deals provoke stakeholders to focus on social–cultural considerations equally. We set out to understand the conditions under which such reactions are agitated or attenuated. Our findings from three studies on cross-border acquisitions confirm our hypotheses that the provocation of social–cultural considerations and related reactions is likely when individuals are induced to consider these transactions through a categorization mindset (i.e., focusing on categorizing and comparing things) instead of a transactional mindset (i.e., focusing on cost–benefit calculations)—even if they encounter the exact same piece of information. Such effects, however, tend to occur when the two transacting parties are perceived to be dissimilar, and when the individuals in question identify closely with the culture being "infiltrated" by foreigners. In other words, stakeholders are likely to get involved when they perceive that one of their own is being threatened by an alien entity.

Taken together, our findings suggest that cross-border acquisitions are hardly pure economic events that involve the transacting parties. First, the general public, though often not directly affected by business transactions, is anything but trivial in specific circumstances. Hence, it may be quite costly to overlook these stakeholders when planning and executing cross-border transactions. Second, how organizations communicate their international transactions will have tremendous implications. If an announcement is preceded by the induction of a transactional mindset, organizations can nudge people toward more rational reactions; if the deal is introduced with languages that sensitize people toward categorizing people and cultures, then impulsive reactions are likely to ensue. In other words, it is usually not what is being expressed to the public, but how it is communicated that matters. The initial framing of an international transaction can go a long way in encouraging discussions and decisions based on reasons rather than emotions.

The lack of strong emotional reactions by non-Singaporeans in Study 1 and by those with low identification to the host countries in Study 3 provided insight for an alternative way to attenuate irrational and exclusionary responses in face of foreign acquisition—by altering how people self-categorize themselves. Intergroup emotions are the results of belonging to, and deriving identity from, one social group instead of another (i.e., the self-categorization and identification of people). Such self-categorization and identification processes are, however, highly malleable. Most people belong to multiple social groups at any point of time in their lives. People can be prodded to think of themselves as members of a political party, members of a country, or a consumer without party or country affiliation altogether, simply through their exposure to different discourses (Tienari, Vaara, & Björkman, 2003). By framing an acquirer as member of one country (e.g., Sweden), people may be pushed to identify themselves as member of another (e.g., Norwegian); but by framing the acquirer as member of a common region (e.g., Europe), people may be prompted to identify themselves as fellow members (e.g., fellow Europeans; Gaertner & Dovidio, 2000). Shifting discourses alter the self-categorization of people. Depending on the social group they identify themselves with, they experience different emotions (Mackie, Smith, & Ray, 2008; Smith, Seger, & Mackie, 2007). For example, in the face of a proposed rise in tuition fees at a state-run college, people thinking in the shoes of university students would react angrily, but if they are swayed to consider themselves as state taxpayers, they would feel less anger as less is asked of their tax money (who benefits by subsidizing the college less; Gordijn, Yzerbyt, Wigboldus, & Dumont, 2006). By guiding the public to identify with a social group that is on neutral ground between the two transacting parties (e.g., cost-conscious consumers), organizations can diffuse some of the irrational outbursts that may snowball into significant obstacles for international transactions. We believe that this is a concept that can be further explored in future research.

The participants in the present research are university students. Thus, it is unclear whether the feelings and perceptions toward the acquisitions are specific to college students, who may be relatively inclined to think rationally when they are induced to adopt a transactional mindset. Thus, further research on other samples should be conducted to investigate the generalizability of our results.

Although our studies were conducted in the context of cross-border acquisitions, we are convinced that the priming of interpretational mindsets is a useful tool to deploy in other settings involving international transactions. Recent events, including the development of some countries and the financial crisis, have seen the waxing of some economies and the waning of others. As people in the countries with falling financial fortunes perceive threats to their well-being, international transactions between their countries and others become charged with nationalistic emotions and protectionist posturing that are oftentimes irrational and unproductive economically. From the stalling of trade negotiations to lower trade barriers at the World Trade Organization talks, the difficulties of reaching agreements during international climate change dialogs, to the all too familiar overtures of Chinese or Indian businesses threatening the welfare of citizens in the United States and Europe, discussions on international transactions are often fraught with social–cultural considerations, hindering cool-headed and rational reflections that will truly benefit everyone. As globalization binds the fortunes of different nations tighter together than ever, these less than rational reactions no longer belong to the sideline of our research. By understanding what can push people to react more or less impulsively, we can begin to find ways to steer these discussions away from irrational fears and toward fruitful collaborations based on reasons.

References

Chiu, C.-y., Gries, P., Torelli, C. J., & Cheng, S. Y. Y. (2011). Toward a social psychology of globalization. *Journal of Social Issues, 67*, 663–676. doi:10.1111/j.1540-4560.2011.01721.x

Chiu, C.-y., & Hong, Y.-y. (2006). *Social psychology of culture.* New York, NY: Psychology Press.

Chiu, C.-y., Mallorie, L., Keh, H. T., & Law, W. (2009). Perceptions of culture in multicultural space: Joint presentation of images from two cultures increases ingroup attribution of culture-typical characteristics. *Journal of Cross-Cultural Psychology, 40*, 282–300. doi:10.1177/0022022108328912

Cuddy, A. J. C., Fiske, S. T., & Glick, P. (2007). The BIAS map: Behaviors from intergroup affect and stereotypes. *Journal of Personality and Social Psychology, 92*, 631. doi:10.1037/0022-3514.92.4.631

Fama, E. F. (1998). Market efficiency, long-term returns, and behavioral finance. *Journal of Financial Economics*, 283–306. doi:10.2139/ssrn.15108

Förster, J., Liberman, N., & Shapira, O. (2009). Preparing for novel versus familiar events: Shifts in global and local processing. *Journal of Experimental Psychology: General, 138*, 383–399. doi:10.1037/a0015748

Frijda, N. H., Kuipers, P., & ter Schure, E. (1989). Relations among emotion, appraisal, and emotional action readiness. *Journal of Personality and Social Psychology, 57*, 212–228. doi:10.1037/0022-3514.57.2.212

Gaertner, S. L., & Dovidio, J. F. (2000). *Reducing intergroup bias: The common ingroup identity model.* Philadelphia, PA: Psychology Press.

Gordijn, E. H., Yzerbyt, V., Wigboldus, D., & Dumont, M. (2006). Emotional reactions to harmful intergroup behavior. *European Journal of Social Psychology, 36*, 15–30. doi:10.1002/ejsp.296

Higgins, E. T. (1989). Knowledge accessibility and activation: Subjectivity and suffering from unconscious sources. In J. S. Uleman & J. A. Bargh (Eds.), *Unintended thought: The limits of awareness intention and control* (pp. 75–123). New York: Guilford.

Kirmani, A., Lee, M., & Yoon, C. (2004). Procedural priming effects on spontaneous inference formation. *Journal of Economic Psychology, 25*, 859–875. doi:10.1016/j.joep.2003.09.003

Krugman, P. (2009). How did economists get it so wrong? *The New York Times.* Retrieved from http://www.nytimes.com/2009/09/06/magazine/06Economic-t.html

Liberman, N., & Trope, Y. (1998). The role of feasibility and desirability considerations in near and distant future decisions: A test of temporal construal theory. *Journal of Personality and Social Psychology, 75*, 5–18. doi:10.1037/0022-3514.75.1.5

Mackie, D. M., Smith, E. R., & Ray, D. G. (2008). Intergroup emotions and intergroup relations. *Social and Personality Psychology Compass, 2*, 1866–1880. doi:10.1111/j.1751-9004.2008.00130.x

Morris, M. W., Mok, A., & Mor, S. (2011). Cultural identity threat: The role of cultural identifications in moderating closure responses to foreign cultural inflow. *Journal of Social Issues, 67*, 760–773. doi:10.1111/j.1540-4560.2011.01726.x

Mussweiler, T. (2002). The malleability of anchoring effects. *Experimental Psychology, 49*, 67–72. doi:10.1027/1618-3169.49.1.67

Mussweiler, T., & Epstude, K. (2009). Relatively fast! Efficiency advantages of comparative thinking. *Journal of Experimental Psychology: General, 138*, 1–21. doi:10.1037/a0014374

Navon, D. (1977). Forest before trees: The precedence of global features in visual perception. *Cognitive Psychology, 9*, 353–383. doi:10.1016/0010-0285(77)90012-3

Powell, B. (2009). China says "keep out" to Coca-Cola. *Times*. Retrieved from http://www.time.com/time/business/article/0,8599,1886024,00.html?xid = rss-topstories

Shen, H., & Wyer, R. S. (2008). Procedural priming and consumer judgments: Effects on the impact of positively and negatively valenced information. *Journal of Consumer Research, 34*, 727–737. doi:10.1086/523292

Shiller, R. J. (2005). *Irrational exuberance*. New York, NY: Doubleday.

Smith, E. R. (1994). Procedural knowledge and processing strategies in social cognition. In R. S. Wyer & T. K. Srull (Eds.), *Handbook of social cognition* (pp. 99–152). Hillsdale, NJ: Lawrence Erlbaum Associates.

Smith, E. R., Seger, C. R., & Mackie, D. M. (2007). Can emotions be truly group level? Evidence for four conceptual criteria. *Journal of Personality and Social Psychology, 93*, 431–446. doi:10.1037/0022-3514.93.3.431

Stephan, W. G., & Stephan, C. W. (2000). An integrated threat theory of prejudice. In S. Oskamp (Ed.), *Reducing prejudice and discrimination* (pp. 23–45). Mahwah, NJ: Erlbaum.

Tajfel, H., & Turner, J. (1979). An integrative theory of intergroup conflict. In W. G. Austin & S. Worchel (Eds.), *The social psychology of intergroup relations* (pp. 94–109). Monterey, CA: Brooks-Cole.

Thaler, R. H., & Sunstein, C. R. (2008). *Nudge: Improving decisions about health, wealth, and happiness*. New York, NY: Penguin Books.

Tienari, J., Vaara, E., & Björkman, I. (2003). Global capitalism meets national spirit: Discourses in media texts on a cross-border acquisition. *Journal of Management Inquiry, 12*, 377–393. doi:10.1177/1056492603258975

Torelli, C. J., Chiu, C.-y., Tam, K.-P., Au, K. C., & Keh, H. T. (2011). Exclusionary reactions to foreign cultures: Effects of simultaneous exposure to cultures in globalized space. *Journal of Social Issues, 67*, 716–742. doi:10.1111/j.1540-4560.2011.01724.x

Vallacher, R. R., & Wegner, D. M. (1989). Levels of personal agency: Individual variation in action identification. *Journal of Personality and Social Psychology, 57*, 660–671. doi:10.1037/0022-3514.57.4.660

Yang, D. Y.-J., Chen, X., Cheng, S. Y. Y., Kwan, L., Tam, K.-P., & Yeh, K.-H. (2011). The lay psychology of globalization and its social impact. *Journal of Social Issues, 67*, 677–695. doi:10.1111/j.1540-4560.2011.01722.x

YUK-YUE TONG is an Assistant Professor of Psychology at Singapore Management University. She received her PhD in Psychology from the University of Hong Kong. Her research focuses on cross-cultural person perception process, automatic evaluation and trait inference, and lay belief of personality.

PAMSY PUN-ZEE HUI received her PhD in Organization Science from the University of Texas at Austin and is a Senior Teaching Fellow of Management at Hong Kong Polytechnic University. Her research focuses on interorganizational relationships and stakeholder management in intercultural settings, and agglomeration of firms in information intensive environments.

LETTY Y-Y. KWAN received her PhD from the University of Illinois, Urbana-Champaign. She researches on how individuals perceive their own and others' cultures and the psychological implications of such perceptions. Her research explicates the different social functions of culture, specifically on trust relations and creative processes.

SIQING PENG received his PhD in Social Psychology from the University of Hong Kong and is a Professor of Marketing at the Guanghua School of Management, Peking University. His research interests include consumer–brand relationship, customer's satisfaction management, cross-cultural marketing, and Chinese indigenous social psychology.

Journal of Social Issues, Vol. 67, No. 4, 2011, pp. 760–773

Cultural Identity Treat: The Role of Cultural Identifications in Moderating Closure Responses to Foreign Cultural Inflow

Michael W. Morris[*]
Columbia University

Aurelia Mok
City University of Hong Kong

Shira Mor
Columbia University

Political theorists of globalization have argued that foreign inflows to a society can give rise to collective-identity closure—social movements aiming to narrow the in-group, and exclude minorities. In this research we investigate whether exposure to the mixing of a foreign culture with one's heritage culture can evoke need for closure, a motive that engenders ethnocentric social judgments. On the basis of a proposed identity threat mechanism, we tested the hypothesis that exposure to situations mixing foreign and heritage cultures would evoke need for closure for individuals with low foreign identification but not those with high foreign identification. An experiment with Hong Kong Chinese students varied linguistic and visual cues of Western and Chinese culture and found, as predicted, that exposure to mixed Western/Chinese conditions elevated need for closure for those low in Western identification but not those high in Western identification.

Globalization refers to the recent expansion and acceleration of flows of people, organizations, capital, images, and ideas across different parts of the world (Appadurai, 1996). Although intergroup contact and exchange have occurred throughout human history, global flows across geographic, political, and

---

[*]Correspondence concerning this article should be addressed to Michael Morris, Columbia Business School, 708 Uris Hall, 3022 Broadway, New York, NY 10027 [e-mail: mwm82@columbia.edu].

Data collection was supported by a grant from Columbia University's Center for International Business and Education Research (CIBER).

cultural boundaries have increased in the past several decades owing to political and economic changes, as well as developments in transportation and information technologies (IT; Giddens, 1985). Whereas experiencing multiple cultures once required traveling abroad or to immigrant neighborhoods, nowadays it permeates everyday life (Arnett, 2002). Foreign and local cultural elements mix in classrooms, workplaces, restaurants, concert halls, and on television and the Internet (Appiah, 2006; Fu & Chiu, 2007; Lowman, 2009).

The consequences of globalization have been studied chiefly at the macro level of societal and economic trends. Journalists have called attention to heightened competition from opening of global markets and to convergence of lifestyles in many parts of the world—an Adidas-clad IT worker could stop at a strip mall for McDonalds and Starbucks on the way to the airport, whether in Los Angeles, Jeddah, or Marseilles (see Friedman, 2005). For some, these signs of communication, interaction, and convergence herald a global village (McLuhan & Powers, 1989). However, others note that globalism has been accompanied by renewed tribalism (Barber, 1996). In many societies, inflows of foreign culture have set off reactionary movements to reduce ethnic and religious diversity in the name of restoring traditional social forms (Appadurai, 1990). For example, as the 1970s oil boom infused Saudi Arabia with shopping malls and other icons of Western consumerism, Saudi clerics countered this Westernization through puritanical Wahhabism, supplanting more inclusive forms of Islam (Commins, 2006). Likewise, in 1980s France as Islamic people and practices became more visible features of everyday life, Le Pen gained surprising support in his political efforts to refashion the French national identity in racially and religiously restrictive terms (Bayart, 2005). Whether fundamentalist or fascist, these social movements are reactions to the blurring of boundaries and overlapping of categories that globalization brings; they seek to clarify the collective identity or purify the community by narrowing its boundaries, narrowing that is typically framed as restoring the rules of an earlier, simpler (and often more fictional than real) halcyon era (Paxton, 2004; Salzman, 2008). This narrowing denies the multiplicity of identity and leads inexorably to the exclusion of people and ideas that complicate the mainstream heritage identity category, such as religious and ethnic minorities (Sen, 2006). Although, scholars have described examples of this societal dialectic of global inflow and collective-identity closure (Bayart, 2005), little is known about the psychological motives that propel these social movements. Geschiere and Meyer (1998) note that "Global flows seem to trigger a search for fixed orientation points and action frames, as well as determined efforts to affirm old and construct new boundaries" (p. 602). Yet how does this reaction work psychologically and what types of people are most susceptible to it?

In this article, we investigate responses to global inflows on the psychological level, hoping to elucidate what types of people are more prone to defensive, closure-oriented responses. We build on the pioneering work of Chiu and colleagues (Torelli, Chiu, Tam, Au, & Keh, 2011) on psychological responses to mixed-culture exposure. Their studies find that priming a mix of the heritage culture and a foreign culture evokes a cultural-difference mindset. On problem solving tasks this can result in complex, integrative creative thinking (Leung & Chiu, 2010). Yet in social judgments it can engender rigid and exclusionary judgments, such as stereotyping members of cultural groups and exaggerating the incompatibility of different traditions (Chiu, Mallorie, Keh, & Law, 2009). These judgments reflect an essentialistic mindset of construing one's cultural group as defined by sharp boundaries and distinctive consensual traits (Shore, 2002). Yet there remains much to learn about how dual cultural priming evokes this mindset and the conditions under which it occurs.

To fill this explanatory gap, we propose that the exclusionary response hinges on heightened need for closure. Need for cognitive closure is an epistemic motive for clear categories and firm decisions and rather than continuing uncertainty or ambiguity (Kruglanski, 1989). This motivational state is evoked by various kinds of threats (Orehek et al., 2010), particularly threats to the ideas central to the person's sense of meaning, such as identity categories (Proulx & Heine, 2010; Van Tongeren & Green, 2010). Exposure to mixes of an inflowing foreign culture with the heritage culture may threaten cultural identity and thereby trigger needs for epistemic certainty and security. It is also plausible on the basis of past research that need for closure underlies exclusionary social judgments. Cognitive closure gives rise to cultural self-stereotyping (Chiu et al., 2000; Fu et al., 2007) as well as prejudicial behaviors toward out-groups (Kruglanski & Freund, 1983). Hence, the essentialistic and exclusionary judgments that follow exposure to mixed heritage/foreign cultural priming could be explained in terms of threat to participants' heritage identity and their ensuing need for closure.

If threat to cultural identity is indeed the mechanism involved, then we can predict which kind of individuals are more and less likely to exhibit closure-oriented social judgments after heritage/foreign priming. This response would be less likely for individuals who identify with the inflowing foreign culture as well as their heritage culture, as such individuals should not feel identity threat from the juxtaposition of the heritage and foreign cultures. Individuals vary dramatically in the degree to which they identify with cultures other than their heritage culture. Acculturation studies have documented that some but not all immigrants identify dually with heritage and host cultures (Berry, 1990). Similarly studies of multicultural societies such as Hong Kong, a longtime Western colony and continuing nexus of Western business in East Asia, find that residents identify with both their local heritage (Chinese) and the inflowing global (Western) culture. Bicultural Hong Kong residents switch between Chinese and Western modes of judgment in response to situational cues, such as languages or visual symbols associated with either of the cultures (Briley, Morris, & Simonson, 2005; Hong, Morris, Chiu, & Benet-Martinez, 2000). Even in societies without such an entrenched foreign

cultural presence, young people today increasingly identify both with their local heritage tradition and with inflowing global culture, typically represented by
Western culture or that of a regionally hegemonic culture (Arnett, 2002; Hermans
& Kempen, 1998). The degree to which individuals identify with a foreign tradition
could moderate their feeling of threat when exposed to mixes of that culture with
their heritage culture; high identifiers with the foreign tradition are less likely to
construe the juxtaposition of foreign and local elements as a threatening invasion
or contamination, and hence less likely to feel a compensatory need for closure.
Consistent with this, past research has found that immigrants with dually strong
heritage and host culture identifications are lower in their chronic level of need for
structure (Tadmor, Tetlock, & Peng, 2009), which is a major component of need
for closure (Kruglanski, 1989).

To test the idea that foreign identification moderates the effect of cultural-
mix priming on need for closure, we conducted an experiment varying whether
university students in Hong Kong were exposed to symbols of the heritage (East
Asian) culture, a foreign (Western) culture, or a mix of the heritage and foreign
cultures, adapting past methods of cultural priming in Hong Kong (e.g., Hong et
al., 2000; Yang & Bond, 1980). Across participants, we independently varied the
language of the experimental session and cultural content of a series of visual
scenes, resulting in conditions where linguistic and visual cues aligned on one of
the two cultural traditions (heritage or foreign) or mixed the two. We expected that
the need for closure response would be triggered by exposure to the threatening
mix of foreign and heritage symbols, not simply by exposure to foreign symbols.
Moreover, this response would be attenuated for individuals who identify highly
with the foreign culture.

Method

Participants

We recruited 111 undergraduate students (58 men; mean age $= 19.85$ years;
$SD = 1.25$) from a university in Hong Kong. Self-reported proficiency in English
and Chinese language was 4.68 ($SD = 1.11$) and 5.87 ($SD = 1.05$), respectively,
rated on a scale of 1 (*very poor*) to 7 (*very fluent*). Level of identification with
Western and East Asian culture was 4.31 ($SD = 1.26$) and 4.92 ($SD = 1.31$),
respectively, rated on a 7-point scale ranging from 1 (*very weak*) to 7 (*very strong*).
Participants were paid HK \$20 (roughly equivalent to US \$3).

Materials and Procedure

Participants were run in noninteracting groups of 5 to 15. They received a
survey with a priming manipulation. We employed two types of cultural primes,

language and visual images. Specifically, participants were randomly assigned to complete a survey either in English ($n = 53$) or in Chinese ($n = 58$). The original survey (in English) was translated into Chinese by a bilingual research assistant and another research assistant translated it back into English to ensure equivalent meaning across the language versions (Brislin, 1986).

Within each language condition, individuals were randomly assigned to a visual image condition, either Western scenes ($n = 37$), Asian scenes ($n = 38$), or noncultural scenes ($n = 36$). Participants viewed four pictures of scenes (taken from Morris and Mok, 2011) and wrote down a few thoughts, feelings, or memories that each evoked. Afterwards, participants completed the need for cognitive closure scale (NFC; Webster & Kruglanski, 1994) on a scale of 1 (*strongly disagree*) to 6 (*strongly agree*), followed by a demographic survey.

Analysis of Data

Participants in the culturally mixed conditions received a survey in English with Asian scenes, or in Chinese with Western scenes. Participants in the culturally aligned conditions received a survey in English with Western or noncultural scenes, or a survey in Chinese with Asian or noncultural scenes. We predicted that more need for closure would be evoked in the culturally mixed than aligned conditions for low identifiers with Western culture but not for high identifiers. In other words, Western identification should moderate the effects of the prime condition, which would be reflected in an interaction of language (English vs. Chinese), scene (Western vs. Asian vs. noncultural), and Western identification.

Results

We tested for the above interaction using a general linear model on the NFC score ($\alpha = 0.70$, $M = 3.90$, and $SD = 3.19$). Western identification was mean-centered. There was a main effect of language, $F(1, 99) = 5.02, p < .05, \eta_p^2 = .05$, suggesting that Chinese language elicited higher need for closure than English. This effect was qualified by a significant three-way interaction of language, scene, and Western identification, $F(2, 99) = 5.30, p < .01, \eta_p^2 = 0.10$. (Initial analysis showed that East Asian identification did not interact with any variables so it is not discussed further).

To explore the three-way interaction, we examined whether the language X scene interaction (which reflects the tendency for NFC to differ in culturally mixed vs. aligned conditions) was significant when Western identification was low (centered at 1 *SD* below the mean) and high (centered at 1 *SD* above the mean). In doing so, we first checked for differences between the two kinds of culturally aligned cells within each language condition (i.e., English language

Table 1. Need For Closure (NFC) as a Function of Type of Prime and Western Identification

Prime			
Language	Scene	Low Western identification	High Western identification
English	Western[a]	3.69 (.13)	3.97 (.12)
	Asian[b]	3.99 (.10)	3.67 (.14)
	Noncultural[c]	3.78 (.11)	3.87 (.14)
Chinese	Western[b]	4.12 (.10)	3.92 (.09)
	Asian[a]	3.79 (.10)	4.00 (.09)
	Noncultural[c]	3.94 (.10)	4.01 (.09)

Note. Low and high Western identification is centered at one standard deviation below and above the mean. [a]Culture compatible prime conditions. [b]Culturally mixed prime conditions. [c]Language prime conditions (with noncultural scenes). Standard errors are given in parentheses.

with Western or noncultural scenes; Chinese language with Asian or noncultural scenes). Results showed that within each language condition, and regardless of levels of Western identification, NFC did not differ between these two conditions, all $p > .10$. Hence, we collapsed across the culturally compatible and noncultural scenes for a culturally aligned condition to contrast with the culturally mixed condition. Table 1 displays the means for each condition by levels of Western identification.

Specifically, we created contrasts that pitted NFC in the culturally mixed conditions (English language/Asian scenes, Chinese language/Western scenes) against the aligned conditions, for high and low Western identifiers separately. High Western identifiers did not differ in NFC across the mixed and aligned conditions, $F(1, 99) = 2.86$, $p = .09$, $\eta_p^2 = .03$. This result did not differ by the language condition, $F_{English}(1, 99) = 2.39$, $p = .13$, $\eta_p^2 = .02$, and $F_{Chinese}(1, 99) = 0.67$, $p = .41$, $\eta_p^2 = .01$. In contrast, low Western identifiers exhibited significantly higher NFC in the mixed than aligned conditions, $F(1, 99) = 9.98$, $p < .001$, $\eta_p^2 = .09$. This pattern was robust across language conditions, $F_{English}(1, 99) = 3.97$, $p < .05$, $\eta_p^2 = .04$, and $F_{Chinese}(1, 99) = 4.68$, $p < .05$, $\eta_p^2 = .05$. Hence, our hypothesis is supported. Culturally mixed contexts evoked higher need for closure for low Western identifiers but not for high Western identifiers.

Further analysis revealed that low Western identifiers exhibited similar levels of NFC in a Western context compared to an Asian context; NFC was not significantly different in the English versus Chinese language condition (with noncultural scenes), $F(1, 99) = 0.91$, $p = .34$, $\eta_p^2 = .01$. These results imply that low identifiers are not threatened by a foreign culture per se; rather they are threatened by the *mix* of the foreign and heritage culture.

Discussion

The results of our experiment provide the first evidence linking exposure to mixes of heritage and foreign cultural symbols with elevated need for closure. Hong Kong participants felt increased need for closure after exposure to a mix of Chinese and Western symbols, implemented through language of instruction and visual images. Consistent with an identity threat account, high identifiers with Western culture did not exhibit this defensive response; only low identifiers, who would be threatened by Western influx into their Chinese heritage, exhibited heightened need for closure. To our knowledge, this is the first evidence that identification with a foreign culture moderates exclusionary responses to cultural mixes.

These findings contribute primarily to the literature on exclusionary reactions to cultural mixes. To review, Chiu et al. (Chiu et al., 2009) found that exposure to juxtapositions of foreign and heritage culture images induces in-group mixes sterotyping and exaggerated concerns about the incompatibility of the two cultures. Our study shows that defensive responses can be evoked by more subtle cultural mixes. With Chiu's paradigm of juxtaposing side-by-side visual images of iconic Western and Eastern symbols, a contrastive mindset is virtually implied by the stimuli. When participants respond with stereotypical, contrastive social judgments, they may be following perceived experimenter demand. In our paradigm of crossing linguistic and visual cues, it is not transparent to participants that two cultural traditions are being mixed. As either English or Chinese language is normal in the setting, participants were not aware that language was a cultural cue. Nevertheless, the mixed culture conditions were threatening to participants who were low in Western identification. Hence, our results suggest that exclusionary responses reflect an unconscious response to threat, not conscious acquiescence to perceived experimental demand.

The current findings also complement other contemporary findings in this research program. Torelli et al. (2011) exposed participants to hypothetical advertisements varying brands and product categories associated with foreign and heritage cultures. Cultural mix advertisements featured a foreign brand in an iconic product category of the heritage culture (i.e., exposing American participants to a Chinese brand of jeans) as opposed to other conditions without this foreign infiltration of iconic heritage-culture domains (e.g., an American brand of jeans or Chinese brand of ovens). As expected, cultural mix advertisements evoked stereotyping of the in-group and judgments that American and Chinese values are incompatible. Tong, Hui, Kwan, and Peng (2011) finds similar reactions to acquisitions of iconic local corporations by foreign firms, especially when a prior task activates a categorization mindset. Although these are clever and externally valid instances of cultural mixing, it is worth noting that the foreign inflow in these cases is more than symbolic. Foreign brands entering one's nation's traditional product categories and foreign firms acquiring local firms represent tangible threats to the local economy. Negative exclusionary responses after exposure to such examples may reflect pushback that is driven by economic protectionist concerns rather than identity defense processes. Our findings support an identity protection account by showing that even subtle mixes of cultural symbols can trigger closure responses.

Our account, and this recent evidence, helps to clarify what about cultural mixes provokes exclusionary responses. Our premise is that cultural identities are threatened by the perception of foreign influx to one's heritage culture. On this account, the defensive exclusionary response should not be prompted by other kinds of cultural mixes, such as a mix of two foreign cultures. Nor would it come from priming the idea of heritage culture outflow into other cultures. That is, although Americans would have closure reactions to a Chinese brand of jeans imported to the United States, they would not to an American brand of rice cookers exported to China. Our account suggests closure responses arise when people feel a need to protect their cultural turf; it is not that cultural mixes are inherently overwhelming.

An alternative account would be that people are threatened by any cultural mix or blend that violates the order of their categories. In her classic book *Purity and Danger*, Douglas (1966) contends that people are averse to that which seems out of place or in between categories. As an example of this tendency to regard category exceptions as unclean, she cites kosher laws, which prohibit animals lacking cloven hooves (pigs) or fish without scales (lobster). For Douglas, mixes across categories inherently evoke an encoding as dirty and dangerous. So a person would have this reaction even to a mix of two foreign cultures. To our knowledge, past research on dual culture priming has always involved the heritage culture and an inflowing foreign culture. More research is needed to test whether closure responses to mixes reflect the motive of cultural turf protection or that of maintaining categories.

We find that high identifiers with a foreign culture are less affected by cultural mixes, presumably because their personal social identity is less dependent on the heritage collective identity. However, it is possible that there are alternative explanations for why high foreign identifiers do not show closure responses. Need for closure can be evoked by informational overload such as trying to solve puzzles in a noisy room (Kruglanski & Webster, 1991; Kruglanski, Webster, & Klem, 1993). It is possible that high identifiers are less overwhelmed by cultural mix situations because they are more accustomed to them. It seems likely that high foreign identifiers spend more time in culturally mixed settings than low identifiers. In future research it would be important to rule out this familiarity hypothesis. If the moderating effect on closure responses is seen with regard to inflow mixes and not outflow mixes, then this would suggest that it has to do with identity threats rather than cognitive overload.

Another contribution of the current research is bridging micro and macro level research on responses to globalization. The societal dialectic of foreign inflow leading to collective-identity closure that we described in the introduction involves reactionary social movements centered on essentialized, narrowed in-group identities. The way individual reactions to a cultural mix can grow into social movements toward closure is illustrated by Chiu and Cheng's (2007) example of a Chinese journalists' response to the opening of a Starbucks Café within the Imperial Forbidden City, a screed of essentialistic arguments about Chinese and American cultures that soon attracted hundreds of thousands of readers and thousands of assenting comments. Social movements of this sort emerge when a leader's framing of social problem resonates with the intuitions of some followers (Gamson, 1995; Loseke, 1999). Need for closure responses create a mindset conducive to essentialized views of cultural groups. Hence, we would expect collective-identity closure movements to arise in sectors of a population with low foreign identification. In this way, our research provides a start to understanding when and where the macro level societal dynamic is most likely to play out.

The threat of cultural inflows is also an issue in international marketing. Foreignness is usually a liability for brands. When taking a brand overseas, firms often develop distinct brands in local languages for selling the same product. Likewise, in foreign acquisitions of iconic businesses the local brand names are retained, such as in Lenovo's acquisition of IBM's PC business. It would be interesting to investigate when the efficacy of such strategies by tracking commercial cultural inflows provoke closure movements, such as boycotts. At the same time, the brand context provides opportunities to consider when foreign cultural inflows are regarded positively. Marketers do not mask the foreign origins when they are importing French wine or Swiss chocolate. Sometime brands are even created intentionally to sound foreign (e.g., Haagen Dazs ice cream, made by Pillsbury, with headquarters in Minneapolis). Research suggests that foreign cultural stereotypes enter consumers' processing of their experiences. When brand names are given French pronunciations, for example, consumers perceive them as hedonically richer (Leclerc, Schmitt, & Dube, 1994). Measures of foreign- or global-culture identification may be useful in understanding which kinds of customers are attracted or repelled by foreign or faux-foreign brands.

Another applied domain is military strategy for foreign operations and counterinsurgency. Military strategists have long been aware that reactions to foreign occupation depend very much on iconic cultural symbols. For example, the Allies left the Japanese Emperor Hirohito in place after WWII as they thought it would enable the country to recover its sense of meaning. Foreign inflows often evoke feelings of invasion and contamination. In 1990, the United States set up bases in Saudi Arabia to protect the oil fields at Hama as it prepared to liberate Kuwait from Iraq. This move enraged many Muslims (including Osama Bin Laden, previously an ally of the United States) who saw it as a violation of the Islamic holy land (Commins, 2006). Strader (2006) proposes that in almost any community there are "cultural centers of gravity" that need to be respected to avoid causing "a culturally sensitive situation to erupt." He lists examples of sites such as Najaf's Shiite cemetery, Mecca's Holy Mosque, Madinah's Prophet's Mosque, the Hindu temples in Varansi, Rome's Vatican, or the Buddhist holy sites at Lumbini, Kusinari, or Isipatana. In addition to geographic sites, some symbols are centers of gravity, for example, "desecration of the image of the Prophet Mohammad" (Strader, 2006, p. 58). Unfortunately military strategists have thought not only about avoiding cultural offense, but also about intentionally creating it. PsyOps units have tried to "weaponize" culture by threatening to violate cultural symbols as a means of breaking prisoners who are withholding information. When such tactics become public they deeply undermine trust. As in the findings of Torelli et al. (2011), foreign inflows become upsetting to the degree that they enter culturally iconic domains. A better understanding of which geographic and symbolic spaces are iconic, and which are not, would help in conducing peacekeeping and humanitarian missions without unintended side-effects of cultural offense.

Limitations and Future Directions

Our study suggests that some individuals in Hong Kong are highly identified with Western culture and, consequently, more accepting of the mixing of Western and East Asian culture. This suggests that they are active consumers of globalization and belies polemics that only wealthy Westerners are in a position to enjoy the foreign inflows that globalization brings (see Geschiere & Meyer, 1998). That said, it must be acknowledged that Hong Kong has long been a wealthy society (with a per capita GDP sometimes exceeding that of its colonizer, the United Kingdom). Also, Hong Kong is undoubtedly an economic beneficiary of global flows: it became wealthy as a broker between Western finance and Chinese manufacturing, it relies on guest workers for its nannies and nurses, and it attracts tourists for its cosmopolitan architecture, cuisine, and cinema. Hence, Hong Kong may be more like wealthy Western nations than most non-Western nations in its experience of globalization. It is important to explore a broader sample of countries in different regions that experience globalization differently to test whether foreign-culture identities are prevalent and whether they buffer individuals against defensive, exclusionary responses to cultural mixes. In addition, future research will do well by examining whether the present findings can be generalized urban student populations. For example, research by Chen and Chiu (2010) suggests that globalization experiences trigger differential responses among rural versus city inhabitants.

In this and other studies of reactions to cultural mixes, participants have been tested within the contexts of their own heritage cultures. In these settings, exposure to cultural mixes gives rise to some patterns of essentialistic social judgment, such as heightened tendencies to impute culturally typical traits to in-group members. Recent findings by Kosic et al. (2004) and Chao et al. (2010) illustrate that need for closure pushes people to seek consensus with the salient in-group in the social environment, even if that is not the heritage-culture in-group. Hence, it would be interesting to examine expatriates' responses to cultural mixes. Would they show an inclination toward essentializing their heritage culture and excluding the host culture? Or would they essentialize the host culture and exclude the heritage culture?

Finally, future research should probe the similarities and differences between foreign-culture identification and other international identifications. Global citizen identifications predict individuals' effective functioning on multinational teams (Shokef & Erez, 2008). Integrated bicultural identifications enable frame switching in culturally laden contexts (Benet-Martinez, Leu, Lee, & Morris, 2002; Fu et al., 2007; Mok & Morris, 2009, 2010a, 2010b; Verkuyten & Pouliasi, 2002). Sussman (2000) proposed that intercultural identifications enable people to hold multiple cultural scripts and draw upon them as needed. Some evidence consistent with this notion of global identities as enabling flexible switching comes from a study of MBA students who have worked in several countries. Mor, Morris, Jagiello, Joh (2011) found that global identification predicts culturally integrated decision making, which involves seeking ideas from other cultures and incorporating these into one's solutions to a problem. Interestingly the link between global identification and this approach to solving problems is cultural perspective taking—imagining how the problem looks to an individual from another culture. In sum, emerging evidence suggests that culturally mixed settings can evoke creative, integrative solutions for individuals who chose to feel the other culture and to individual members of the culture.

References

Appadurai, A. (1990). Disjuncture and difference in the global cultural economy. *Public Culture, 2*, 295–310. doi:10.1177/026327690007002017

Appadurai, A. (1996). *Modernity at large: Cultural dimensions of globalization.* Minneapolis, MN: University of Minnesota Press.

Appiah, K. A. (2006). *Cosmopolitanism: Ethics in a world of strangers.* New York: W. W. Norton and Co.

Arnett, J. J. (2002). The psychology of globalization. *American Psychologist, 57*, 744–783. doi:10.1037/0003-066X.57.10.774

Barber, B. R. (1996). *Jihad vs. McWorld.* New York: Ballatine Books.

Bayart, J.-F. (2005). *The illusion of cultural identity.* Chicago: University of Chicago Press.

Benet-Martínez, V., Leu, J., Lee, F., & Morris, M. (2002). Negotiating biculturalism: Cultural frame-switching in biculturals with "oppositional" vs. "compatible" cultural identities. *Journal of Cross-Cultural Psychology, 33*, 492–451. doi:10.1177/00220221102033005005

Berry, J. W. (1990). Psychology of acculturation: Understanding individuals moving between cultures. In R. Brislin (Ed.), *Applied cross-cultural psychology.* CA: Sage.

Briley, D. A., Morris, M. W., & Simonson, I. (2005). Cultural chameleons: Biculturals, conformity motives, and decision making. *Journal of Consumer Psychology, 15*, 351–63. doi:10.1207/s15327663jcp1504_9

Brislin, R. W. (1986). The wording and translation of research instruments. In W. J. Lonner, & J. W. Berry (Eds.), *Field methods in cross-cultural research.* CA: Sage Publications.

Chao, M. M., Zhang, Z-X., & Chiu, C. (2010). Adherence to perceived norms across cultural boundaries: The role of need for cognitive closure and ingroup identification. *Group Processes and Intergroup Relations, 13,* 69–89. doi:10.1177/1368430209343115

Chen, X., & Chiu, C.-y. (2010). Rural-urban differences in generation of Chinese and Western exemplary persons: The case of China. *Asian Journal of Social Psychology, 13,* 9–18. doi:10.1111/j.1467-839X.2010.01296.x

Chiu, C.-y., & Cheng, S. (2007). Toward a social psychology of culture and globalization: Some social cognitive consequences of activating two cultures simultaneously. *Social and Personality Psychology Compass, 1,* 84–100. doi:10.1111/j.1751-9004.2007.00017.x

Chiu, C.-y., Mallorie, L., Keh, H.-t., & Law, W. (2009). Perceptions of culture in multicultural space: Joint presentation of images from two cultures increases in-group attribution of culture-typical characteristics. *Journal of Cross-cultural Psychology, 40,* 282–300. doi:10.1177/0022022108328912

Commins, D. (2006). *The Wahhabi mission and Saudi Arabia.* London: I.B. Taurus.

Douglas, M. (1966). *Purity and danger: An analysis of concepts of pollution and taboo.* New York: Praeger.

Friedman, T. H. (2005). *The world is flat.* New York: Farrar, Straus and Giroux.

Fu, H. J., & Chiu, C. (2007). Local culture's responses to globalization: Exemplary persons and their attendant values. *Journal of Cross-Cultural Psychology, 38,* 636–653. doi:10.1177/0022022107305244

Fu, H. J., Chiu, C., Morris, M. W., & Young, J. M. (2007). Spontaneous inferences from cultural cues: Varying responses of cultural insiders and outsiders. *Journal of Cross-Cultural Psychology, 38,* 58–75. doi:10.1177/0022022106295443

Fu, H. J., Morris, M. W., Lee, S., Chao, M., Chiu, C., & Hong, Y. (2007). Epistemic motives and cultural conformity: Need for closure, culture, and context as determinants of conflict judgments. *Journal of Personality and Social Psychology, 92,* 191–207. doi:10.1037/0022-3514.92.2.191

Gamson, W. A. (1995). Constructing social protest. In H. Johnston & B. Klandermans (Eds.), *Social movements and culture.* Minneapolis: University of Minnesota Press.

Geschiere, P., & Meyer, B. (1998). Globalization and identity: Dialectics of flow and closure. *Development and Change, 29,* 601–615. doi:10.1111/1467-7660.00092

Giddens, A. (1985). *The nation state and violence.* Cambridge: Polity Press.

Hermans, H. J. M., & Kempen, H. J. G. (1998). Moving cultures: The perilous problems of cultural dichotomies in a globalizing society. *American Psychologist, 53,* 1111–1120. doi:10.1037/0003-066X.53.10.1111

Hong, Y. Y., Morris, M. W., Chiu, C. Y., & Benet-Martinez, V. (2000). Multicultural minds: A dynamic constructivist approach to culture and cognition. *American Psychologist, 55,* 709–720. doi:10.1037/0003-066X.55.7.709

Kosic, A., Kruglanski, A. W., Pierro, A., & Mannetti, L. (2004). The social cognitions of immigrants' acculturation: Effects of the need for closure and reference group at entry. *Journal of Personality and Social Psychology, 86,* 796–813. doi:10.1037/0022-3514.86.6.796

Kruglanski, A. W. (1989). *Lay epistemics and human knowledge: Cognitive and motivational bases.* New York: Plenum.

Kruglanski, A. W., & Freund, T. (1983). The freezing and un-freezing of lay inferences: Effects on impressional primacy, ethnic stereotyping, and numerical anchoring. *Journal of Experimental Social Psychology, 19,* 448–468. doi:10.1016/0022-1031(83)90022-7

Kruglanski, A. W., & Webster, D. M. (1991). Group members' reactions to opinion deviates and conformists at varying degrees of proximity to decision deadline and of environmental noise. *Journal of Personality and Social Psychology, 61,* 212–225. doi:10.1037/0022-3514.61.2.212

Kruglanski, A. W., Webster, D. M., & Klem, A. (1993). Motivated resistance and openness to persuasion in the presence or absence of prior information. *Journal of Personality and Social Psychology, 65,* 861–876. doi:10.1037/0022-3514.65.5.861

Leclerc, F., Schmitt, B. H., & Dube, L. (1994). Foreign branding and its effect on product perceptions and attitudes. *Journal of Marketing Research, 31,* 263–270.

Leung, A. K. Y., & Chiu, C. Y. (2010) Multicultural experiences, idea receptiveness, and creativity. *Journal of Cross Cultural Psychology, 41*, 723–741. doi:10.1177/0022022110361707

Loseke, D. (1999). *Thinking about social problems: An introduction to constructionist perspectives.* NY: Aldine De Gruyter.

Lowman, S. (2009). The shrinking of Chinatown: Group is working on a strategy to restore neighborhood's Asian identity. *The Washington Post.* Retrieved from http://www.washingtonpost.com/wpdyn/content/article/2009/01/28/AR2009012801315.html

McLuhan, M., & Powers, B. R. (1989). *The global village: Transformation in world, life and media.* New York: Oxford University Press.

Mok, A., & Morris, M. W. (2009). Cultural chameleons and iconoclasts: Assimilation and reactance to cultural cues in biculturals' expressed personalities as a function of identity conflict. *Journal of Experimental Social Psychology, 45*, 884–889. doi:10.1016/j.jesp.2009.04.004

Mok, A., & Morris, M. W. (2010a). Asian-Americans' creative styles in Asian and American situations: Assimilative and contrastive responses as a function of bicultural identity integration. *Management and Organization Review, 6*, 371–390. doi:10.1111/j.1740-8784.2010.00190.x

Mok, A., & Morris, M. W. (2010b). An upside to bicultural identity conflict: Resisting group-think in cultural in-groups. *Journal of Experimental Social Psychology, 46*, 1114–1117. doi:10.1016/j.jesp.2010.05.020

Mor, S., Morris, W. M., Jagiello, A., & Joh, J. (2011). Thinking global, acting local: Global identity promotes culturally integrative decision making. Manuscript in preparation.

Morris, M. W., & Mok, A. (2011). Isolating effects of cultural schemas: Cultural priming shifts Asian Americans' biases in social description and memory. *Journal of Experimental Social Psychology, 47*, 117–126. doi:10.1016/j.jesp.2010.08.019

Orehek, E., Dossje, B., Kruglanski, A. W., Cole, A., Saddler, T., & Jackson, J. (2010). Need for closure and the social response to terrorism. *Basic and Applied Social Psychology, 32*, 279–290. doi:10.1080/01973533.2010.519196

Paxton, R. O. (2004). *The anatomy of Fascism.* London: Penguin Books.

Proulx, T., & Heine, S. J. (2010). The frog in Kierkegaard's beer: Finding meaning in the threat-compensation literature. *Social and Personality Psychology Compass, 4*, 889–905. doi:10.1111/j.1751-9004.2010.00304.x

Salzman, M. B. (2008). Globalization, religious fundamentalism and the need for meaning. *International Journal of Intercultural Relations, 32*, 318–327. doi:10.1016/j.ijintrel.2008.04.006

Sen, A. (2006). *Identity and violence: The illusion of destiny.* New York: Norton.

Shokef, E., & Erez, M. (2008). Cultural intelligence and global identity in multicultural teams. *Handbook of Cultural Intelligence: Theory, Measurement, and Applications,* 177–191.

Shore, B. (2002). Taking culture seriously. *Human Development, 45, 226–228.* doi:10.1159/000064982

Strader, K. (2006). *Culture: The new key terrain integrating cultural competence into JIPB.* Ft. Leavenworth, KS: School of Advanced Military Studies [Monograph].

Sussman, N. M. (2000). The dynamic nature of cultural identity throughout cultural transitions: Why home is not so sweet. *Personality and Social Psychology Review, 4*, 355–373. doi:10.1207/S15327957PSPR0404_5

Tadmor, C. T., Tetlock, P. E., & Peng, K. (2009). Acculturation strategies and integrative complexity: The cognitive implications of biculturalism. *Journal of Cross-Cultural Psychology, 40*, 105–39. doi:10.1177/0022022108326279

Tong, Y.-y., Hui, P. P.-Z., Kwan, L., & Peng, S. (2011). National feelings or rational dealings? The role of procedural priming on the perceptions of cross-border acquisitions. *Journal of Social Issues, 67*, 743–759. doi:10.1111/j.1540-4560.2011.01725.x

Torelli, C. J., Chiu, C.-Y., Tam, K.-p., Au, A. K. C., & Keh, H. T. (2011). Exclusionary reactions to foreign cultures: Effects of simultaneous exposure to cultures in globalized space. *Journal of Social Issues, 67*, 716–742. doi:10.1111/j.1540-4560.2011.01724.x

Van Tongeren, D. R., & Green, J. D. (2010). Combating meaninglessness: On the automatic defense of meaning. *Personality and Social Psychology Bulletin, 36*, 1372–1384. doi:10.1177/0146167210383043

Verkuyten, M., & Pouliasi, K. (2002). Biculturalism among older children: Cultural frame switching, attributions, self-identification, and attitudes. *Journal of Cross-Cultural Psychology, 33*, 596–609. doi:10.1177/0022022102238271

Webster, D. M., & Kruglanski, A. W. (1994). Individual differences in need for cognitive closure. *Journal of Personality and Social Psychology, 67*, 1049–1062. doi:10.1037/0022-3514.67.6.1049

Yang, K. S., & Bond, M. H. (1980). Ethnic affirmation by Chinese bilinguals. *Journal of Cross Cultural Psychology, 11*, 411–425. doi:10.1177/0022022180114002

MICHAEL MORRIS is the Chavkin-Chang Professor at Columbia University in the Business School and the Psychology Department. Previously he worked at Stanford University and, as a visitor, at universities in China, Japan, Korea, and Spain. He studies cultural differences in conflict management, justice judgments, and social interaction and relationship patterns. Increasingly he researches the dynamics of individuals, negotiating dyads, and teams that span multiple cultures. Morris is a founding editor of *Management and Organization Review*, an executive editor of the *Journal of Trust Research*, and an editorial board member at *Social and Personality Science*.

AURELIA MOK is an assistant professor of Management at the City University of Hong Kong. She received her Ph.D. in Management at Columbia Business School and her research examines how individuals negotiate between dual cultural identities and the implications for judgment, decision making and behavior. She is also interested in intercultural relations, cross-cultural management and consumer behavior.

SHIRA MOR is currently a Ph.D. candidate in Management at Columbia Business School. She graduated from Columbia University with a B.A in psychology and sociology (magna cum laude). Shira's research lies at the intersection of cultural psychology, organizational behavior, and conflict resolution research.

Journal of Social Issues, Vol. 67, No. 4, 2011, pp. 774–786

Psychological Consequences of Postindustrial Anomie on Self and Motivation Among Japanese Youth

Vinai Norasakkunkit*

Minnesota State University–Mankato

Yukiko Uchida

Kyoto University

Due to economic structural changes in Japan, an increasing population of youth are "Not engaged in Employment, Education, or Training" (NEET). We argue that this state of anomie is associated with a lack of motivation in conforming to inter-dependent norms. To illustrate this type of "deviant" motivation, we conducted a study in which high- and low risk Japanese students were given either success or failure feedback upon completing a challenging task. Low risk Japanese students were more likely to persist on the challenging task upon being given negative feedback compared to being given positive feedback. This motivational pattern is consistent with that of the prototypical Japanese (Heine et al.). In contrast, the op-posite pattern was found with high risk Japanese students. High risk students were also lower on levels of interdependence relative to low risk students according to both explicit and implicit measures of self-construal.

In Japan, people love working at Sony, and people who go out of Sony want to come back. . .sometimes that makes you slightly frustrated [because] you think, 'please let us get more young people in'. But that is the nature of [Japanese] society. Japanese believe that there is more to society than making money. . . It's a different environment. The company is family. They are not motivated by money in Japan. They're really not. No senior executive has ever come into my office and said, 'I want a raise.' Never! Never! Never!. . .Often they won't even take the raise because they say they are not 'senior' to 'that' person. He is

*Correspondence concerning this article should be addressed to Vinai Norasakkunkit at the Department of Psychology, Minnesota State University–Mankato, Mankato, MN 56001 [e-mail: vinai.norasakkunkit@mnsu.edu].

This study was supported by grants from the Kokoro Research Center, Kyoto University, and the Japan Society for the Promotion of Science (JSPS). The authors would also like to thank Beth Morling for her useful comments on an earlier version of this draft. The authors would like to thank Shozo Kishimoto and Midori Fujiwara of *Takatsuki Orange No Kai*, a hikikomori outreach program in Takatsuki, Japan, for their consultation on this project.

older than me. He came in before I did. —Sony's Chairman Sir Howard Stringer on CNN's
Fareed Zakaria GPS, (March 20, 2011).

This quote encapsulates what is well documented in the cultural psychological literature about Japanese society (Markus & Kitayama, 1991). Namely, that
Japanese society tends to be a seniority-based, interdependent society where one's
measure of success is largely determined by whether one has secured a permanent
position in a large company like Sony. Doing so would allow individuals to reap
the benefits of being associated with an elite organization and the stability of the
network of tight social ties that the organization can offer (Nakane, 1970). In much
of the industrialized world, globalization and digitalization have enabled possi-
bilities for individuals to find alternative paths to success by capitalizing on their
own idiosyncrasies that afford the emergence of innovative companies like Facebook and Google. Yet, in Japan, securing a permanent position in well-recognized,
large companies like Sony still remains the socially sanctioned "legitimate" path
to success. As Sir Howard Stringer implied, success in Japan is not only about
making money but also about finding a secure workplace to be socially embedded
in (see Brinton, 2011).

Globalization and Anomie

Traditionally, most cross-cultural psychological studies have examined segments of the population that represent society's center: middle class, occupationally functional adults. However, those who are most affected by economic
structural change due to globalization pressures are likely to be segments of the
population who move away from the center of society due to changing circumstances in their society. As these individuals move to the periphery of society, they
may no longer be under the pressure to internalize the dominant psychological
orientations; they may instead maintain or develop more "atypical" psychological
tendencies. For research purposes, this marginalized segment of the population
can be used as a comparison group to assess the impact of globalization and/or
cultural change.

According to Toivonen, Norasakkunkit, and Uchida (2011), globalization and
the transition to a postindustrial economy for economically developed societies
have exerted enormous pressures on such societies to highlight individualism, mer-
itocracy, competitiveness, commercialism, and innovation. In turn, these pressures
have promoted a shift toward deregulated, flexible labor markets. Consequently,
competition for the best and most secure jobs has intensified and necessary labor
market restructuring has converted what were once considered regular jobs to in-
expensive, precarious ones. In Japan, however, due to the seniority system that is
still very much in place in most organizations, the costs of labor restructuring have
been unevenly distributed across generations by confining labor reforms to those

who are relatively new to the labor market (i.e., the youth). Those who are protected from labor reforms are the senior elites and the fortunate university graduates who were able to secure "good" jobs during the narrow window of opportunity before graduation based on the particular Japanese recruitment system.

The resistance to liberalizing the labor market more evenly so that both short-term employment systems and long-term employment systems are equally permeable to qualified candidates can be described as exclusionary reactions to globalization pressures (Chiu, Gries, Torelli, & Cheng, 2011). Given that the protection of core institutions within the long-term employment system comes at a cost, the brunt of that cost is absorbed asymmetrically by the youth outside the protective bubble of the long-term employment system. The youth who are left out are rendered second class citizens who become marginalized in society and face little prospects of ever securing a desirable job that can offer a sense of belonging (Brinton, 2011).

Many of these marginalized youth are unable to fend for themselves in the face of uncertainty, instability, and a fierce competition for a spot inside the protective bubble of the long-term employment system. These people then often have no choice but to take indefinite refuge in the care of their immediate families because public aid in Japan is not only associated with immense negative stigma but can only to be made available if self-help and family support are not sufficient (Vij, 2007). As they resort to relying on their immediate families for financial support, many of them may choose to completely withdraw from employment, education, or training and are therefore referred to as NEETs (i.e., Not in Employment, Education, or Training) a term originally coined by the British government to describe British youth who were temporarily not participating in society (DfEE, 2001).

According to the Japanese government's classification of NEET, the individuals who fall into the NEET category in Japan must be between 15 and 34 years of age, unmarried, not enrolled in school or engaged in housework, and not seeking work or the technical training needed for work (Kosugi & Horii, 2003). Those who are marginally involved in employment are part-time freelance workers called *Freeters* who live with their parents (like most other NEETs) but who occasionally earn some money with low skilled and low paying jobs. A subcategory of NEETs called *hikikomori* (social isolates) not only completely withdraws from participating occupationally but also withdraws from participating socially. They isolate themselves into their own bedrooms from 6 months to decades at a time without interacting with others, sometimes including their own families. According to Zielenziger (2007), an estimated five million marginalized youth are partially or fully withdrawn from Japanese society. Also, according to a leading Japanese psychiatrist, Saito (1998), the number of people who classify as hikikomori who, by Saito's definition, do not suffer from any other Diagnostic and Statistical Manual-IV (DSM-IV) psychological disorder is estimated at one million. More recently, the Cabinet Office of the Japanese Government (2010) reported an estimate of about 700,000 hikikomoris. Furthermore the rate of "school refusal," a precursor to hikikomori, has doubled since 1990 (Jones, 2006).

It is important to note here that the consequences of marginalization due to globalization pressures will depend on the social structures that are in place and the predominant mode of agency afforded by the society. Hence, we should not expect that marginalization will take the same form in every society. In the United States, for example, marginalization will probably not take the form of social withdrawal but may take form more as alternative routes to empowering one's agency (e.g., participating in a protests, engaging in criminal activities, joining a gang, etc.; see Merton, 1938).

Given that the increasing population of marginalized youth is the direct result of social structural changes in Japanese society due to globalization pressures, we argue that studying the psychology of NEETs and hikikomoris offers a viable way to investigate some of the psychological consequences of globalization in an interdependent, seniority-based cultural system like Japan. Specifically, we are interested in trying to explain why Japanese media and researchers have portrayed the NEETs and hikikomoris in Japan as having low motivation, including describing them as having a "psychopathology characterized by impaired motivation" (Koyama et al., 2010, p. 72). We argue that the NEETs should endorse lower levels of explicit and implicit interdependent attitudes and therefore have a motivational style that deviates from one that is oriented toward participating in an interdependent cultural system precisely because they have been forced to drop out of that system as a consequence of the asymmetric reforms in the Japanese labor markets. At the same time, they may not necessarily be moving toward an alternative model of agency or alternative pathways to success given their general lack of familiarity with such alternatives (Zielenziger, 2006).

Motivational Processes of NEETs

To assess how "deviant" the motivational processes of NEETs are from mainstream Japanese youth, one has to understand the motivational processes associated with an interdependent self-construal, the predominant orientation of self in the Japanese cultural context (Markus & Kitayama, 1991). According to Morling, Kitayama, and Miyamoto (2002), the interdependent self-construal tends to be more adjustable (or malleable) than the Western-based, independent self-construal. A more malleable view of self allows for a greater capacity for adjusting to different relationships, roles, and situations, which then helps the individual to conform to socially expected standards of behavior and maintain social harmony (see also Kitayama, Markus, Matsumoto, & Norasakkunkit, 1997). The nature of a relatively malleable self-structure among Japanese suggest that Japanese are more likely to work harder and persist in response to failure than North Americans, whereas North Americans are more likely to work harder and persist in response to success than Japanese (Heine et al., 2001). Although the Japanese pattern here describes occupationally and socially functional Japanese individuals, the motivational pattern for NEETs, including hikikomoris, may very well deviate from this pattern.

To illustrate this type of deviant motivation among NEETs, we conducted an experiment on motivation. Because it was deemed impractical to recruit a large number of true NEETs to come to a research laboratory at a university setting to participate in a controlled experiment, we recruited a sample of Japanese students who were high risk or low risk of becoming NEET according to a NEET risk factor scale. Specifically, the motivational style associated with students at risk of becoming NEET was compared with that of low risk students to see if deviation from an interdependent-oriented motive is one psychological consequence of being marginalized due to globalization pressures being exerted on an interdependent cultural system like Japan.

The NEET risk factor scale (Uchida & Norasakkunkit, 2011, in preparation) has been found to discriminate between high risk Japanese students, low risk Japanese students, hikikomoris and non-hikikomori NEETs, and North American students. Specifically, high risk students were no different from hikikomoris and non-hikikomori NEETs in terms of NEET tendencies, according to the NEET risk factor scale. Also as expected, low risk Japanese students scored lower on NEET tendencies than the high risk Japanese students and the other two NEET groups. Furthermore, NEET tendencies were more likely to be found in the Japanese population and less likely to be found in the North American population. In sum, Uchida and Norasakkunkit suggest that, although not ideal, high risk Japanese students can serve as a reasonable proxy for real NEETs in experimental studies at university labs.

In this study, we used Heine et al.'s (2001) cross-cultural study in which they investigated the motivation to persist on a challenging task upon receiving success or failure feedback. Specifically, we randomly assigned high risk and low risk Japanese students to receive either success feedback or failure feedback upon performing a creativity test called the Remote Associates Test (RAT). It was expected that the motivational pattern for low risk Japanese students would replicate the Japanese pattern in Heine et al.'s study of persisting for longer periods of time upon receiving failure feedback relative to receiving success feedback, because a habit of being more responsive to failure feedback is more useful in knowing how to adjust oneself to fit in and maintain social harmony. We then expected that the high risk students, given their lack of incentive to have to fit in and maintain social harmony, would have a motivational pattern that deviated from this prototypical Japanese pattern. Furthermore, given NEETs' marginalized position in Japanese society, it was expected that high risk students would endorse lower levels of explicit and implicit interdependent self-construal relative to low risk students.

One caveat to our approach is that participants were university students at Kyoto University, an elite institution, rather than real NEETs or hikikomoris. One can easily argue then that such individuals, given their elite status, are not likely to be marginalized in Japanese society. However, NEETs are most commonly found in middle class families who tend to send their high school graduates to universities (Cabinet Office of the Japanese Government, 2010) and even an increasing number of young adults who earn doctoral degrees end up marginalized and working in unstable part-time academic positions while essentially leading a freeter lifestyle (Mizuki, 2007). Moreover, as mentioned earlier, in the process of validating the NEET risk factor scale, the students at risk of becoming NEET, even at an elite institution, were found to be more similar to real NEETs and hikikomoris and different from low risk students in terms of psychological risk factors (Uchida & Norasakkunkit, 2011, in preparation).

Method

Participants

Participants were undergraduate students recruited from Kyoto University and were paid 1,500 yen (about US $15) each for their participation. After removing six participants who did not complete the study, 106 participants (55 males and 51 females) completed both the experimental portion and an online test portion of the study. The age ranged from 18 to 23 ($M = 19.22$, $SD = 1.15$). All participants were Japanese citizens. The participants were divided into low to moderate risk (referred to as the "low risk" group henceforth) of becoming NEET ($N = 84$) and high risk of becoming NEET ($N = 23$) according to the cut off score of the NEET risk factor scale (see Materials section for details).

Materials

Materials were either originally created in Japanese or an existing Japanese version of the measure was used.

NEET risk factor scale (Uchida & Norasakkunkit, 2011, in preparation). This scale was developed by compiling common attitudes and values held by NEETs according to other investigators. These items used a 7-point Likert scale. Initial analyses identified 27 meaningful survey items that measured the risk of becoming NEET. Furthermore, three distinct risk factors emerged in the initial exploratory factor analysis. Factor 1 was labeled "freeter lifestyle preference," which refers to the tendency of becoming a "freeter" who consciously chooses not to work despite opportunities and job availabilities. An example of an item from this factor is, "After graduation, if there is something at work that I cannot tolerate, it is better to not force myself and instead just quit." Indeed, Uchida and Norasakkunkit (2011, in preparation) found that the freeter-type NEETs scored higher than hikikomori-type NEETs on this particular factor. The next factor that emerged, Factor 2, has to do with a "lack of self competence" (i.e., not feeling competent in accomplishing interdependent cultural tasks). An example of an item from this factor is, "My social skills are low, and I am not good at relating to others." Factor 3 has to do with an "unclear ambition for the future" (i.e., having unclear or unrealistic goals for what they want to do in the future). An example of an item from this factor is, "I don't quite know what I want to do in the future."

These three risk factors represent at least three different types of NEET subcategories. Although these subcategories are relatively distinct from each other, a reliability analysis also revealed that an overall score, combining all the items, could be calculated to represent overall risk of becoming NEET, as indicated by a Cronbach's alpha of .87 for the current sample. Uchida and Norasakkunkit (2011, in preparation) also found that Cronbach's alpha was .85 for hikikomori-type NEETs, .85 for freeter-type NEETs, and .91 for North Americans. A score of 104 separates high risk of becoming NEET from everybody else (i.e., low risk of becoming NEET).

Self-construal scale (Singelis, 1994). This 24-item self-report instrument on a 7-point Likert scale attempts to measure the two images of self that are conceptualized as reflecting the emphasis on connectedness and relations often found in non-Western cultures (interdependent) and the separateness and uniqueness of the individual (independent) stressed in the West. The Cronbach's alpha internal consistency for independent self-construal items and interdependent self-construal items were .57 and .76, respectively.

Implicit Association Test of self-construal (Self-Construal IAT; Uchida, Park & Kitayama, 2008). This test measured reaction time and accuracy for a categorization task as indices of independent and interdependent attitudes at the implicit or automatic level. The procedure involved having participants categorize numerous verbs and adjectives to the following categories; (1) relational verbs or positive adjectives versus nonrelational verbs or negative adjectives; (2) relational verbs or negative adjectives versus nonrelational verbs or positive adjectives. The test was designed as a word association task in which the participant is said to be more implicitly interdependent the faster s/he is at associating a relational verb (e.g., visit) with a positive adjective (e.g., good) and slower and less accurately s/he is at associating a nonrelational verb (e.g., run) with a positive adjective (e.g., good) when asked to do so. On the other hand, the participant is said to be more implicitly independent if this pattern is reversed.

Remote Association Test (RAT; Mednick, 1962). This is a test that was used to examine persistence in response to failure by Heine et al. (2001). The test was used in this research study for the same reason, and it involves having participants read three words that represent three hints. After reading the three hints, the participant is prompted to come up with the one correct word that relates to the three hints. For example, if "chocolate," "fortune," and "tin" is a set of hints, then the one correct word which relates to these hints is "cookie" because the word "cookie" can be combined with each hint in the set to create a meaningful phrase (i.e., chocolate cookie, fortune cookie, and cookie tin). There were three versions of this test varying in difficulty: (a) the very difficult test; (b) the very easy test; and (c) the moderately difficult test. There was also an answer sheet with a bogus standardized ranking of scores for only the difficult test and the easy test to be given after the participant completes the corresponding test.

Procedure

Replicating Heine et al.'s (2001) experimental procedure, participants were randomly assigned to either the difficult test condition or the easy test condition and were given instructions about the RAT before taking the test on their own. After 8 minutes, the participants were asked to stop taking the test and were given the answer key and the bogus standardized ranking of scores sheet. They were asked to score their own tests and indicate where they ranked according to the standardized scoring sheet. The bogus scoring sheet was designed so that those assigned to the difficult test condition would learn they scored below the 50th percentile (i.e., failure feedback condition) while those in the easy test condition ended up ranking above the 50th percentile (i.e., success feedback condition).

Once participants completed and scored the initial RAT, they were told to take another test on a computer that required a password to open. After a number of failed attempts at entering the correct password, the experimenter asked the participant to wait alone in the lab while the experimenter went out to get the password information from the primary investigator. Before leaving the lab, the experimenter placed a moderately difficult version of the RAT in front of the participant, saying that although the test was not a part of the study, the participant had the option of attempting the test while waiting for the experimenter to return. At that point, the experimenter left the lab and went to an observation room next door to observe the participant through a hidden wireless camera that was placed above the participant. The experimenter watched for whether the participant attempted the moderately difficult test and recorded the time that the participant persisted on the moderately difficult test for up to fifteen minutes. After fifteen minutes, the experimenter returned to the lab and told the participant that the primary investigator was nowhere to be found and that the participant needed to take the web version of the computer test on any computer with an Internet access. Before leaving the lab, the participant was given a handout with instructions on how to access the online test.

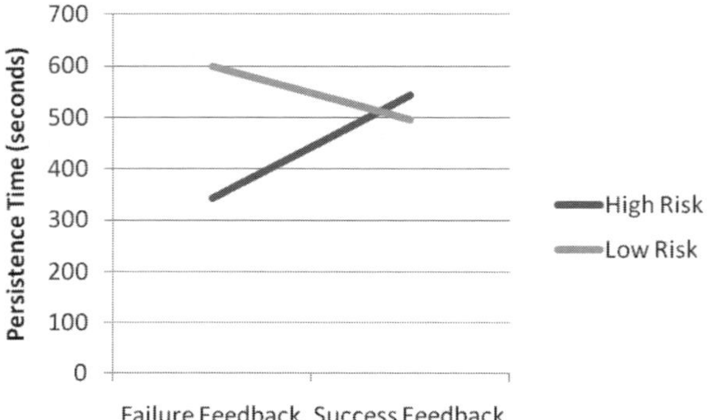

Fig. 1. Interaction effect between risk and feedback.

The online version of the test included the Singelis self-construal scale and the self-construal IAT, among other measures for a separate study. After the participants completed the online version of the test, they returned to the lab within a month of participating in the experiment to be debriefed and compensated.

Results

As expected, independent samples t-tests suggested that high risk students scored lower on self-reported interdependent self-construal ($M = 4.16$, $SD = 0.78$) than low risk students ($M = 4.60$, $SD = 0.70$), as indicated by $t(109) = 2.63$, $p = .01$. There was no difference in levels of self-reported independent self-construal. Consistent with this finding on the self-report measure, high risk students scored higher on self-construal IAT ($M = 0.22$, $SD = 0.78$), which is associated with lower implicit interdependence, than low risk students ($M = 0.06$, $SD = 0.69$), as indicated by $F(1, 104) = 4.00$, $p < .05$, controlling for order effects.

A risk (high vs. low risk) by feedback (success vs. failure feedback) analysis of variance with persistence time (in seconds) as the dependent variable confirmed, as expected, the hypothesized interaction, as indicated by $F(1, 103) = 5.85$, $p < .02$ (Figure 1). Specifically, the low risk pattern replicated the Japanese pattern in Heine et al.'s (2001) study where persistence was greater in the failure feedback condition ($M = 598.22$, $SD = 256.70$) relative to the success feedback condition ($M = 495.98$, $SD = 259.18$). In contrast, the high risk pattern was reversed ($M = 343.00$, $SD = 315.50$ vs. $M = 542.98$, $SD = 267.52$). There was no main effect of risk or condition. Also, there was no gender main effect, nor did gender interact with any other variable. Simple slope analysis in the failure feedback condition suggested that NEET tendencies were inversely associated with persistence time

($\beta = -5.87$, $SE = 1.83$, $p < .01$). In the success feedback condition, however, NEET tendencies were positively but not significantly associated with persistence time ($\beta = 0.55$, $SE = 1.87$, ns). Thus, these simple slope analyses suggest that NEET tendencies were associated with reduced motivation in response to failure feedback but not necessarily associated with increased motivation in response to success feedback.

Implicit self-construal was also found to be significantly associated with persistence time after controlling for order effects in the failure feedback condition ($\beta = -0.22$, $p = .05$). This finding suggested that as implicit independence decreased (or as implicit interdependence increased), persistence time increased in the failure feedback condition.

Discussion

This study investigated the consequences of success (positive) and failure (negative) feedback on levels of motivation to persist on a challenging task for students with high risk of becoming NEET versus students with low risk of becoming NEET. Heine et al.'s (2001) cross-cultural findings suggest that because Japanese generally have to adjust the self to others and the situation to maintain social harmony, they are more likely to attend to their own shortcomings to make the necessary adjustments in themselves. Behaviorally, this translates into being more persistent in response to negative feedback rather than positive feedback in the current experimental conditions. This study hypothesized and found that whereas this pattern was replicated among low risk Japanese students, it was reversed for high risk Japanese students. High risk students also scored lower on levels of self-reported interdependence and implicit interdependence.

Although we only investigated high risk students in this study and future research is needed to confirm our results in NEET samples, the preliminary results from this study have important implications for understanding how individuals who harbor attitudes and values that represent those of a growing population of Japanese NEETs, probably do not perceive strong incentives to conform to interdependent norms associated with mainstream Japanese middle class values. We believe this is because many Japanese youth today are no longer able to count on the long-term mutual commitment and stable bonds shared between employees and employers, a privilege enjoyed by the Japanese youth of previous generations. Therefore, the incentive to improve oneself by being responsive to negative feedback to meet social expectations, fit in, and maintain social harmony may be significantly diminished for the younger Japanese generation, especially for those who are outside the protective bubble of the long-term employment system. In this sense, the aversion that NEETs/hikikomoris have toward having to conform to social pressures and standards may simply represent a more extreme version of a growing attitude among Japanese youth in general.

Although globalization can afford new opportunities for growth and creativity (see Leung, Maddux, Leung, Galinsky, & Chiu, 2008), the marginalization of Japanese youth reminds us that there is also a dark side to globalization. Specifically, when "global values" of individualism, egalitarianism, competitiveness, commercialism, and innovation exert pressures on a fundamentally incompatible seniority-based, male-dominated, interdependent-oriented labor force like that found in Japan, one can expect core institutions to resist such pressures. Japanese youth today face a dualized social structure as a result of one employment system being protected from globalization pressures although shifting the cost of that social choice to the individuals who lie outside that system. In the protected long-term employment system, interdependent norms and expectations prevail. For the growing number of people who fall outside that system (i.e., precariat workers, NEETs, and hikikomoris), the incentive to conform to interdependent norms and expectations are much less compelling. Consequently, the motivational processes associated with constant self-improvement for the sake of fitting into an in-group are probably unsustainable for marginalized groups in Japan. Although marginalized groups such as NEETs and hikikomori can also be distinguished from each other by other factors such as family dynamics and socioeconomic status (Uchida & Norasakkunkit, 2011, in preparation), we agree with Zielenziger (2006) that, at the macro level, both NEET and hikikomori are afforded by the same societal processes that make Japanese youth bear the brunt of the cost of institutional protections from globalization pressures.

Although we have primarily focused on the motivational consequences of the costly exclusionary or "hot" reactions to globalization pressures in Japan, future research can perhaps examine the cognitive and emotional consequences of such reactions as well. Although hikikomori itself does not seem to be associated with any particular psychopathology (Koyama et al., 2010; Uchida & Norasakkunkit, 2011, in preparation), perhaps there is a way in which the kind of institutional hot reactions found in Japan affects mental health in profound ways. Thus, the mental health consequences of such reactions remain to be fully explored. It is also likely that incorporating cool, integrative reactions at the individual level in an institutional context that is essentially hostile to cool reactions requires such reactions to be manifested very tactfully and strategically so as not to be a nail that sticks out only to be pounded down (Toivonen et al., 2011). Future research can also focus on identifying individuals who are able to accomplish such a task and elaborating on their psychological characteristics.

If core institutions within an interdependent and economically developed cultural system continue to practice protective strategies rather than reform itself to be more compatible with a more permeable and horizontal system of a postindustrial economy, then those who find themselves outside the protected bubble may experience being caught in the growing rift between cultural practices and societal changes, thereby causing them to feel lost and confused. This state of "anomie" may be perceived to be so hopelessly irreconcilable that they may actively reject interdependent goals and values but not necessarily have anything else to replace them with for now.

References

Brinton, M. (2011). *Lost in transition: Youth, work, and instability in postindustrial Japan.* New York: Cambridge University Press.

Cabinet Office, Japanese Government. (2010). *Hikikomori ni kansuru jittai chosa [An investigation of the nature of hikikomori].* Retrieved from http://www8.cao.go.jp/youth/kenkyu/hikikomori/pdf_index.html

Chiu, C. Y., Gries, P. H., Torelli, C., & Cheng, S. (2011). Toward a social psychology of globalization. *Journal of Social Issues, 67*(4), 663–676. doi:10.1111/j.1540-4560.2011.01721.x

DfEE. (2001). *Transforming youth work.* London, UK: Department for Education and Employment.

Heine, S. J., Kitayama, S., Lehman, D. R., Takata, T., Ide, E., Leung, C., & Matsumoto, H. (2001). Divergent consesequences of success and failure in Japan and North America. An investigation of self-improving motivations and malleable selves. *Journal of Personality and Social Psychology, 81*, 599–615. doi:10.1037/0022-3514.81.4.599

Jones, M. (2006). Shutting themselves in. *The New York Times,* January 15, 46–52.

Kitayama, S., Markus, H. R., Matsumoto, H., & Norasakkunkit, V. (1997). Individual and collective processes in the construction of the self: Self-enhancement in the United States and self-criticism in Japan. *Journal of Personality and Social Psychology, 72*(6), 1245–1267. doi:10.1037/0022-3514.72.6.1245

Kosugi, R., & Hori, Y. (2003). *Gakkō kara Shokugyō e no Ikō wo Shien Suru Shokikan eno Hiaringu Chōsa Kekka: Nihon ni okeru NEET Mondai no Shozai to Taiō* [Results from a Survey of Institutions that Support the School-to-Work Transition: The Nature of the NEET Problem in Japan and Relevant Responses], JIL Discussion Paper Series 03-001: Japan Institute of Labour Policy and Training.

Koyama, A., Miyake, Y., Kawakami, N., Tsuchiya, M., Tachimori, H., & Takeshima, T. (2010). Lifetime prevalence, psychiatric comorbidity and demographic correlates of "hikikomori" in a community population in Japan. *Psychiatry Research, 176*, 69–74.

Leung, A. K.-y., Maddux, W. W., Galinsky, A. D., & Chiu, C.-y. (2008). Multicultural experience enhances creativity: The when and how? *American Psychologist, 63*, 169–181.

Markus, H. R., & Kitayama, S. (1991). Culture and the self: Implications for cognition, emotion, and motivation. *Psychological Review, 98*(2), 224–253. doi:10.1037/0033-295X.98.2.224

Mednick, S. A. (1962). The associative basis of the creative process. *Psychological Review, 26*, 220–232.

Merton, R. K. (1938). Social structure and anomie. *American Sociological Review, 3*, 672–682.

Mizuki, S. (2007). *Kougakureki waakingu pua: Seisan koujo to shite no daigakuin* [The educated working poor: Graduate schools as freeter manufacturing factories]. Tokyo: Koubunsha.

Morling, B., Kitayama, S., & Miyamoto, Y. (2002). Cultural practices emphasize influence in the U.S. and adjustment in Japan. *Personality and Social Psychology Bulletin, 28*, 311–323. doi:10.1177/0146167202286003

Nakane, C. (1970). *Japanese society.* Berkley: University of California Press.

Saito, T. (1998). *Shakaiteki Hikikomori: Owaranai Shishunki* [Social Withdrawal: Unending Adolescence]. Tokyo: PHP Shuppan.

Singelis, T. M. (1994). The measurement of independent and interdependent self-construals. *Personality and Social Psychology Bulletin, 20*(5), 580–591. doi:10.1177/0146167294205014

Toivonen, T., Norasakkunkit, V., & Uchida, Y. (2011). Unable to conform, unwilling to rebel? Youth, culture and motivation in globalizing Japan. *Frontiers in Cultural Psychology, 2*, 207. doi:10.3389/fpsyg.2011.00207

Uchida, Y., & Norasakkunkit, V. (2011). *Hikikomori/NEET keikou to taijinkankei no kentou* (The NEET Risk Factor Scale and special considerations to interpersonal factors). Unpublished manuscript [Manuscript in preparation].

Uchida, Y., Park, J., & Kitayama, S. (2008). Explicit and implicit social orientations: Independence and interdependence in Japan and the U.S. *Paper presented at the 9th Annual Conference of the Society of Personality and Social Psychology,* February, Albuquerque, New Mexico.
Vij, R. (2007). *Japanese modernity and welfare.* Hampshire: Palgrave Macmillan.
Zielenziger, M. (2006). *Shutting out the sun: How Japan created its own lost generation.* New York: Nan A. Talese.
Zielenziger, M. (2007). Japan's Lost Generation. *Lecture at World Affairs Council of the Monterey Bay,* April, Monterey, California.

VINAI NORASAKKUNKIT is an associate professor in the Psychology department at Minnesota State University, Mankato. His research has focused on examining clinical topics such as social anxiety and emotional well-being from a cultural psychological perspective.

YUKIKO UCHIDA is an associate professor in the Kokoro Research Center at Kyoto University. Her research has focused on emotions, relationships and subjective well-being from a cultural psychological perspective.

Journal of Social Issues, Vol. 67, No. 4, 2011, pp. 787–805

When Knowledge Is a Double-Edged Sword: Contact, Media Exposure, and American China Policy Preferences

Peter Hays Gries* and **H. Michael Crowson**
The University of Oklahoma

Huajian Cai
The Chinese Academy of Sciences

Globalization affords greater opportunities to learn about foreign peoples than in the past. What impacts do interpersonal contact, media exposure to and knowledge about China have on the American people's China policy preferences? Two large surveys of U.S. citizens were conducted in the summers of 2008 and 2009 to explore whether knowledge about China and prejudice against the Chinese people and the Chinese government would mediate the relationship between contact and media exposure on the one hand, and U.S. China policy preferences on the other. Results show that while knowledge played the expected mediating roles between contact and media exposure on the one hand, and prejudice against the Chinese people on the other, greater knowledge of China was actually associated with greater negativity toward the Chinese government, which in turn contributed to desires for tougher China policies. Both media exposure and interpersonal contact thus had mixed effects on China policy preferences.

Globalization involves the experiential compression of time and space (Giddens, 1985). Airplane travel and new communications technologies such as e-mail and Skype now allow peoples once separated by oceans and continents to interact more directly and frequently with one another than ever before. Furthermore, indirect contact in the form of increasing exposure to different cultures and international events through media such as television and the Internet has also risen dramatically in recent years, affording greater opportunities to learn about

---

*Correspondence concerning this article should be addressed to Peter Hays Gries, Institute for U.S.–China Issues, University of Oklahoma, 729 Elm Ave., Hester Hall, Room 120, Norman, Oklahoma, 73019–2105 [e-mail: gries@ou.edu].

foreign peoples than in the past. What impact do these growing interactions have on how the citizens of different countries feel and think about each other? And do these thoughts and feelings impact their foreign policy preferences?

This article explores these questions in the context of U.S.–China relations, arguably the most important bilateral relationship of the 21st century. China's dramatic recent economic and military rise has engendered significant anxiety around the world, America included. This makes understanding the determinants of mutual perception in U.S.–China relations particularly important, especially under conditions of rapid globalization.

The Chinese government recognizes that fears about "China's rise" could lead to the emergence of counterbalancing alliances among other countries that would undermine Chinese security. China has therefore sought to allay foreign fears by shifting the discursive terrain from one of "China's rise" first to "peaceful rise" and then to the even more innocuous "peaceful development" (e.g., Glaser & Medeiros, 2007). And China is seeking to manage China's international image in other ways as well. Since 2004, more than 300 Confucius Institutes have been launched around the world, aggressively promoting Chinese language education, as well as renewed international academic and cultural exchange. The underlying assumption appears to be that increased contact with and knowledge about China will improve foreign attitudes toward China.

This is reminiscent of Gordon Allport's (1954) intergroup contact hypothesis, in which he proposed that increased contact between ethnic groups living in close proximity would increase their knowledge about each other and thereby decrease prejudice. Allport's influential hypotheses not only led to a flourishing of social psychological research on the effects of intergroup contact on prejudice, but also to actual social policy, as busing, affirmative action, and other social policies were implemented during the U.S. civil rights movement in the attempt to reduce prejudice between American racial groups.

Decades of research and policy experiments have revealed that increased intergroup contact, under the right conditions, can lead to reductions in prejudice (Binder et al., 2009; Pettigrew & Tropp, 2006). Increased contact under the wrong conditions, however, can exacerbate conflict and prejudice. This literature is of great relevance to students of both the social psychology of globalization and U.S.–China relations. Of particular relevance to China's recent globalization strategy, Pettigrew and Tropp (2008) have noted in a recent meta-analysis that increased knowledge does serve as a mediator of the relationship between intergroup contact and prejudice reduction.

Can we utilize theories from the social psychology of intergroup relations to better understand the dynamics of mutual perception in U.S.–China relations? If so, it may very well have implications for understanding the broader social psychology of globalization. Specifically, this article addresses the following questions, which are exploratory in nature. First, what impact does globalization have, not just on attitudes toward foreign peoples, but on attitudes toward foreign governments? Unfortunately, when the Chicago Council on Global Affairs regularly surveys American attitudes toward foreign countries, it asks for ratings of "your feelings toward some countries and peoples," conflating the two. Little is therefore known about the relationship between attitudes toward foreign peoples and their governments. Recent research on China, however, has suggested that Americans are much more positive toward the Chinese people than they are about its government (e.g. Gries, Crowson & Cai, 2011). Is it possible that the increased exposure that accompanies globalization fosters empathy between peoples but not necessarily between governments? For instance, will increased contact with Chinese people and knowledge about China be associated with more positive American attitudes toward the Chinese government, or more negative attitudes?

Second, might media exposure act as a type of indirect contact, increasing knowledge and improving attitudes? Third, is knowledge about China the panacea for American attitudes toward China, as Chinese policymakers appear to assume? Fourth and finally, will contact, media exposure, knowledge, prejudice, and attitudes toward the Chinese government have a significant impact on American China policy preferences?

To explore these questions, two large surveys of Americans were conducted in the summers of 2008 and 2009. Structural equation modeling (SEM) was employed to study whether knowledge, prejudice against the Chinese people, and negative attitudes toward the Chinese government would mediate the relationship between contact and media exposure on the one hand, and American China policy preferences on the other. Whereas SEM is often utilized to deductively test theory, we use it in the current research to model relationships inductively. We adopt this exploratory approach with the goal of providing researchers interested in the links between psychology and globalization with a "starting point" for thinking about how contact, knowledge, prejudice, and policy attitudes might fit together in the context of international relations.

STUDY 1

Method

Procedures and participants

During the first week of August 2008, 2,785 members of a middle-American state university community completed an Internet survey. Participants were given the option of entering a draw to win tickets to home football games. The 2,584 in the final sample did not include 201 participants who completed the survey improperly, were not U.S. citizens, or were Chinese Americans (excluded because some may have only recently emigrated from China). The online survey began with a consent form that explained to participants the nature of the study, its voluntary nature, and the anonymity of the data collected.

The final sample included 1,310 undergraduates, 460 graduate students, 200 faculty, and 614 university staff (57 of whom did not attend college). There was a remarkable balance of women ($N = 1,289$) and men ($N = 1,295$), and Republicans ($N = 988$) and Democrats ($N = 940$) (656 chose "Independent or none"). Ages ranged from 18 to 72, with a mean age of 29.72 ($SD = 12.78$). In terms of ethnicity, the sample was 81% White, 3% African American, 4% non-Chinese Asian American, 4% Latino/a, 6% Native American, and 3% "other."

Measures

Unless otherwise noted, the questions that composed the following scales were on 7-point Likert scales, ranging from 1 (*strongly disagree*) to 7 (*strongly agree*). They were largely balanced in terms of positively and negatively worded items.

Prejudice Scale. A scale composed of four "*The Chinese people are...*" statements. Two were positive (*friendly* and *trustworthy*) and reverse coded, and two were negative (*devious* and *dishonest*). Higher values on the scale indicate greater "prejudice" or negative attitudes toward the Chinese people.

Negative Attitudes toward the Chinese Government Scale. A scale composed of four "*The Chinese government is...*" items, using the same four adjectives (*friendly, trustworthy, devious, dishonest*) used in the prejudice scale. Higher values indicate greater prejudice against or negativity toward the Chinese government.

Containment Policies toward China Scale. A three-item scale tapping respondents' preferred U.S. China policy. It included "The best way to deal with China is to build up our military to counter Chinese power," and two reverse coded items, "Our government should adopt a friendlier foreign policy toward China" and "The U.S. government should engage China through an active diplomacy that seeks to improve the relationship between our two countries." Higher values on "containment" indicate a preference for tougher U.S. policies toward China.

Contact quality was measured with two items. "On the whole, my past experiences with Chinese people have been pleasant" was measured on a 7-point scale, while "How many close Chinese friends do you have?" had four response options, "none," "a few," "many," and "very many." Scores on the two items were summed to form a 2–11 scale, with higher values indicating greater contact quality.

Knowledge about China was measured with three multiple choice questions (correct answers underlined): "The man who began China's economic

Table 1. Descriptive Statistics and Zero-Order Correlations (Study 1)

Variable	1	2	3	4	5	M	SD	α	N
1. Contact quality	–	.12	−.39	−.11	−.27	7.23/7.37[a]	1.39/1.37	.34/.37	2
2. Knowledge	.06	–	−.12	.13	−.14	.47/.48[b]	.33/.33	.44/.41	3
3. Prejudice: Chinese people	−.42	−.08	–	.09	.36	2.63/2.63	.98/.96	.86/.85	4
4. Negative attitude: Chinese Government	−.13	.06[n]	.1	–	.12	4.74/4.76	1.02/1.03	.85/.83	4
5. Containment policy: China	−.22	−.13	.28	.16	–	2.76/2.73	.95/.94	.66/.61	3

Notes. Development sample (min $N = 1{,}281$) figures are first and above the diagonal; Cross-validation sample (min $N = 1{,}279$) figures are second and below the diagonal.
[n] Correlation is not significant. All other correlations are significant at $p < .001$ (2-tailed).
[a] Sum of 4- and 7-point scales. Values range from 2–11.
[b] Values range from 0–1.
N refers to the number of items in the scale.

development policy of "Reform and Opening" was (Mao Zedong/Hu Jintao/Deng Xiaoping/Jiang Zemin)," "The dominant ethnicity/race in China is the (Hui/Manchu/Han/Zhuang)," and "The Tiananmen Massacre occurred in (1969/1979/1989/1999)." The sequence of the four response categories to each question was randomized. Correct answers were coded 1 and incorrect answers 0, and the three items were averaged to form a scale from 0 to 1 in which higher numbers indicate greater knowledge about China.

Results

Replication is a fundamental principle of the scientific method. We therefore decided to randomly divide our large sample ($N = 2{,}582$) into two samples of $N = 1{,}292$ and $N = 1{,}290$. The first would be used for model development, and the second to cross-validate our final model.

Descriptive statistics

Table 1 displays the scale alphas and number of scale items for both 2008 samples. The alphas for the containment scale were fair for both samples, while the alphas for the prejudice and negative attitudes toward the Chinese government scales were both good. Our contact quality and knowledge scales had poor internal reliabilities, however. This may be due in part to the low number of items utilized to measure these factors. To help compensate for these poor alphas, we used

SEM in our statistical analyses, allowing us to model not just prediction but also measurement error.

Table 1 reports the means and standard deviations for the five scales in both samples. The table also includes the correlations among these variables. The means on contact quality and knowledge were just above and below the scale midpoints of 7 and 0.5 respectively. While the means on negative attitudes toward the Chinese government were above the scale midpoint, the prejudice and containment scales were lower. Given that the prejudice and negative government scales included the exact same four items, differing only on the subject of each sentence—Chinese "people" versus "government"—the mean differences were remarkably large, t $(1284) = -55.92, p < .001$. The low scores on containment indicate that while our American participants as a whole were ambivalent about the Chinese government, they did not advocate tougher China polices.

Structural equation models

How should we interpret the pattern of associations also reported in Table 1? Given that the correlations are zero-order, and do not account for collinearity, we need to be careful about interpreting them. And there is the additional issue of mediation: are knowledge, prejudice, and negative attitudes toward the Chinese government mediating the impact of contact on China policy preferences? We decided to use SEM to find out. SEM has a number of advantages over multiple regression, such as modeling mediated relationships among variables and evaluating the global fit of a model containing those mediated relationships. As noted above, it also has the advantage of allowing for the modeling of both prediction and measurement error. We used AMOS 17.0 (IBM: Armonk, NY, USA) with full information maximum likelihood estimation to first test measurement and structural models on our development sample, and then to cross-validate our final structural model on our replication sample.

We first created five latent variables with two to four indicator variables and measurement error terms for each. For instance, our prejudice latent variable was indicated by our four prejudice items, with the two positive items (*friendly* and *trustworthy*) reverse coded. The error terms for the two reverse coded items were allowed to covary to address a possible method effect. We then allowed all five of our latent variables to covary. The first row of Table 2 reveals that this measurement model was a good fit to the data. We examined the fit of all of our models based on the χ^2 test and p value, the Comparative Fit Index (CFI), Tucker-Lewis Index (TLI), the Normed Fit Index (NFI), and the Root Mean Square Error of Approximation (RMSEA). Nonsignificant χ^2 values are considered a good indicator of close model fit, although with large sample sizes such as ours a significant p value is acceptable. Also, conventional cutoffs for close model fit

Table 2. Fitness Statistics

Model	χ^2	P	df	CFI	NFI	TLI	RMSEA
Study 1 development sample ($N = 1,292$)							
1. Measurement	422.83	.000	92	.952	.940	.930	.053
2. Final structural	427.21	.000	93	.952	.940	.930	.053
Study 1 replication sample ($N = 1,290$)							
3. Cross-validation	501.41	.000	93	.935	.922	.905	.058
Study 2 development sample ($N = 1,342$)							
4. Measurement	1002.55	.000	204	946	.934	.928	.054
5. Fully saturated structural	1006.59	.000	205	946	.943	.928	.054
6. Final structural	1019.83	.000	212	946	.933	.929	.053
Study 2 replication sample ($N = 1,306$)							
7. Cross-validation	945.30	.000	212	.944	.929	.927	.051
"Good fit" conventions		0		$\geq$.95	$\geq$.95	$\geq$.95	$\leq$.06

Notes. χ^2 = chi-square; p = significance level; df = degrees of freedom; CFI = comparative fit index; NFI = normed fit index; TLI = Tucker-Lewis Index; RMSEA = root mean square error of approximation.

are CFI, TLI, and NFI values greater than .95, and RMSEA values less than .06 (Kline, 2005; Schumacker & Lomax, 2004).

Since the measurement model was a good fit to the development data, we proceeded to test a fully saturated structural model in which contact quality served as the lone exogenous variable, containment as the final dependent variable, and knowledge and the two attitudes variables as mediators. The path from contact quality to negative attitudes toward the Chinese government was not statistically significant so was trimmed. The final structural model, displayed in Figure 1, also exhibited good model fit, as can be seen in the fitness statistics displayed in the second row of Table 2.

Figure 1 confirms the contact literature's finding that contact directly and negatively predicts prejudice ($\beta = -.36$), and that knowledge plays a weak mediating role (indirect effect $= -.016$) in the relationship as well. Contact quality was positively, though weakly, associated ($\beta = .12$) with knowledge, which was in turn associated with decreased prejudice ($\beta = -.13$). These findings are consistent with Pettigrew and Tropp's (2008) meta-analysis of the contact literature mentioned above, which found knowledge to be a weak but significant mediator of contact on prejudice.

Although knowledge about China was associated with *reduced* prejudice, it was associated with an *increase* in negative attitudes toward the Chinese government ($\beta = .17$). In other words, the more our American participants knew about China, the less they liked the Chinese government. However, knowledge was

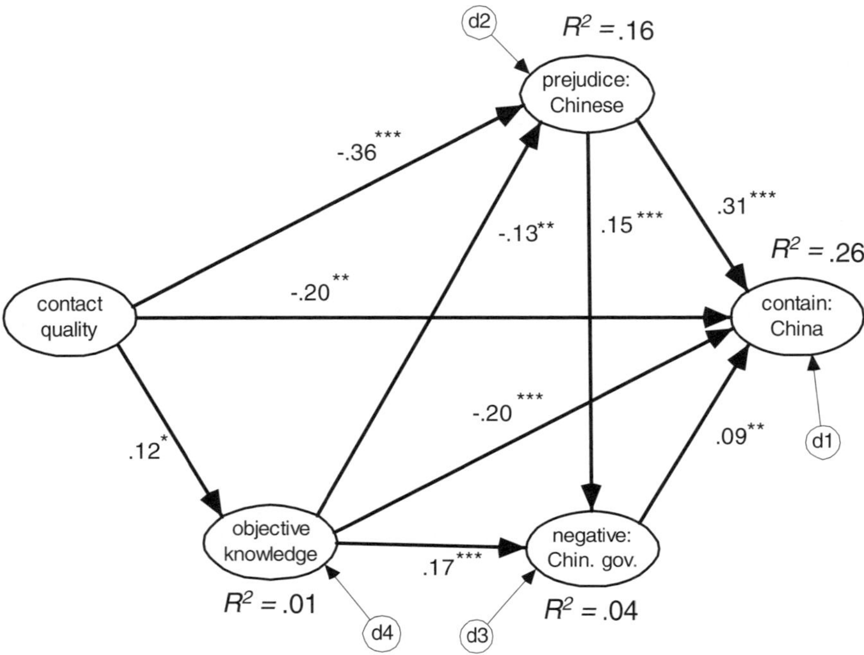

Fig. 1. Final structural model, Study 1 development sample ($N = 1,292$).

Note. 16 indicator variables and their measurement error terms are not displayed. Standardized regression coefficients are presented in the figure.
*$p < .05$; **$p < .01$; ***$p < .001$.

associated with decreased prejudice, which was positively associated with negative attitudes toward the Chinese government ($\beta = .15$). The indirect path from knowledge to attitudes toward the Chinese government via prejudice toward the Chinese people was negative (indirect effect $= -.04$). This indicated that persons scoring higher on knowledge were less likely to voice stronger containment attitudes when considered through the mediating factor of prejudice.

Perhaps most impressively, our model explains a full 26% of the variance in China policy preferences. Figure 1 reveals that all four of the other variables in the model were statistically significant predictors of containment policy preferences. It is noteworthy that of the four predictors, prejudice was the strongest ($\beta = .31$) and negative attitudes toward the Chinese government was the weakest ($\beta = .09$) predictor of policy preferences. This is surprising: our containment variable measured preferred policies toward China as a country, and yet it was attitudes toward the Chinese people (prejudice) rather than attitudes toward their government that had far greater explanatory power.

To cross-validate our final structural model, we ran it again on our replication sample ($N = 1{,}290$), which had not been used during model development. The third line of Table 2 displays the resulting fit statistics, which, while not quite as good as those of the development sample, were still adequate. The R-squared values and path coefficients from the replication model, furthermore, were largely identical to those from the development sample displayed in Figure 1. A few minor differences worth noting were that the overall R-squared for containment decreased from 26% to 23%, the path from knowledge to prejudice decreased from $-.13$ to $-.07$, becoming statistically nonsignificant, and the path from prejudice to contain increased from .21 to .31. Overall, these fitness statistics, path coefficients, and R-squared values from our cross-validation sample give us greater confidence in the replicability of the model displayed in Figure 1.

Discussion

Study 1 confirmed the prediction from the contact hypothesis that objective knowledge about China would mediate the relationship between interpersonal contact quality and prejudice toward the Chinese people. It also extended the contact hypothesis by demonstrating that increased knowledge does not improve all kinds of attitudes: attitudes toward the Chinese government actually *worsened* as knowledge about China increased. Study 1 also showed that both attitudes toward the Chinese people and government partially mediated the relationship between contact quality and China policy preferences in the expected directions: the more negative the attitudes toward the Chinese people and government, the more our American participants desired a tougher policy of containing China.

Given that international relations theorists devote most of their attention to the state, and largely ignore issues like prejudice, we were surprised to find that prejudice against Chinese people had a greater impact on China policy preferences than negative attitudes toward the Chinese government. But given that overall levels of prejudice toward the Chinese people were quite low in both of our samples (a mean of just 2.63 out of seven for both), it is also heartening to find that positive American attitudes toward the Chinese people appear to have a greater impact on China policy preferences than negative attitudes toward the Chinese government. Contact quality and knowledge about China, furthermore, were directly associated with desires for friendlier U.S. China policies.

One possible empirical weakness of Study 1 was that our measure of objective knowledge about China included just three multiple choice questions about China, and one of the three asked the date of the Tiananmen Square Massacre (1989). Given the normative valence of this item, it may have influenced our finding that increased knowledge about China was positively associated with more negative attitudes toward the Chinese government. A lengthier and more content-neutral test of knowledge about China is needed.

Secondly, our knowledge about China variable sought to tap objective knowledge. Perhaps a more subjective measure of knowledge as reflected in a self-report of perceived knowledge would play a different mediating role between contact and China attitudes and policy preferences.

Third and finally, Study 1 only tapped the direct interpersonal contact our American participants had with Chinese people. What about their indirect contact with China through the increased media exposure via television and the Internet that has accompanied globalization? Does media exposure act as a kind of indirect contact, improving American attitudes toward China? To address these issues and questions, and to further replicate the findings above, we conducted a follow-up survey in 2009.

STUDY 2

Method

Procedures and Sample

On August 12–14, 2009, 2,819 members of a mid-American state university community completed a 10-minute online Internet survey in exchange for the opportunity to enter a raffle for football tickets. Participants were informed about the topic of the study, its voluntary nature, and the protection of their privacy.

Data from 126 non-U.S. citizens, 35 Chinese Americans (who may have only recently emigrated from China), and ten respondents who did not follow instructions were dropped from further analysis. The final sample ($N = 2,648$) included 614 staff, 213 faculty, 441 graduate students, and 1,380 undergraduates. It included slightly more women ($N = 1,426$) than men ($N = 1,222$), and slightly more Democrats ($N = 1,059$) than Republicans ($N = 906$) or Independents ($N = 683$). However, the mean score on a 7-point liberal-conservative self-placement scale was very close to the scale midpoint of 4 ($M = 3.78$, $SD = 1.77$), suggesting ideological balance. The mean age of the sample was 29.49 ($SD = 13.03$). 83% of the respondents were in-state, but the remaining 17% came from every state in United States; 78.4% were Caucasian/White, 3.9% were African American, 3.5% were Asian American (non-Chinese), 3.6% were Latino/Latina, and 7.6% were Native American.

Measures

As in the first study, unless otherwise noted, all questions were on 7-point Likert scales. Questions were again largely balanced and question order was randomized on each page.

Contact quality was measured with two items that differed slightly from those used in Study 1: "My contacts with Chinese people have been friendly" and "When you have interacted with Chinese people, has the contact been pleasant?" Both were scored on 4-point Likert-type scales.

Media exposure. Participants were asked, "Do you read or watch many news stories about China? How much media exposure do you have to the following types of news stories about China?" The three categories were "news about Chinese (culture / economics; trade / politics; the Chinese military)." The 7-point Likert scale for each was anchored by *none at all* and *a great deal*. Note that this is a self-report and thus subjective measure of media exposure.

Objective knowledge about China was measured with 10 multiple choice questions. A sample question was "Which of the following is a current leader of China?" (Hu Jintao/Jiang Zemin/Mao Zedong/Deng Xiaoping). The sequence of the four response choices was again randomized. The Tiananmen Massacre item from the first study was dropped so that all 10 questions were value neutral.

Subjective knowledge. Participants were asked, "How much do you know about China?" The three categories of knowledge were: "I am knowledgeable about Chinese (culture / economics; trade / politics; the Chinese military)."

The *Prejudice* and *Negative Attitudes toward the Chinese Government scales* used in the current study were identical to those used in Study 1.

Containment Policies toward China Scale. Four items were similar to the three-item scale used in Study 1. Two new items were: "The U.S. government should engage China through an active diplomacy that seeks to improve the relationship between our two countries" (reverse coded) and "The U.S. government should pursue a tougher China policy." Higher values indicate a desire for a tougher U.S. China policy.

Results

We again began by dividing our large sample ($N = 2,648$) into two random samples. The first ($N = 1,342$) was used for model development, the second ($N = 1,306$) for model replication.

Descriptive Statistics

The scale alphas and number of items for both 2009 samples are displayed in Table 3. As in Study 1, the internal reliabilities for the Containment Scale were

Table 3. Descriptive Statistics and Zero-Order Correlations (Study 2)

Variable	1	2	3	4	5	6	7	M	SD	α	N
1. Contact quality	–	.17	.17	.20	−.46	−.07*	−.26	3.35/3.35[a]	.51/.49	.69/.64	2
2. Media exposure	.15	–	.36	.71	−.16	.11	−.19	3.04/3.02	1.20/1.24	.85/.84	3
3. Objective knowledge	.13	.31	–	.37	−.11	.09	−.18	44.96/44.68[b]	22.43/21.92	.60/.58	10
4. Subjective knowledge	.13	.69	.32	–	−.20	.12	−.19	3.54/3.51	1.42/1.39	.88/.86	3
5. Prejudice: Chinese people.	−.41	−.17	−.10	−.14	–	.10	.35	2.69/2.66	1.02/.94	.88/.85	4
6. Negative attitude: Chinese Government	−.03[n]	.15	.05[n]	.15	.05[n]	–	.22	4.67/4.73	1.02/1.03	.86/.85	4
7. Containment policy: China	−.23	−.13	−.17	−.10	.34	.20	–	3.15/3.18	.87/.87	.67/.66	4

Notes. Development sample (min $N = 1{,}323$) figures are first and above the diagonal; Cross-validation sample (min $N = 1{,}287$) figures are second and below the diagonal.

N refers to the number of items in the scale. Unless otherwise noted, all correlations are significant at $p \leq .001$ (2-tailed); *$p < .01$.

[n] Correlation is not significant.

[a] 4-point scale; [b] 100-point quiz scale.

fair, in the mid .60s, and very good for our Prejudice and Negative Attitudes toward the Chinese Government Scales, again in the mid to high .80s. The biggest differences from Study 1 were our contact and objective knowledge variables, whose internal reliabilities both improved dramatically. The alphas for our contact quality items doubled from the .30s to the .60s, which is really quite good for a two-item scale. The alphas for our Objective Knowledge Scale also increased dramatically, from the low .40s to around .60. The two new three-item scales for Media Exposure and Subjective Knowledge had very good internal reliabilities in the mid to high .80s.

The means and standard deviations reported in Table 3 again reveal low average levels of prejudice (an average of just 2.7 on a 7-point scale) but slightly negative attitudes toward the Chinese government (an average of 4.7). On average, 2009 participants still preferred a friendlier policy toward China (3.2 out of 7), but not as much as participants had in Study 1 (2.7 out of 7). Average interpersonal contact quality was quite high (3.4 out of 4), and media exposure somewhat low (3 out of 7). Participants scored slightly below the scale midpoint (3.5 out of 7) on Subjective Knowledge. Finally, both samples averaged 45 out of 100 on the 10-item objective knowledge multiple choice quiz. Given that there were only four response choices for each of the ten questions, and pure chance would have resulted in a score of 25%, our respondents on average cannot be said to be very objectively knowledgeable about China. Fortunately, a healthy standard deviation of 22 ensures that we have sufficient variation in our Objective Knowledge scale for it to constitute a useful measure.

Structural equation models

The zero-order correlations reported in Table 3 reveal that the data in the current study largely replicates Study 1 findings in regard to the possible effects that contact has on prejudice, negative attitudes toward the Chinese government, and preferences toward containment. We again used AMOS 17.0 with full information maximum likelihood estimation to perform SEM, exploring the pattern of relationships among the seven variables.

We first created seven latent variables with indicator variables and measurement error terms for each. Because our Objective Knowledge variable is based on a 10-item quiz, we first created three parcels of three or four averaged quiz items each to better manage the overall number of parameters in the model. We again allowed the error terms for the pairs of reverse coded items in the Prejudice, and Negative Attitudes toward the Chinese Government, and Containment Policy toward China scales to covary to address a method effect. Because we suspected a method effect due to the similar wordings and high correlations between our new Subjective Knowledge and Media Exposure scales, we also allowed the error terms for the pairs of culture, economics and trade, and politics and military items to covary. We then allowed all seven of our completed latent variables to covary. The fourth line in Table 2 reveals that this measurement model was a good fit to the data.

We then proceeded to test a fully saturated structural model in which Contact Quality and Media Exposure were the exogenous variables, Containment Policy the final dependent variable, and the two knowledge and two attitudes variables acted as sequential mediators. Line five of Table 2 reveals that this fully saturated structural model was also a good fit to the development sample data. Nevertheless, six statistically nonsignificant paths were then trimmed. The final structural model, displayed in Figure 2, had slightly better model fit, as can be seen in the sixth line of Table 2.

Figure 2 reveals dual paths from direct and indirect contact to China policy preferences. Direct interpersonal contact was again associated with reduced prejudice toward the Chinese people, and had no impact on attitudes toward the Chinese government. And indirect media exposure to China had a greater indirect impact on policy preferences via negative attitudes toward the Chinese government than through prejudice.

Surprisingly, media exposure had *both* positive and negative impacts on China policy preferences in the model. On the positive side, the direct path from media exposure to containment policy was small and negative ($\beta = -.11$), indicating that greater media exposure was associated with less desire for tougher containment policies against China. Furthermore, the indirect path from media exposure to subjective knowledge to prejudice also reduced desires to contain China. On the negative side, however, media exposure was associated with greater objective

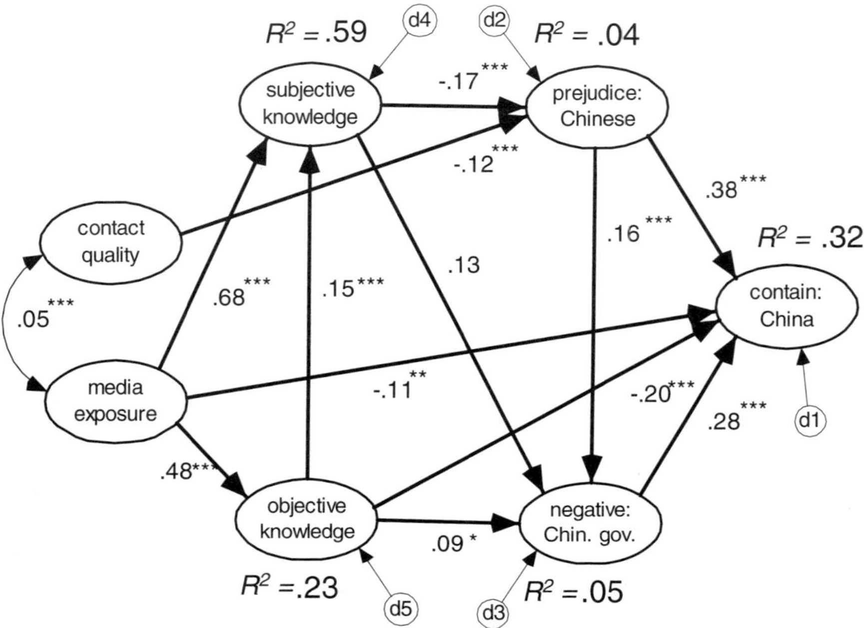

Fig. 2. Final structural model, Study 2 development sample ($N = 1,342$).

Note. 23 indicator variables and their measurement error terms are not displayed. (Ten objective knowledge items were parceled into three indicator variables, to reduce the overall number of parameters in the model). Standardized regression coefficients are presented in the figure.
$^*p < .05$; $^{**}p < .01$; $^{***}p < .001$.

knowledge of China, which was again associated with slightly more negative views of the Chinese government, which in turn was associated with greater preference for a tougher China policy. A similar path via subjective knowledge and attitudes toward the Chinese government was also associated with greater containment scores.

Figure 2 also reveals that objective and subjective knowledge were not that strongly related ($\beta = .15$), and that subjective knowledge had a greater impact on prejudice reduction than did objective knowledge. In other words, when it comes to prejudice, it is not what the respondents actually know but what they think they know.

Like media exposure, knowledge was associated with both positive and negative impacts on China policy preferences. The only direct relationship was a negative one, with objective knowledge associated with a reduction of desires to contain China ($\beta = -.20$). Also on the positive side, subjective knowledge was associated with reduced prejudice ($\beta = -.17$), which was accompanied by desires for a friendlier China policy ($\beta = .38$). On the negative side, both objective and subjective knowledge were associated with small increases ($\beta = .09$ and .13) in negative attitudes toward the Chinese government, which were connected to increased desires for tougher China policies ($\beta = .28$).

Finally, it is worth noting that, as with Study 1 data, our explanatory variables were once again able to account for a considerable amount of the overall variance in China policy preferences. Indeed, our R-squared for containment increased from 26% in Study 1 to a full 32% in the current study. It is also worth noting that prejudice was again a stronger predictor of China policy preferences than negative attitudes toward the Chinese government.

Finally, we sought to replicate the final 2009 structural model in the current study by running it on our replication sample, which had not been used during model development. The seventh and final line of Table 2 displays the resulting fit statistics, which while not quite as good as those from the development sample, were still adequate. The R-squared values and path coefficients from the replication model were remarkably similar to those from the development sample. The only noteworthy difference was that subjective knowledge became a much stronger predictor of negative attitudes toward the Chinese government than objective knowledge, with the former path increasing from $\beta = .13$ to $\beta = .20$, and the latter falling from $\beta = .09$ to $\beta = .00$ and statistical nonsignificance. This suggests that not just prejudice but also attitudes toward the Chinese government are more impacted by what we think we know than by what we actually know.

Discussion

Study 2 both replicated and extended the findings from Study 1. In all four data sets, contact quality was associated with decreased prejudice, which in turn powerfully predicted China policy preferences in a positive direction. This finding not only aligns with the extensive contact literature, but also suggests that to the extent that Confucius Institutes can promote *high-quality exchanges* between American and Chinese *people*, they will have a positive impact on U.S.–China relations.

Study 2 also extended the findings from Study 1. First, media exposure appears to act as a type of extended or indirect contact impacting knowledge, attitudes, and policy preferences. However, the impact of media exposure on China policy preferences in the current study was mixed. The direct impact of increased media exposure was a small but significant desire for a *friendlier* U.S. China policy. This finding should serve as an important rebuttal to those Chinese who claim that the American media is unambiguously negative about China and that this is why Americans do not support friendlier China policies. In fact, the over 5,000 Americans in all four of our samples on average did desire friendlier China policies, and greater media exposure appears to have directly contributed to this preference. That said, increased media exposure was associated with greater objective and subjective knowledge about China, both of which were positively associated with more *negative* attitudes toward the Chinese government.

Second, our measures of objective and subjective knowledge were significantly, though weakly, associated with more negative views of the Chinese government. Knowledge was thus associated with greater desires for *tougher* China policies via participants' attitudes toward the Chinese government. Like media exposure, however, increased knowledge had mixed effects, also contributing to desires for *friendlier* China policies, both directly from objective knowledge, and indirectly via prejudice reduction.

General Discussion

Do the increased interpersonal contact and media exposure accompanying globalization, and greater knowledge about China lead to more positive American attitudes toward the Chinese people and government, and preferences for a more accommodating American China policy? The Chinese government appears to be betting heavily that they do, investing a tremendous amount of time and money into cultivating increased contact between Chinese and Americans through international interpersonal exchanges, and greater knowledge about China through Confucius Institutes.

The evidence from our 2008 and 2009 surveys is mixed, however. On the positive side, contact quality is associated with dramatic reductions in prejudice against the Chinese people, as predicted by the contact hypothesis (Allport, 1954). And decreased prejudice, in turn, is strongly associated with desires for a friendlier China policy. Furthermore, as predicted by the contact literature, the impact of interpersonal contact on prejudice was mediated by knowledge. The impact of knowledge was small but in the expected direction: the more a participant knew (or believed he/she knew) about China, the less prejudice the person felt toward the Chinese people.

On the negative side, knowledge also mediated the impact of contact on attitudes toward the Chinese government, but in the opposite direction: more knowledge about China was accompanied by more *negative* attitudes toward the Chinese government. Given the strong impact of ideology on American attitudes toward China (Gries, et al., 2011; Gries, Cai, & Crowson, 2010), this finding may not be surprising. It does, however, suggest that extensions of the contact hypothesis beyond attitudes toward social groups (i.e., prejudice) to other types of attitudes (such as attitudes toward governments) need to be sensitive to the specific intergroup context. Greater knowledge can be a double-edged sword.

On balance, however, our surveys suggest that the Chinese government has made a good investment in international exchange and education about China. Contact quality and knowledge reduced prejudice, which is accompanied by desires for a friendlier China policy. This positive effect on policy preferences counteracts the negative impact of knowledge on attitudes toward the Chinese government, and their negative impact on policy preferences. As noted above, we find it surprising that prejudice had such a strong impact on China policy preferences. Although this finding requires further confirmation, it is heartening, as on average Americans have a very favorable view of the Chinese people.

All survey designs have their strengths and weaknesses. Our survey respondents were all from one university community, and the majority was from a single mid-American state (many students were from other states, however). We therefore need to be cautious about generalizing from such data about levels of say, anti-Chinese prejudice, to all Americans. However, our core interest is not in the *absolute* levels of specific opinion, for which nationally representative survey data would be more appropriate. Instead, our interest is in the "patterns of associations" among different variables. Our design therefore emphasizes construct or internal validity. Nonetheless, we believe we have also achieved a reasonable degree of external validity. This is not a small student-only sample, but a large, diverse sample of American adults well balanced in terms of age, gender, and ideology.

This study has focused on purely situational determinants of American attitudes toward China. Previous scholarship has demonstrated that individual differences in identity and ideology have a major impact on American attitudes toward China. For instance, Americans higher in nationalism or cultural conservatism are on average more negative about China than their compatriots who are low on those traits (Gries & Crowson, 2010). Indeed, the powerful role of ideology in shaping American attitudes toward China may help explain how it is that Americans who know so little about China nonetheless have coherent attitudes toward China. Gries, Crowson, Sandel, and Cai (2010) found that both individual differences variables such as personality and ideology and situational variables such as media exposure impacted changing American attitudes toward China before and after the 2008 Beijing Olympics. Future scholarship, however, could take the next step to explore person by situation interactions. For instance, does increased media exposure to China contribute to greater negativity toward the Chinese government equally among all Americans, or might it differentially impact those high and low in nationalism? Similarly, does increased interpersonal contact with Chinese reduce prejudice among American cultural conservatives and cultural liberals alike? Future work should seek to combine the analysis of such individual differences and situational variables.

We hope that these inductive findings can serve as the basis for future theorizing in the social psychology of globalization. Specifically, we believe our empirical results have implications for addressing the broad issues of what social psychological factors contribute to the positive and negative effects of globalization (Chiu, Gries, Torelli, & Cheng, 2011). Our normative desire is that such scholarship can help *increase* integrative and *decrease* exclusionary reactions to foreign cultures (Chiu & Cheng, 2007). Defensive and exclusionary reactions to foreign cultures perceived as threats to one's own culture will only contribute to xenophobia and the likelihood of increased international conflict. Inclusionary responses to globalization, by contrast, will increase intercultural understanding and learning, and promote cooperation in the 21st century.

References

Allport, G. W. (1954). *The nature of prejudice*. Reading, MA: Addison-Wesley.

Binder, J., Zagefka, H., Brown, R., Funke, F., Kessler, T., Mummendey, A., . . . Leyens, J. (2009). Does contact reduce prejudice or does prejudice reduce contact? A longitudinal test of the contact hypothesis among majority and minority groups in three European countries. *Journal of Personality and Social Psychology, 96*(4), 843–856. doi:10.1037/a0013470

Chiu, C.-y., & Cheng, S. Y.-y. (2007). Toward a social psychology of culture and globalization: Some social cognitive consequences of activating two cultures simultaneously. *Social and Personality Psychology Compass, 1*, 84–100. doi:10.1111/j.1751-9004.2007.00017.x

Chiu, C.-y., Gries, P. H., Torelli, C., & Cheng, S. Y.-y. (2011). Toward a social psychology of globalization. *Journal of Social Issues, 67*, 663–676. doi:10.1111/j.1540-4560.2011.01721.x

Giddens, A. (1985). *The nation state and violence*. Cambridge: Polity Press.

Glaser, B. S., & Medeiros, E. (2007). The changing ecology of foreign policymaking in China: The ascension and demise of the theory of "peaceful rise". *The China Quarterly, 190*, 291–310. doi:10.1017/S0305741007001208

Gries, P. H., Cai, H., & Crowson, H. M. (2010). The spectre of Communism in US-China Policy: Bipartisanship in the American subconscious. *The Chinese Journal of International Politics, 3*, 397–413. doi:10.1093/cjip/poq014

Gries, P. H., & Crowson, H. M. (2010). Political orientation, party affiliation, and American attitudes towards China. *Journal of Chinese Political Science, 15*, 219–244. doi:10.1007/s11366-010-9115-1

Gries, P. H., Crowson, H. M., & Cai, H. (2011). God, guns, and. . . China? How ideology impacts American attitudes and policy preferences toward China. *International Relations of the Asia-Pacific*. doi:10.1093/irap/lcr012

Gries, P. H., Crowson, H. M., Sandel, T., & Cai, H. (2010). The Olympic effect on American attitudes towards China: Beyond personality, ideology, and media exposure. *Journal of Contemporary China, 19*, 213–231. doi:10.1080/10670560903444181

Kline, R. B. (2005). *Principles and practice of structural equation modeling* (2nd ed.). New York, NY: Guilford Press.

Pettigrew, T. F., & Tropp, L. R. (2006). A meta-analytic test of intergroup contact theory. *Journal of Personality and Social Psychology, 90*, 751–783. doi:10.1037/0022-3514.90.5.751

Pettigrew, T. F., & Tropp, L. R. (2008). How does intergroup contact reduce prejudice? Meta-analytic tests of three mediators. *European Journal of Social Psychology, 38*(6), 922–934. doi:10.1002/ejsp.504

Schumacker, R. E., & Lomax, R. G. (2004). *A beginner's guide to structural equation modeling*. Mahwah, NJ: Lawrence Erlbaum.

PETER HAYS GRIES is the Harold J. & Ruth Newman Chair in U.S.-China Issues and Director of the Institute for U.S.-China Issues at the University of Oklahoma. He is author of *China's New Nationalism* (University of California Press, 2004), and co-editor (with Stanley Rosen) of *Chinese Politics* (Routledge 2010) and *State and Society in 21st Century China* (Routledge 2004).

H. MICHAEL CROWSON is an Associate Professor in the Department of Educational Psychology at the University of Oklahoma. His research focuses on conceptualization and measurement of classroom need for closure; the role of classroom need for closure in student learning and achievement; predictors of preservice teachers' diversity-related attitudes, with particular emphasis on their attitudes toward students with disabilities; dispositional factors associated with prejudice and noninclusive attitudes and behaviors in society; and measurement-related issues in moral judgment and personal epistemology research.

HUAJIAN CAI is a Professor at the Institute of Psychology, Chinese Academy of Sciences. His research involves mainly cultural differences in self-evaluation motives and particularly the causes and manifestations as well as meanings of cultural difference in self-esteem. He is also interested in some methodological issues such as response bias in self-report measures.

Journal of Social Issues, Vol. 67, No. 4, 2011, pp. 806–824

Going Beyond the Multicultural Experience—Creativity Link: The Mediating Role of Emotions

Chi-Ying Cheng* **and Angela K.-y. Leung**
Singapore Management University

Tsung-Yu Wu
National Taiwan University of Science and Technology

This research examines the mediating role of emotions implicated in the multicultural experience—creativity link. We propose that when individuals are dealing with apparent cultural contradictions upon encountering two cultures simultaneously, mentally juxtaposing dissonant cultural stimuli could lower positive affect or increase negative affect, which could in turn induce a deeper level of cognitive processing of cultural discrepancies and inspire creativity. Two studies compared dual cultural exposure versus single cultural exposure among bicultural Singaporeans (Study 1) and compared self-relevant (jointly presenting local and foreign cultures) versus self-irrelevant (jointly presenting foreign cultures only) dual cultural exposure among monocultural Taiwanese (Study 2). As in past research, dual cultural exposure promotes creativity, particularly if one presented culture is self-relevant. Further, this effect was mediated by a less positive or a more negative emotional state. These findings illuminate the underlying influence of emotions activated by simultaneous exposure to diverse cultures.

With the expansive scale of connectivity and global competition among different nations, more individuals will meet with foreign cultures that are strikingly

---

*Correspondence concerning this article should be addressed to Chi-Ying Cheng or Angela K.-y. Leung, Singapore Management University, Level 4, 90 Stamford Road, Singapore 178903, Singapore [e-mails: cycheng@smu.edu.sg or angelaleung@smu.edu.sg].

This research was partially supported by grants awarded to Chi-Ying Cheng and Angela K.-y. Leung from the Behavioral Sciences Institute and the Office of Research of the Singapore Management University.

The authors contributed equally to this work.*

different from their own. At times, such cultural encounters pull individuals out of their cultural comfort zone and trigger exclusionary emotional reactions such as fear of cultural conflicts or anger against foreign cultural intrusion. Nonetheless, exposure to foreign cultures, when coupled with a cultural learning mindset, can also elicit integrative emotional reactions such as admiration for desirable qualities or achievements of a foreign culture (Chiu, Gries, Torelli, & Cheng, 2011). These integrative responses can enhance creativity, resulting in important cognitive benefits of immersing in another culture in this globalizing era.

In this research, we seek to extend this dual reaction model to globalization by explicating the facilitative role of emotions—particularly negative emotions—implicated in people's integrative responses to foreign cultures, focusing on increased creativity as an important outcome following intercultural integrative reactions. Specifically, our findings in two studies revealed that the positive relationship between simultaneous exposure to two cultures and creativity could be mediated by the experience of a less positive or a more negative emotional state.

The Multicultural Experience—Creativity Link

The *creative cognition approach* suggests that the acquisition of different knowledge traditions can facilitate the generation of creative ideas (Finke, Ward, & Smith, 1992; Ward, Smith, & Vaid, 1997). This account credits the critical process of synthesizing seemingly incompatible ideas made available by different knowledge traditions as an important cognitive catalyst for creativity (see also Campbell, 1960; Royce, 1898; Simonton, 1988). The acceleration of globalization has created ample opportunities for cultural navigators to acquire new cultural knowledge (Chiu & Cheng, 2007). Expansion of cultural knowledge can confer important creative benefits for two major reasons. First, individuals with more multicultural experience, given their richer knowledge of different cultures, are at a better position to make connections among disparate ideas originated from different cultural sources (Cheng, Sanchez-Burks, & Lee, 2008; Leung, Maddux, Galinsky, & Chiu, 2008). Second, extensive exposure to multiple cultures entails extensive exposure to multiple perspectives. The awareness of these multiple, sometimes contradictory, perspectives helps individuals break mental set from structured and routinized ways of approaching problems, which is conducive to developing out-of-the-box thinking (Maddux & Galinsky, 2009; Maddux, Leung, Chiu, & Galinsky, 2009).

Accumulating evidence buttresses the multicultural experience—creativity link, showing that individuals with richer multicultural experiences more readily engage in cognitive processes implicated in creative thinking; they more readily sample ideas from diverse cultures for creative idea expansion and more spontaneously retrieve from memory unconventional knowledge (Leung & Chiu, 2010). In addition, there is both correlational and experimental evidence that individuals with more exposure to foreign cultures perform better in creative idea generation and creative insight tasks (Leung, Chen, & Chiu, 2010; Leung & Chiu, 2008, 2010; Maddux & Galinsky, 2009).

Research also shows that resisting cultural conformity is a precondition for realizing the creative advantages of multicultural experience. Therefore, environments that discourage conformity to readily available and established ideas from one's own culture—such as those that lower the need for cognitive closure and release individuals from mortality concerns—foster the creative benefits of multicultural experiences (Leung & Chiu, 2010). Further, individuals who are more open to experiences tend to appraise their multicultural encounters more positively, and thus are more prepared to learn from these experiences and become creative (Leung & Chiu, 2008).

The Role of Cognitive and Emotional Reactions to Foreign Cultures in Creativity

Existing research explains the positive relationship between intercultural contacts and creativity mostly in terms of the display of emotionally neutral cognitive responses to foreign cultures (Chiu & Cheng, 2007). Such responses include engagement in cognitive juxtaposition of culturally diverse ideas, adoption of a cultural learning mindset (Leung et al., 2008), openness to new experiences, and deemphasizing the need for firm answers and existential security (Leung & Chiu, 2008, 2010). Research to date, however, has not examined the facilitative role of emotional responses—particularly negative emotions—to foreign cultures in creative performance. Researchers have theorized that people may exhibit exclusionary or integrative reactions to foreign cultures (Chiu et al., 2011). To elaborate, simultaneous exposure to two cultures can sharpen the perceived cultural contours, making salient the contrast between the two cultural traditions (Chiu & Cheng, 2007). Such heightened attention to cultural contrast, when coupled with strong identification with one's own culture, can lead to closing of the mind to knowledge inflow from foreign cultures and lower creative performance (Morris, Mok, & Mor, 2011). In contrast, when the same heightened attention to cultural contrast is accompanied by an appreciation of ideas from diverse cultures as potentially enriching intellectual resources, this can facilitate an integrative reaction toward the foreign culture, producing enduring creative advantages (Chiu & Cheng, 2007; Leung et al., 2008).

Accordingly, negative affect such as fear and withdrawal is expected to mediate exclusionary reactions to foreign cultures, whereas positive affect such as admiration and delight is implicated in integrative reactions (Chiu et al., 2011). We propose a different, and perhaps a more dynamic view on the role of negative emotions in the multicultural experience—creativity link, focusing on how individuals make sense of and resolve culturally discrepant ideas. We propose that the effortful process of combining seemingly incompatible cultural knowledge can lower positive affect or increase negative affect, which can in turn motivate a deeper level of cognitive processing of cultural discrepancies and inspire creativity. On the basis of this reasoning, in this research, we seek to extend the dual reactions model to globalization by expounding the previously overlooked facilitative role of negative affect in the multicultural experience—creativity link.

The Mediating Role of Emotions in the Multicultural Experience—Creativity Relationship

There is growing evidence for the role of moods/emotions in creativity (Baas, De Dreu, & Nijstad, 2008), although it is still unclear which mood/emotional state benefits creativity the most (Amabile, 1996; Vosburg & Kaufmann, 1999). Some research shows that positive versus neutral moods facilitate creative problem solving across a broad range of settings (see Ashby, Isen, & Turken, 1999). Other research, however, has shown that negative moods (vs. positive or neutral moods) foster creative performance (e.g., Bartolic, Basso, Schefft, Glauser, & Titanic-Schefft, 1999; Gasper, 2003). These mixed results have led many scholars to concur that the effects of mood states on creativity are context-dependent (see Martin & Stoner, 1996).

In this article, we argue that exposure to two cultures, particularly when one of them is one's own culture, will motivate people to make sense of, reconcile, and synthesize cultural discrepancies. With accelerating globalizing forces, it is highly common for individuals to constantly encounter their own local culture and foreign culture simultaneously (e.g., a Taiwanese student reading Taiwan news on the Internet and checking Facebook in an American café). Such a culturally rich environment is conducive to a mindset that actively compares and juxtaposes the different cultural representations that are exposed. When individuals face ideas from diverse cultures, they are confronted with apparent contradictions among these ideas and would experience cognitive dissonance. Such experience may elicit unpleasant emotional states, which in turn motivate the individuals to engage in deeper cognitive processing or even develop higher integrative complexity (Tadmor, Tetlock, & Peng, 2009), which presumably can instigate creativity. Integrative complexity highlights two creativity-supporting capacities: *Differentiation* refers to the willingness to acknowledge competing perspectives on the same issue and *integration* refers to the ability to forge conceptual links between these perspectives (Suedfeld, Tetlock, & Streufert, 1992). The contention that the experience of negative emotions facilitates cognitive complexity is consonant with findings in mood research. For example, under negative moods, individuals are more likely to produce eyewitness accounts not misled by constructive bias (Fielder, Asbeck, & Nickel, 1991), formulate higher quality and more effective persuasive messages (Forgas, 2007), and engage in more exhaustive information processing (Isen, Daubman, & Nowicki, 1987) and more accurate information acquisition (Sinclair, 1988).

Together, the cognitive experience of juxtaposing and resolving discrepant ideas from different cultural sources could potentially lower positive emotions or increase negative ones, and these emotional states are associated with higher cognitive complexity and are creativity-enhancing. In short, our analysis suggests that following exposure to two or more cultures, an ensuing negative or less positive emotional state may accompany higher creative performance.

Overview

We reported two studies that explored for the first time the mediating role of negative emotional states in the multicultural experience—creativity link. These studies were conducted in Singapore and Taiwan because both regions have appropriated global and Western ideas and practices to globalize their economies, and Singaporean and Taiwanese share similar attitudes toward globalization (Yang et al., 2011). Study 1 examined the effects of presenting a single culture (Chinese or American) or two cultures (Chinese and American) on the emotional experiences and creative performance of Singaporean Chinese. We predict that the experience of negative emotions will mediate the relationship between dual cultural exposure (vs. single cultural exposure) and creative performance.

Study 2 extended Study 1 by studying the mediating effect of negative emotions with a sample of Taiwanese Chinese, and more importantly, by manipulating the degree of self-relevance of the presented cultures. Thus, in one condition of Study 2, we presented to Taiwanese participants a self-relevant local culture (Taiwanese culture) and a less self-relevant foreign culture (American culture). In another condition, we presented two low self-relevance foreign cultures (American and Indian cultures). Exposure to a self-relevant local culture and a foreign culture as opposed to two low self-relevant foreign cultures could evoke more negative emotions because the self-relevance of local culture increases the motivation to reconcile cultural discrepancies and/or to attain cultural syntheses—a mental state that is emotionally unpleasant but conducive to deep cognitive processing and creative performance. We predict incremental creative benefits of local and foreign cultural exposure over dual foreign cultural exposure and that negative emotions will mediate the hypothesized incremental benefits.

STUDY 1

Method

Participants

The participants were 113 Singaporean Chinese students (36 males, 77 females; mean age = 21.96 years) at a university in Singapore, who took part in the study in exchange for S$10 (~US$7.5).

Procedure and Materials

Participants first watched a 10-minute Powerpoint slideshow depicting different characteristic aspects of (a) both Chinese and American cultures (dual cultural exposure) or (b) Chinese *or* American culture (single cultural exposure). A total of 72 slides were presented that covered different cultural aspects including apparel, architecture, arts, cuisine, entertainment, furniture, home decorations, landscape, life, literature, movies, music, recreation, and scenery. In the dual cultural exposure condition, one Chinese picture and one American picture matched in content were shown side by side on each slide (e.g., a picture of roasted turkey for Thanksgiving on the left and a picture of hot-pot for the Chinese New Year's Eve on the right); in the single cultural exposure condition, one picture of either culture was shown (e.g., either a picture of roasted turkey for Thanksgiving or a picture of hot-pot for the Chinese New Year's Eve was shown at the center). This part of the study was disguised as a pretest for pilot testing the slideshow materials; as part of the cover story, participants were then asked to write down briefly their personal thoughts or comments about the slideshow.

Emotion Measure

Next, in an ostensibly unrelated study, participants filled out a short survey that consisted of an emotion assessment, a creativity task, and some demographic items. The emotion measure assessed both positive and negative emotions (Elliot & Devine, 1994). We presented 24 emotion terms (e.g., frustrated, optimistic) and participants answered on a 7-point scale the extent to which each emotion term reflected how they were feeling at that particular moment (1 = *does not apply at all at this moment*, 7 = *applies very much at this moment*).

The Unusual Uses Test

Participants were given 10 minutes to complete an Unusual Uses Test (Guilford, 1959)—a widely used creativity task that measures people's ability to generate divergent ideas and to devise different strategies for using a common object. In the current study, participants were asked to list as many uses for garbage bags as possible. They were instructed not to limit themselves to any kind of garbage bag or to the uses they had seen or heard about before.

We created two measures of creativity based on the Unusual Uses Test. The first measure, *fluency*, refers to the total number of unusual uses participants generated after eliminating repetitive responses. The second measure, *flexibility*, refers to the total number of categories of unusual uses generated. Two independent coders grouped the responses into different categories (e.g., containers, waterproof materials, arts, and furniture) and then counted the number of categories of unusual uses for each participant. Inter-judge reliability for the flexibility score was high, $r = .78, p < .0001$. Coding inconsistencies were resolved through discussion with the authors.

Results and Discussion

Factor Structure of the Emotion Measure

We performed a principal component analysis on the 24 emotion items. The scree plot clearly indicated a three-factor solution. A follow-up maximum-likelihood factor analysis with oblimin rotation showed that the first factor accounted for 43.53% of the total variance and had significant loadings ($>.40$) from 11 emotions related to negative feelings: annoyed, frustrated, disappointed, concerned, anxious, bothered, tense, distressed, angry, negative, and critical. The second factor accounted for 16.21% of the total variance and had significant loadings ($>.40$) from six positive emotions: optimistic, good, energetic, friendly, happy, and content. The last factor accounted for 6.55% of the total variance and had significant loadings ($>.40$) from seven emotions related to negative self-reflections: shamed, guilty, embarrassed, disgusted, regretful, uneasy, and uncomfortable. We took the mean of the respective items to form three measures: negative emotions ($\alpha = .93$), positive emotions ($\alpha = .91$), and negative self-reflections ($\alpha = .89$). Negative emotions were positively correlated with negative self-reflections ($r = .77, p < .0001$), and positive emotions were negatively correlated with negative emotions ($r = -.22, p = .02$) and negative self-reflections ($r = -.27, p = .004$).

Dual Cultural Exposure and Creativity

We first checked if the two single cultural exposure conditions (Chinese or American) differed significantly from each other in predicting creativity and emotions. Regression analyses revealed that these two conditions did not differ on the total number of unusual garbage bag uses participants generated ($M_{\text{Chinese}} =$ 10.40, $SD_{\text{Chinese}} = 4.42$ vs. $M_{\text{American}} = 10.24$, $SD_{\text{American}} = 4.11$; $\beta = -0.17$,

$SE = 1.06$, $t = -0.16$, $p = .88$), the number of different categories used ($M_{Chinese} = 7.72$, $SD_{Chinese} = 2.91$ vs. $M_{American} = 7.50$, $SD_{American} = 2.76$; $\beta = -0.22$, $SE = 0.73$, $t = -0.30$, $p = .76$), and the three emotion indexes (negative emotions: $M_{Chinese} = 2.37$, $SD_{Chinese} = 1.23$ vs. $M_{American} = 2.37$, $SD_{American} = 1.12$; $\beta = -0.002$, $SE = 0.32$, $t = -0.01$, $p = .10$; positive emotions: $M_{Chinese} = 4.02$, $SD_{Chinese} = 1.23$ vs. $M_{American} = 4.17$, $SD_{American} = 1.04$; $3 = 0.15$, $SE = 0.34$, $t = 0.45$, $p = .65$; negative self-reflections: $M_{Chinese} = 1.83$, $SD_{Chinese} = 1.26$ vs. $M_{American} = 1.71$, $SD_{American} = 0.77$; $\beta = -0.12$, $SE = 0.26$, $t = -0.45$, $p = .65$). For the following analyses, we collapsed these two single cultural exposure conditions.

Across the two creativity measures of fluency and flexibility, we replicated the previous finding that dual cultural exposure enhances creativity (Leung & Chiu, 2008, 2010). Specifically, simultaneous exposure to both Chinese and American cultures as opposed to exposure to a single culture significantly increased fluency ($M_{Dual} = 12.19$, $SD_{Dual} = 3.78$ vs. $M_{Single} = 10.31$, $SD_{Single} = 4.20$; $\beta = 1.93$, $SE = 0.77$, $t = 2.52$, $p = .01$) and flexibility ($M_{Dual} = 8.81$, $SD_{Dual} = 2.72$ vs. $M_{Single} = 7.59$, $SD_{Single} = 2.80$; $\beta = 1.29$, $SE = 0.53$, $t = 2.46$, $p = .02$).

Dual Cultural Exposure and Emotions

We examined the effects of dual versus single cultural exposure on the three emotion indexes. Unexpectedly, participants in the dual and single cultural exposure conditions did not differ in their experience of negative emotions ($M_{Dual} = 2.17$, $SD_{Dual} = 1.25$ vs. $M_{Single} = 2.37$, $SD_{Single} = 1.16$; $\beta = -0.16$, $SE = 0.23$, $t = -0.72$, $p = .47$) and negative self-reflections ($M_{Dual} = 1.71$, $SD_{Dual} = 0.99$ vs. $M_{Single} = 1.76$, $SD_{Single} = 1$; $\beta = 0.06$, $SE = 0.18$, $t = 0.32$, $p = .75$). However, participants in the dual (vs. single) cultural exposure condition experienced fewer positive emotions ($M_{Dual} = 3.43$, $SD_{Dual} = 1.43$ vs. $M_{Single} = 4.11$, $SD_{Single} = 1.12$; $\beta = -0.66$, $SE = 0.25$, $t = -2.67$, $p = .01$). Thus, upon encountering both Chinese and American cultures, participants reported feeling less positively than did their peers who encountered only one culture.

Emotion Mediated the Dual Cultural Exposure—Creativity Relationship

Next, we tested whether experiencing less positive emotions mediated the effects of dual cultural exposure on fluency and flexibility. Following Baron and Kenny (1986), we regressed each of the two creativity measures on the cultural exposure conditions, and results reported above indicated a significant effect of cultural exposure on creativity. Next, we predicted the two creativity measures from both cultural exposure and positive emotions. In this analysis, positive emotions were a significant predictor of flexibility ($\beta = -0.46$, $SE = 0.20$, $t = -2.29$, $p = .02$), but dual cultural exposure was not ($\beta = 0.99$, $SE = 0.53$, $t = 1.86$, $p = .07$; Figure 1). This suggests that positive emotions mediated the dual cultural

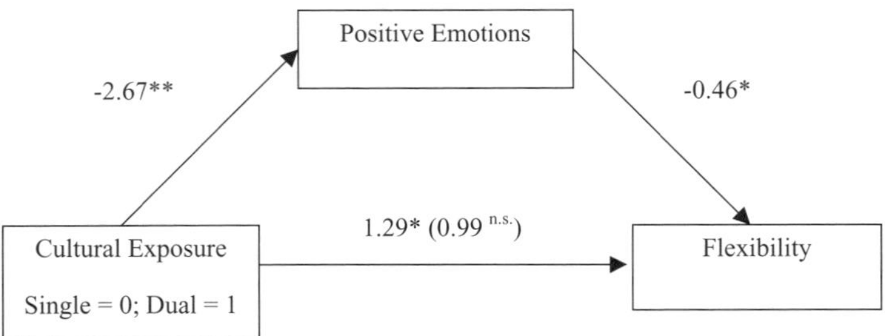

Fig. 1. Mediation analyses for positive emotions and flexibility, Study 1. Numbers represent standardized regression coefficients. $*p < .05; **p < .01$.

exposure–creativity relationship. Exposure to two cultures is associated with the experience of less positive emotions, which in turn predicts greater flexibility. A Sobel test provided further support for this mediation ($Z = -1.94, p = .05$). However, positive emotions did not predict fluency ($\beta = -0.37, SE = 0.30, t = -1.23, p = .22$).

Overall, the findings of Study 1 replicated previous research results (Leung & Chiu, 2010). Individuals encountering two cultures simultaneously have higher creative performance than do those encountering a single culture. Aside from replicating this important finding, Study 1 also revealed for the first time that dual cultural exposure is associated with a less positive emotional state, which in turn predicts greater flexibility in a creativity test. Although we predicted that negative emotions would mediate the dual cultural exposure—creativity relationship, the current finding showed that only the experience of less positive emotions mediated the relationship. We speculate that Singaporeans, with their rich multicultural experiences, may be fairly experienced in coping with ambivalence arising from dual exposure to Chinese and American cultures (Chen, Ng, & Rao, 2005), given that Singapore is a multiethnic nation. When they cognitively process Chinese and American cultures, they may not find ideas from two cultures to be highly incompatible. Nonetheless, being aware of a moderate level of cultural incompatibility when encountering both cultures simultaneously may still elicit a less positive emotional state, which in turn leads to higher creative performance. We will return to this issue in the General Discussion.

STUDY 2

To extend Study 1 results, in Study 2 we included a different Chinese sample (Taiwanese Chinese), a cultural group with less extensive multicultural experience than Singaporean Chinese. With the Taiwanese sample, we hypothesize that a negative emotional state will mediate the dual cultural exposure–creativity relationship, because Taiwanese with generally fewer multicultural experiences when encountering seemingly incompatible cultures may need to expend more cognitive effort on making sense of and reconciling apparent contradictions between Taiwanese and American cultures. In addition, we compared the effects of presenting a local and a foreign culture against presenting two foreign cultures in order to determine whether encountering a self-relevant local culture and a foreign culture would have incremental creative benefits.

Method

Participants

The participants were 63 Taiwanese students (45 males, 18 females; mean age = 20.02 years) at a university in Taiwan, who participated in exchange for NTD$150 (~US$5.0).

Procedure and Materials

Participants first watched a 10-minute Powerpoint slideshow depicting different characteristic aspects of (a) Taiwanese *and* American cultures (local and foreign cultural exposure) or (b) Indian *and* American cultures (dual foreign cultural exposure). We chose Indian culture in the dual foreign culture exposure condition because like Taiwan, India is a rapidly globalizing Asian country and most Taiwanese have limited exposure to Indian culture and do not consider it to be a culture of high personal relevance. A total of 72 slides were presented covering different cultural aspects similar to those in Study 1. In the local and foreign cultural exposure condition, one Taiwanese picture and one American picture matched in content were shown side by side on each slide (e.g., a picture of American cheese on the left and a picture of stinky tofu on the right); in the dual foreign cultural exposure condition, one Indian picture and one American picture matched in content were shown side by side (e.g., a picture of White House on the left and a picture of Taj Mahal on the right). This part of the study was again disguised as a pretest for pilot testing the slideshow materials; as part of the cover story, participants were then asked to write down briefly their personal thoughts or comments about the slideshow.

Measures

Next, participants completed the identical emotion assessment and Unusual Uses Test used in Study 1. Again, we created two measures of creativity: fluency (number of unusual uses generated after eliminating repetitive responses) and flexibility (number of distinct categories of ideas). Two independent coders coded the number of categories of unusual uses for each participant. Interjudge reliability for the flexibility score was high, $r = .81, p < .0001$. Coding inconsistencies were resolved through discussion with the authors. Finally, as a manipulation check, we had participants report their levels of identification and familiarity with the three cultures, both measured by a 9-point Likert scale.

Results and Discussion

Manipulation Check for Dual Cultural Exposure

To ensure that our participants indeed had higher identification and familiarity with Taiwanese culture than with American and Indian cultures, we compared participants' self-reported identification and familiarity with the three cultures. Participants had significantly stronger identification with Taiwanese culture than with American or Indian culture [$M_{\text{Taiwan}} = 6.73, SD_{\text{Taiwan}} = 1.60; M_{\text{America}} = 5.76, SD_{\text{America}} = 1.55; M_{\text{India}} = 4.43, SD_{\text{India}} = 1.29; F(1, 62) = 48.06, p < .0001$]. They also had significantly higher familiarity with Taiwanese culture than the other two cultures [$M_{\text{Taiwan}} = 7.11, SD_{\text{Taiwan}} = 1.25; M_{\text{America}} = 5.21, SD_{\text{America}} = 1.38; M_{\text{India}} = 3.44, SD_{\text{India}} = 1.38; F(1, 62) = 211.37, p < .0001$]. These results indicated that the two cultures in the local and foreign cultural exposure condition include a more self-relevant local culture and a less self-relevant foreign culture.

Factor Structure of the Emotion Measure.

We again performed a principal component analysis on the 24 emotion items. As in Study 1, the screen plot indicated a three-factor solution. A follow-up maximum-likelihood factor analysis with oblimin rotation showed that the first factor accounted for 33.91% of the total variance and had significant loadings ($>.40$) from the same 11 negative emotions as in Study 1; the second factor accounted for 13.74% of the total variance with significant loadings ($>.40$) from the same 6 positive emotions; and the last factor accounted for 4.77% of the total variance with significant loadings ($>.40$) from the same 7 negative self-reflection emotions. The reliabilities for the three emotion measures were high: negative emotions ($\alpha = .89$), positive emotions ($\alpha = .91$), and negative self-reflections ($\alpha = .87$). Negative emotions were positively correlated with negative self-reflections ($r = .62, p < .0001$), and positive emotions were negatively correlated with negative emotions ($r = -.26, p = .03$) and negative self-reflections ($r = -.17, p = .17$).

Dual Cultural Effects on Creativity

We compared the two cultural exposure conditions on fluency and flexibility and found that simultaneous exposure to Taiwanese and American cultures versus simultaneous exposure to Indian and American cultures significantly enhanced fluency ($M_{\text{Taiwan and America}} = 8.09$, $SD_{\text{Taiwan and America}} = 3.80$ vs. $M_{\text{India and America}} = 6.26$, $SD_{\text{India and America}} = 3.40$; $\beta = 1.84$, $SE = 0.91$, $t = 2.22$, $p = .048$). Although the result for flexibility was not significant ($M_{\text{Taiwan and America}} = 6.22$, $SD_{\text{Taiwan and America}} = 2.76$ vs. $M_{\text{India and America}} = 5.19$, $SD_{\text{India and America}} = 2.87$; $\beta = 1.03$, $SE = 0.71$, $t = 1.45$, $p = .15$), the means were in the predicted direction. As hypothesized, relative to dual foreign cultural exposure, local and foreign cultural exposure increases creativity, particularly in ideational fluency.

Dual Cultural Effects on Emotions

Next, we compared the three emotion indexes across the two cultural exposure conditions. Due to skewed distributions of the emotion indexes, we log-transformed these scores. Regression analyses revealed that relative to their peers in the dual foreign cultural exposure condition, participants in the local and foreign cultural exposure condition experienced more negative emotions ($M_{\text{Taiwan and America}} = 3.49$, $SD_{\text{Taiwan and America}} = 1.29$ vs. $M_{\text{India and America}} = 2.78$, $SD_{\text{India and America}} = 1.27$; $\beta = 0.13$, $SE = 0.05$, $t = 2.71$, $p = .009$) as well as more negative self-reflections ($M_{\text{Taiwan and America}} = 2.49$, $SD_{\text{Taiwan and America}} = 0.82$ vs. $M_{\text{India and America}} = 1.97$, $SD_{\text{India and America}} = 0.91$; $\beta = 0.11$, $SE = 0.05$, $t = 2.31$, $p = .02$); participants across the two dual cultural exposure conditions, however, did not differ in their experience of positive emotions ($M_{\text{Taiwan and America}} = 4.24$, $SD_{\text{Taiwan and America}} = 1.10$ vs. $M_{\text{India and America}} = 4.19$, $SD_{\text{India and America}} = 1.30$; $\beta = 0.01$, $SE = 0.04$, $t = 0.34$, $p = .74$). Thus, simultaneous exposure to one's own culture and a foreign culture elicits more negative emotions than exposure to two foreign cultures.

Emotion Mediated the Dual Cultural Exposure—Creativity Relationship

We then tested whether negative emotions and negative self-reflections mediated the effects of dual cultural exposure on fluency and flexibility with a series of regression analyses. Following Baron and Kenny (1986), we have already reported the findings supporting the effects of dual cultural exposure on fluency, as well as a trend on flexibility. Next, we regressed each creativity measure on both cultural exposure and negative emotions. As predicted, negative emotions predicted fluency and flexibility ($\beta = 6.04$, $SE = 2.28$, $t = 2.65$, $p = .01$ and $\beta = 4.43$, $SE = 1.79$, $t = 2.48$, $p = .02$, respectively), whereas dual cultural exposure did not ($\beta = 1.04$, $SE = 0.92$, $t = 1.13$, $p = .26$ and $\beta = 0.44$, $SE = 0.72$, $t = 0.61$, $p = .54$, respectively; Figure 2a). Sobel test results confirmed the significant mediation effects ($Z_{\text{Fluency}} = 2.07$, $p = .02$; $Z_{\text{Flexibility}} = 1.79$, $p = .04$). We also repeated the same procedures for negative self-reflections. Again, as predicted,

(a)

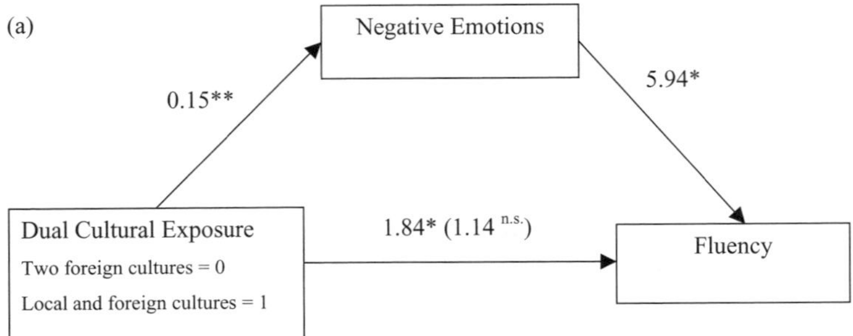

(b)

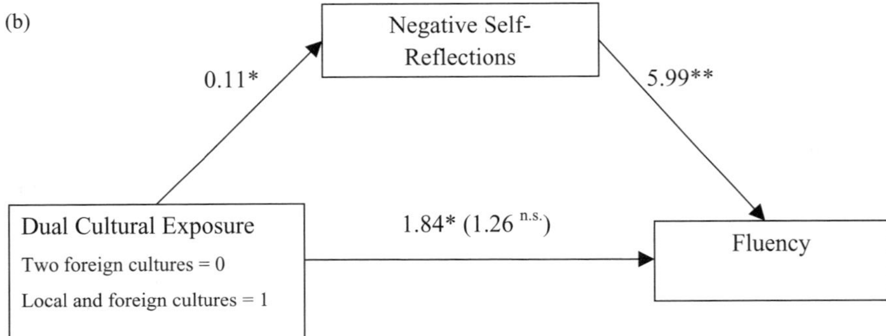

Fig. 2. (a) Mediation analyses for negative emotions and fluency, Study 2. Numbers represent standardized regression coefficients. $^*p < .05$; $^{**}p < .01$. (b) Mediation analyses for negative self-reflections and fluency, Study 2. Numbers represent standardized regression coefficients. $^*p < .05$; $^{**}p < .01$.

negative self-reflections predicted both fluency and flexibility ($\beta = 5.10$, $SE = 2.30$, $t = 2.22$, $p = .03$ and $\beta = 3.91$, $SE = 1.79$, $t = 2.18$, $p = .03$, respectively), but dual cultural exposure did not ($\beta = 1.26$, $SE = 0.92$, $t = 1.36$, $p = .18$ and $\beta = 0.58$, $SE = 0.72$, $t = 0.81$, $p = .42$, respectively; Figure 2b). Furthermore, Sobel test results supported the predicted mediation effects ($Z_{\text{Fluency}} = 1.79$, $p = .04$; $Z_{\text{Flexibility}} = 1.71$, $p = .04$).

Together, findings of Study 2 suggest that negative emotions and negative self-reflections mediate the dual cultural exposure—creativity relationship: Exposure to local and foreign cultures has incremental creative benefits over exposure to two foreign cultures, with the experience of a negative emotional state mediating this effect.

General Discussion

Our two studies extended the previous finding that individuals presented with two cultures simultaneously would have higher creative performance than do those presented with a single culture. Aside from replicating this important finding, we explored for the first time the emotional underpinning of the effect of dual cultural exposure on creativity. Study 1 showed that dual cultural exposure is associated with a less positive emotional state, which in turn predicts higher creative performance. In Study 2, we found incremental creative benefits of exposure to a self-relevant local culture and a foreign culture over exposure to two foreign cultures. As hypothesized, the experience of negative emotional states (negative emotions and negative self-reflections) mediates the incremental creative benefits of exposure to local and foreign cultures. Taken together, the current research provides initial evidence that a less positive or a more negative emotional state is a possible mediator of the positive relationship between simultaneous exposure to two cultures and creative performance.

The current research provides new perspectives to the multicultural experience—creativity link by illuminating its mediating emotional states with participants from two cultures. Singaporean Chinese have richer multicultural experiences and seem to be more adept at coping with cultural ambivalence and dissonance that emerges from simultaneous exposure to Chinese and American cultures. This quality may have prepared Singaporeans well for dealing with cultural disparities and contradictions that they frequently experience in the living environment (Cheng et al., 2008). Thus, they experience only a decrease in positive emotions when they face conflicting ideas from Chinese and American cultures. By comparison, Taiwanese Chinese have less extensive exposure to American culture. They may feel more cognitively challenged when they seek to reconcile or integrate conflicting ideas from Chinese and American cultures. Thus, they experience more negative emotions upon simultaneously encountering these two cultures. The differing levels of bicultural experiences may explain why less positive emotions and more negative emotions mediate the link between dual cultural exposure and creativity for Singaporean and Taiwanese participants, respectively.

Our findings also provide a substantial implication on the kind of multicultural experience that is particularly beneficial. Consistent with a recent study (Leung & Chiu, 2010), Study 1 showed that exposure to a single culture does not produce as much creative advantage as exposure to two cultures simultaneously, possibly because exposure to a single culture does not motivate active comparison and cognitive juxtaposition of different cultural representations. Further, in Study 2, we showed that creative advantage is more likely to be realized upon simultaneous exposure to local and foreign cultures as opposed to two foreign cultures, suggesting that increased self-relevance of the presented cultures in bicultural exposure can further enhance creativity. More research is needed to achieve a nuanced understanding of how factors such as cultural identification and personal involvement with a given culture affect the way individuals respond to and incorporate inputs from multicultural experiences (see Cheng et al., 2008; Morris et al., 2011).

Furthermore, we recruited college students as participants and future research is required to replicate the current findings with nonstudent samples.

Nonetheless, we want to acknowledge that Taiwanese are relatively unfamiliar with American and Indian cultures. Their lack of knowledge about the two cultures might have prevented them from recognizing meaningful cultural discrepancies and experiencing cognitive dissonance. This could explain why Taiwanese reported a lesser amount of negative emotions and performed less creatively when they were exposed to American and Indian cultures simultaneously (vs. Chinese and American cultures simultaneously). Future research can explore the levels of familiarity or knowledge necessary for people to recognize meaningful dissonance between two cultures that inspires creativity.

Notably, creativity is a multifaceted construct. In the present research, we used the same Unusual Uses Test across the two studies and focused on measuring idea novelty as indicated by fluency and flexibility. Creativity is typically defined as the process of creating something both novel and useful (Amabile, 1996). Cultural differences have been identified such that Westerners weigh novelty more in creativity whereas East Asians weigh usefulness more (Morris & Leung, 2010). Although cultural difference in different evaluation criteria of creativity is not a major concern in our studies, future research can replicate our findings with a creativity measure that balances demands for both novelty and usefulness. Relatedly, future research can explore the role of emotions in creative performance in other creativity facets such as creative insight that requires recognition of correct solutions to problems after overcoming some sort of cognitive impasse (Gilhooly & Murphy, 2005; e.g., Duncker Candle Task, Remote Associates Test) and creative recombination that requires discerning relationships among distinct concepts and forming a new combination that links these concepts together (Royce, 1898).

Implications for Globalization Research

The growing cultural enclaves resulting from globalization offer unprecedented opportunities for expanding individuals' cultural knowledge repertoire and stretching their cultural comfort zone. Encountering icons of local and foreign cultures in the same globalized space creates a rich multicultural environment that increases the salience of culture as a schema for organizing perceptions (Chiu, Mallorie, Keh, & Law, 2009; Torelli, Chiu, Kam, Au, & Keh, 2011).

In this context of rapid globalization, the study of emotional reactions toward foreign and global cultures is timely. Whereas some individuals are wary about the hegemonic dominance of foreign or global cultures leading to an eventual erosion of local cultures, others welcome and appreciate the infusion of foreign cultural ideas. Researchers theorize that people who hold a nationalistic, exclusionary attitude toward foreign cultures may feel such negative intercultural emotions such as anger, fear, and disgust (Chiu et al., 2011). The present research, however, provides initial evidence that people who hold an integrative attitude toward foreign cultures may also experience negative emotions, which can possibly energize cognitive transformations that are conducive to creativity. This finding is particularly relevant to understanding the psychological reactions of global citizens who are constantly in contact with multiple cultural demands, which can be emotionally taxing to cope with (Kramer, Lau-Gesk, & Chiu, 2009). The emotional distress accompanied with multicultural encounters can potentially be transferred to instigating creative thinking. Indeed, this idea is consonant with the finding that the best performing expatriates working overseas tend to be those who experience the most severe cultural shock (Thomas, 1998). Relatedly, the current finding has important implications for expatriate training and coaching as most training programs aim to reduce the discomfort and cultural shock caused by exposure to discrepancies between local and host cultures (Lublin, 1992). Organizational personnel may want to recognize the beneficial effects of negative emotions induced by multicultural experiences.

In this light, it would be illuminating to distinguish negative emotions that may paralyze creativity (e.g., fear, anger, disgust) from negative emotions that may catalyze creativity (e.g., puzzled, confused). Similarly, it would be useful to investigate whether there is an optimal amount of negative emotions to be experienced in order to enhance creative performance. We, however, do not mean to discount the beneficial effects of positive moods on creativity (e.g., Baas, De Dreu, & Nijstad, 2008). Rather, our research adds to multicultural research by showing that mentally juxtaposing conflicting ideas from different cultural sources may elicit negative moods, which can facilitate cognitive complexity and creative problem solving.

Conclusion

Extending the dual reactions model to globalization, we proposed and found that less positive or negative emotional states are also implicated in integrative responses toward foreign or global cultures. With globalization greatly speeding up transnational circulation of ideas, popular cultures, languages, and resources, people are faced with unprecedented opportunities of cultural learning. Cultural learning, similar to other kinds of learning, may also reflect the wisdom of "no pain, no gain," an important gauge of learning outcomes and effectiveness. A certain degree of emotional negativity can beneficially instigate greater cognitive complexity in the experiential learning of different cultures. We hope that the current research has represented another step that brings us closer to understanding the potential benefits of our multicultural experiences in this globalized era.

References

Amabile, T. (1996). *Creativity in context*. Boulder, CO: Westview Press.

Ashby, F. G., Isen, A. M., & Turken, A. U. (1999). A neuropsychological theory of positive affect and its influence on cognition. *Psychological Review, 106*(3), 529–550. doi:10.1037/0033-295X.106.3.529

Baas, M., De Dreu, C. K. W., & Nijstad, B. A. (2008). A meta-analysis of 25 years of mood-creativity research: Hedonic tone, activation, or regulatory focus? *Psychological Bulletin, 134*(6), 779–806. doi:10.1037/a0012815

Baron, R. M., & Kenny, D. A. (1986). The moderator-mediator variable distinction in social psychological research: Conceptual, strategic, and statistical considerations. *Journal of Personality and Social Psychology, 51*(6), 1173–1182. doi:10.1037//0022-3514.51.6.1173

Bartolic, E. I., Basso, M. R., Schefft, B. K., Glauser, T., & Titanic-Schefft, M. (1999). Effects of experimentally-induced emotional states on frontal lobe cognitive task performance. *Neuropsychologia, 37*(6), 677–683. doi:10.1016/S0028-3932(98)00123-7

Campbell, D. T. (1960). Blind variation and selective retention in creative thought as in other knowledge processes. *Psychological Review, 67*(6), 380–400. doi:10.1037/h0040373

Chen, H., Ng, S. L., & Rao, A. K. (2005). Cultural differences in consumer impatience. *Journal of Marketing Research, 42*(3), 291–301. doi:10.1509/jmkr.2005.42.3.291

Cheng, C.-Y., Sanchez-Burks, J., & Lee, F. (2008). Connecting the dots within: Creative performance and identity integration. *Psychological Science, 19*(11), 1178–1184. doi:10.1111/j.1467-9280.2008.02220.x

Cheng, C.-Y., Darling, E., Lee, F., Molina, K., Sanchez-Burks, J., Sanders, M, & Zhao, L. (2008). Reaping the rewards of cultural diversity: The role of identity integration. *Personality and Social Psychology Compass, 2*(3), 1182–1198. doi:10.1111/j.1751-9004.2008.00103.x

Chiu, C.-y., & Cheng, S. Y.-y. (2007). Toward a social psychology of culture and globalization: Some social cognitive consequences of activating two cultures simultaneously. *Social and Personality Psychology Compass, 1*(1), 84–100. doi:10.1111/j.1751-9004.2007.00017.x

Chiu, C.-y., Gries, P., Torelli, C. J., & Cheng, S. Y.-y. (2011). Toward a social psychology of globalization. *Journal of Social Issues, 67*, 663–676. doi:10.1111/j.1540-4560.2011.01721.x

Chiu, C.-y., Mallorie, L., Keh, H.-t., & Law, W. (2009). Perceptions of culture in multicultural space: Joint presentation of images from two cultures increases in-group attribution of culture-typical characteristics. *Journal of Cross-cultural Psychology, 40*, 282–300. doi:10.1177/0022022108328912

Elliot, A. J., & Devine, P. G. (1994). On the motivational nature of cognitive dissonance: Dissonance as psychological discomfort. *Journal of Personality and Social Psychology, 67*(3), 382–394. doi:10.1037/0022-3514.67.3.382

Fiedler, K., Asbeck, J., & Nickel, S. (1991). Mood and constructive memory effects on social judgment. *Cognition and Emotion, 5*(5–6), 363–378. doi:10.1080/02699939108411048

Finke, R. A., Ward, T. B., & Smith, S. M. (1992). *Creative cognition: Theory, research, and applications*. Cambridge, MA: MIT Press.

Forgas, J. P. (2007). When sad is better than happy: Negative affect can improve the quality and effectiveness of persuasive messages and social influence strategies. *Journal of Experimental Social Psychology, 43*(4), 513–528. doi:10.1016/j.jesp.2006.05.006

Gasper, K. (2003). When necessity is the mother of invention: Mood and problem solving. *Journal of Experimental and Social Psychology, 39*(3), 248–262. doi:10.1016/S0022-1031(03)00023-4

Gilhooly, K. J., & Murphy, P. (2005). Differentiating insight from non-insight problems. *Thinking and Reasoning, 11*(3), 279–302. doi:10.1080/13546780442000187

Guilford, J. P. (1959). Traits of creativity. In H. H. Anderson (Ed.), *Creativity and its cultivation* (pp. 142–161). New York: Harper.

Isen, A. M., Daubman, K. A., & Nowicki, G. P. (1987). Positive affect facilitates creative problem solving. *Journal of Personality and Social Psychology, 52*(6), 1122–1131. doi:10.1037//0022-3514.52.6.1122

Kramer, T., Lau-Gesk, L., & Chiu, C.-y. (2009). Biculturalism and mixed emotions: Managing cultural and emotional duality. *Journal of Consumer Psychology, 19*, 661–672. doi:10.1016/j.jcps.2009.03.001

Leung, A. K.-y., Chen, J., & Chiu, C.-y. (2010). Multicultural experience fosters creative conceptual expansion. In A. K.-y. Leung, C.-y. Chiu, & Y.-y. Hong (Eds.), *Cultural processes: A social psychological perspective* (pp. 263–285). New York: Cambridge University Press.

Leung, A. K.-y., & Chiu, C.-y. (2008). Interactive effects of multicultural experiences and openness to experience on creativity. *Creativity Research Journal, 20*(4), 376–382. doi:10.1080/10400410802391371

Leung, A. K.-y., & Chiu, C.-y. (2010). Multicultural experiences, idea receptiveness, and creativity. *Journal of Cross-Cultural Psychology, 41*(5–6), 723–741. dci:10.1177/0022022110361707

Leung, A. K.-y., Maddux, W. W., Galinsky, A. D., & Chiu, C.-y. (2008). Multicultural experience enhances creativity: The when and how? *American Psychologist, 63*(3), 169–181. doi:10.1037/0003-066X.63.3.169

Lublin, J. S. (1992). Younger managers learn global skills. *Wall Street Journal*, March 31.

Maddux, W. W., & Galinsky, A. D. (2009). Cultural borders and mental barriers: The relationship between living abroad and creativity. *Journal of Personality and Social Psychology, 96*(5), 1047–1061. doi:10.1037/a0014861

Maddux, W. W., Leung, A. K.-y., Chiu, C.-y., & Galinsky, A. (2009). Toward a more complete understanding of the link between multicultural experience and creativity. *American Psychologist, 64*(2), 156–158.

Martin, L. L., & Stoner, P. (1996). Mood as input: What we think about how we feel determines how we think. In L. L. Martin & A. Tesser (Eds.), *Striving and feeling: Interactions among goals, affect and self-regulation* (pp. 279–301). Mahwah, NJ: Erlbaum.

Morris, W. M., & Leung, K. (2010). Creativity east and west: Perspectives and parallels. *Management and Organization Review, 6*(3), 313–327. doi:10.1111/j.1740-8784.2010.00193.x

Morris, M. W., Mok, A., & Mor, S. (2011). Cultural identity threat: The role of cultural identifications in moderating closure responses to foreign cultural inflow. *Journal of Social Issues, 67*, 743–759. doi:10.1111/j.1540-4560.2011.01726.x

Royce, J. (1898). The psychology of invention. *Psychological Review, 5*(2), 113–144. doi:10.1037/h0074372.

Simonton, D. K. (1988). Creativity, leadership, and chance. In R. J. Sternberg (Ed.), *The nature of creativity* (pp. 386–426). Cambridge, England: Cambridge University Press.

Sinclair, R. C. (1988). Mood, categorization breadth, and performance appraisal: The effects of order of information acquisition and affective state on halo, accuracy, information retrieval and evaluations. *Organizational Behavior and Human Decision Processes, 42*(1), 22–46. doi:10.1016/0749-5978(88)90018-0

Suedfeld, P., Tetlock, P. E., & Streufert, S. (1992). Conceptual/integrative complexity. In C. P. Smith, J. W. Atkinson, D. C. McClelland, & J. Veroff (Eds.), *Motivation and personality: Handbook of thematic content analysis* (pp. 393–400). New York: Cambridge University Press.

Tadmor, C. T., Tetlock, P. E., & Peng, K. (2009). Acculturation strategies and cognitive complexity. *Journal of Cross-Cultural Psychology, 40*(1), 105–139. doi:10.1177/0022022108326279

Thomas, D. C. (1998). The expatriate experience: A critical review and synthesis. *Advances in International Comparative Management, 12*, 237–273

Torelli, C. J., Chiu, C.-Y., Tam, K.-p., Au, A. K. C., & Keh, H. T. (2011). Exclusionary reactions to foreign cultures: Effects of simultaneous exposure to cultures in globalized space. *Journal of Social Issues, 67*, 716–742. doi:10.1111/j.1540-4560.2011.01724.x

Vosburg, S., & Kaufmann, G. (1999). Mood and creativity research: The view from a conceptual organizing perspective. In S. W. Russ (Ed.), *Affect, creative experience, and psychological adjustment* (pp. 19–39). Philadelphia: Taylor & Francis.

Ward, T. B., Smith, S. M., & Vaid, J. (1997). Conceptual structures and processes in creative thought. In T. B. Ward, S. M. Smith, & J. Vaid (Eds.), *Creative thought: An investigation of conceptual structures and processes* (pp. 1–27). Washington, DC: American Psychological Association Books.

Yang, D. Y.-J., Chen, X., Cheng, S. Y. Y., Kwan, L., Tam, K.-P., & Yeh, K.-H. (2011). The lay psychology of globalization and its social impact. *Journal of Social Issues, 67*, 677–695. doi:10.1111/j.1540-4560.2011.01722.x

CHI-YING CHENG is Assistant Professor of Psychology at the Singapore Management University. She received her PhD from the University of Michigan. Her research examines the underlying psychological mechanisms and behavioral outcomes of dual identity integration with special focus on culture. She also investigates the influence of multiple identity integration on organizational outcomes such as creativity, leadership, cultural competence, and negotiation.

ANGELA KA-YEE LEUNG is Assistant Professor of Psychology at the Singapore Management University. She received her PhD from the University of Illinois. Her research seeks to understand how people participate actively in dynamic cultural processes and the psychological implications for multicultural competence. She is also interested in the role of embodiment (bodily interactions with the environment) in the acquisition and endorsement of cultural values.

TSUNG-YU WU is an associate professor in the Department of Business Administration at the National Taiwan University of Science and Technology. He received his PhD from National Taiwan University in 2003. His research interests focus on the relationship between emotional labor and abusive supervision, authoritarian leadership in Chinese context, uncertainty management theory and its implications for stress and leadership, creativity in the workplace, and trickle-down model and its application to supportive leadership behaviors.

Journal of Social Issues, Vol. 67, No. 4, 2011, pp. 825–840

Beyond General Intelligence (IQ) and Emotional Intelligence (EQ): The Role of Cultural Intelligence (CQ) on Cross-Border Leadership Effectiveness in a Globalized World

Thomas Rockstuhl*
Nanyang Technological University

Stefan Seiler
Swiss Military Academy at ETH Zurich

Soon Ang
Nanyang Technological University

Linn Van Dyne
Michigan State University

Hubert Annen
Swiss Military Academy at ETH Zurich

Emphasizing the importance of cross-border effectiveness in the contemporary globalized world, we propose that cultural intelligence—the leadership capability to manage effectively in culturally diverse settings—is a critical leadership competency for those with cross-border responsibilities. We tested this hypothesis with multisource data, including multiple intelligences, in a sample of 126 Swiss military officers with both domestic and cross-border leadership responsibilities. Results supported our predictions: (1) general intelligence predicted both domestic and cross-border leadership effectiveness; (2) emotional intelligence was a stronger predictor of domestic leadership effectiveness, and (3) cultural intelligence was a stronger predictor of cross-border leadership effectiveness. Overall,

*Correspondence concerning this article should be sent to Thomas Rockstuhl, Block S3, 01C-108 Nanyang Business School, Nanyang Technological University, Nanyang Avenue, Singapore 639798 [e-mail: thom0003@e.ntu.edu.sg].

825

results show the value of cultural intelligence as a critical leadership competency in today's globalized world.

Globalization is a reality in the 21st century workplace. As a consequence, leaders must function effectively in cross-border situations as well as in domestic contexts. Leaders working in cross-border contexts must cope effectively with contrasting economic, political, and cultural practices. As a result, careful selection, grooming, and development of leaders who can operate effectively in our globalized environment is a pressing need for contemporary organizations (Avolio, Walumbwa, & Weber, 2009).

To date, research on leadership effectiveness has been dominantly domestic in focus, and does not necessarily generalize to global leaders (Gregersen, Morrison, & Black, 1998; House, Hanges, Javidan, Dorfman, & Gupta, 2004). Hence, there is a critical need for research that extends our understanding of how differences in context (domestic vs. cross-border) require different leadership capabilities (Johns, 2006). As we build our arguments, we emphasize the importance of matching leadership capabilities to the specific context.

Global leaders, like all leaders, are responsible for performing their job responsibilities and accomplishing their individual goals. Accordingly, general effectiveness, defined as the effectiveness of observable actions that managers take to accomplish their goals (Campbell, McCloy, Oppler, & Sager, 1993), is important for global leaders. We use the term "general" in describing this type of effectiveness because it makes no reference to culture or cultural diversity. Thus, it applies to all leader jobs.

Going beyond general effectiveness, it is crucial to recognize the unique responsibilities that leaders have when their jobs are international in scope and involve cross-border responsibilities (Spreitzer, McCall, & Mahoney, 1997). Leadership in cross-border contexts requires leaders to (1) adopt a multicultural perspective rather than a country-specific perspective; (2) balance local and global demands which can be contradictory; and (3) work with multiple cultures simultaneously rather than working with one dominant culture (Bartlett & Goshal, 1992). Thus, we define cross-border effectiveness as the effectiveness of observable actions that managers take to accomplish their goals in situations characterized by cross-border cultural diversity. This aspect of global leaders' effectiveness explicitly recognizes and emphasizes the unique challenges of heterogeneous national, institutional, and cultural contexts (Shin, Morgeson, & Campion, 2007).

Effective leadership depends on the ability to solve complex technical and social problems (Mumford, Zaccaro, Harding, Jacobs, & Fleishman, 2000). Given important differences in domestic and cross-border contexts, it is unlikely that leadership effectiveness is the same in domestic contexts as in cross-border contexts. In this article, we aim to shed light on these differences by focusing on ways that leadership competencies are similar and different in their relevance to different contexts (domestic vs. cross-border).

Cultural Intelligence and Cross-Border Leadership Effectiveness

When leaders work in cross-border contexts, the social problems of leadership are especially complex because cultural background influences prototypes and schemas about appropriate leadership behaviors. For example, expectations about preferred leadership styles (House et al., 2004), managerial behaviors (Shin et al., 2007), and the nature of relationships (Yeung & Ready, 1995) are all influenced by culture. Thus, effective cross-border leadership requires the ability to function in culturally diverse contexts.

Although general intelligence (Judge, Colbert, & Ilies, 2004) as well as emotional intelligence (Caruso, Meyer, & Salovey, 2002) have been linked to leadership effectiveness in domestic contexts, neither deals explicitly with the ability to function in cross-border contexts. To address the unique aspects of culturally diverse settings, Earley and Ang (2003) drew on Sternberg and Detterman's (1986) multidimensional perspective on intelligence to develop a conceptual model of cultural intelligence (CQ). Ang and colleagues (Ang & Van Dyne, 2008; Ang et al., 2007) defined CQ as an individual's capability to function effectively in situations characterized by cultural diversity. They conceptualized CQ as a multidimensional concept comprising metacognitive, cognitive, motivational, and behavioral dimensions.

Metacognitive CQ is an individual's level of conscious cultural awareness during intercultural interactions. It involves higher level cognitive strategies—such as developing heuristics and guidelines for social interaction in novel cultural settings—based on deep-level information processing. Those with high metacognitive CQ are consciously aware of the cultural preferences and norms of different societies prior and during interactions. They question cultural assumptions and adjust their mental models about intercultural experiences (Triandis, 2006).

Whereas metacognitive CQ focuses on higher order cognitive processes, cognitive CQ is knowledge of norms, practices, and conventions in different cultures acquired from education and personal experience. This includes knowledge of cultural universals as well as knowledge of cultural differences. Those with high cognitive CQ have sophisticated mental maps of culture, cultural environments, and how the self is embedded in cultural contexts. These knowledge structures provide them with a starting point for anticipating and understanding cultural systems that shape and influence patterns of social interaction within a culture.

Motivational CQ is the capability to direct attention and energy toward learning about and operating in culturally diverse situations. Kanfer and Heggestad (1997, p. 39) argued that motivational capacities "provide agentic control of affect, cognition, and behavior that facilitate goal accomplishment." Expectations and the value associated with successfully accomplishing a task (Eccles & Wigfield, 2002) influence the direction and magnitude of energy channeled toward that task. Those with high motivational CQ direct attention and energy toward cross-cultural situations based on their intrinsic interest in cultures (Deci & Ryan, 1985) and confidence in intercultural effectiveness (Bandura, 2002).

Finally, behavioral CQ is the capability to exhibit culturally appropriate verbal and nonverbal actions when interacting with people from other cultures. Behavioral CQ also includes judicious use of speech acts—using culturally appropriate words and phrases in communication. Those with high behavioral CQ demonstrate flexibility in their intercultural interactions and adapt their behaviors to put others at ease and facilitate effective interactions.

Rooted in differential biological bases (Rockstuhl, Hong, Ng, Ang, & Chiu, 2011), metacognitive, cognitive, motivational, and behavioral CQ represent qualitatively different facets of overall CQ—the capability to function and manage effectively in culturally diverse settings (Ang & Van Dyne, 2008; Ang et al., 2007). Accordingly, the four facets are distinct capabilities that together form a higher level overall CQ construct.

Offermann and Phan (2002) offered three theoretical reasons for why leaders with high CQ capabilities are better able to manage the culturally diverse expectations of their followers in cross-border contexts (Avolio et al., 2009). First, awareness during intercultural interactions allows leaders to understand the impact of their own culture and background. It gives them insights into how their own values may bias their assumptions about behaviors in the workplace. It enhances awareness of the expectations they hold for themselves and others in leader–follower relationships. Second, high CQ causes leaders to pause and verify the accuracy of their cultural assumptions, consider their knowledge of other cultures, and hypothesize about possible values, biases, and expectations that may apply to intercultural interactions. Third, leaders with high CQ combine their rich understanding of self and others with motivation and behavioral flexibility in ways that allow them to adapt their leadership behaviors appropriately to specific cross-cultural situations.

In addition to managing diverse expectations as a function of cultural differences, leaders in cross-border contexts also need to effectively manage the exclusionary reactions that can be evoked by cross-cultural contact (Torelli, Chiu, Tam, Au, & Keh, 2011). Social categorization theory (Tajfel, 1981; Turner, 1987) theorizes that exclusionary reactions to culturally diverse others are initially driven by perceptions of dissimilarity and viewing others as members of the out-group. Research demonstrates, however, that those with high CQ are more likely to develop trusting relationships with culturally diverse others and less likely to engage in exclusionary reactions (Rockstuhl & Ng, 2008). Consistent with our earlier emphasis on matching capabilities to the context, their results also demonstrated that CQ did not influence trust when partners were culturally homogeneous.

An increasing amount of research demonstrates the importance of CQ for performance effectiveness in cross-border contexts (for reviews, see Ang, Van Dyne, & Tan, 2011; Ng, Van Dyne, & Ang, in press). This includes expatriate performance in international assignments (Chen, Kirkman, Kim, Farh, & Tangirala, 2010), successful intercultural negotiations (Imai & Gelfand, 2010), leadership potential (Kim & Van Dyne, 2011), and leadership effectiveness in culturally diverse work groups (Groves & Feyerherm, 2011).

To summarize, theory and research support the notion that leaders with high CQ should be more effective at managing expectations of culturally diverse others and minimizing exclusionary reactions that can occur in cross-border contexts. Thus, we hypothesize that general intelligence will predict leadership effectiveness in domestic contexts and in cross-border contexts; emotional intelligence will be a stronger predictor of leadership effectiveness in domestic contexts; and cultural intelligence will be a stronger predictor of leadership effectiveness in cross-border contexts.

Method

We tested our hypotheses with field data from 126 military leaders and their peers studying at the Swiss Military Academy at ETH Zurich. CQ has special relevance to leadership in military settings because armed forces throughout the world are increasingly involved in international assignments (Ang & Ng, 2007). We obtained data from professional officers in a 3-year training program that focused on developing domestic and cross-border leadership capabilities. Thus, the sample allows comparison of leadership effectiveness across contexts. During the program officers completed domestic assignments (e.g., physical education, group projects, and general military and leadership military training) as well and cross-border assignments (e.g., international support operations for the UN in former Yugoslavia and international civil-military collaboration training with U.S., EU, and Croatian armed forces). Military contexts represent high-stakes settings where leadership effectiveness has broad implications for countries, regions, and in some cases, the world. Poor-quality leadership can exacerbate tensions and heighten conflict between groups. In addition, it is essential that military leaders overcome initial exclusionary reactions that can be triggered when interacting with people from different cultures in high-stress situations. As a result, gaining a better understanding of general and cross-border leadership effectiveness in this setting should have important practical implications.

All 126 participants (95% response rate) were male Caucasians with average previous leadership experience of 6.44 years ($SD = 4.79$). On average, they had lived in 1.45 different countries ($SD = .91$). They had been studying and working together on a daily basis for at least 7 months prior to the study.

Procedure

Two peers in the program, selected based on cultural diversity, provided ratings of general and cross-border leadership effectiveness, such that those with French, Italian, or Rhaeto-Romansh background were rated by peers who had a German background and vice versa. We designed the data collection using peers for the assessment of leadership effectiveness for four reasons. First, all participants had extensive previous leadership experience in the military and were knowledgeable observers in these contexts. Second, military mission goals were clearly specified, and thus peers could readily observe both domestic and cross-border effectiveness in terms of mission completion. Third, participants worked closely together and had numerous opportunities to observe peers' leadership effectiveness across general and cross-border contexts. Finally, Viswesvaran, Schmidt, and Ones (2002) showed in their meta-analysis of convergence between peer and supervisory ratings that leadership is one job performance dimension for which ratings from these two sources are interchangeable.

Participants provided data on cultural intelligence, emotional intelligence, and demographic background. In addition, we obtained archival data on general mental ability and personality. This multisource approach is a strength of the design.

Measures

Peers assessed general leadership effectiveness and cross-border leadership effectiveness with six items each ($1 = $ *strongly disagree*; $7 = $ *strongly agree*). Existing leadership effectiveness measures (e.g., Ng, Ang, & Chan, 2008; Offermann, Bailey, Vasilopoulos, Seal, & Sass, 2004) do not distinguish explicitly between general and cross-border effectiveness. Thus, we reviewed the literature on general leadership effectiveness, developed six general leadership items, and then wrote parallel items that focused specifically on leadership effectiveness in culturally diverse contexts.

Independent ratings by three subject matter experts ($1 = $ *not at all representative*, $2 = $ *somewhat*, $3 = $ *highly representative*) provided face validity for the items (intraclass correlation $= .83$). Exploratory factor analysis (pilot sample #1: $n = 95$) showed two distinct factors (74.49% explained variance), and confirmatory factor analysis (CFA) (pilot sample #2: $n = 189$) demonstrated acceptable fit: χ^2 ($53df$) $= 94.69$, $p < .05$, RMSEA $= .066$. In the substantive sample, interrater agreement ($r_{WG(J)} = .71 - 1.00$) supported aggregation of peer ratings for general ($\alpha = .91$) and cross-border leadership effectiveness ($\alpha = .93$).

We assessed CQ with the previously validated 20-item CQS (Cultural Intelligence Scale: Ang et al., 2007), which is highly reliable and generalizable across samples and cultures (Van Dyne, Ang, & Koh, 2008). Sample items include: I check the accuracy of my cultural knowledge as I interact with people from different cultures; and I alter my facial expressions when a cross-cultural inter-action requires it ($\alpha = .89$). CFA analysis of a second-order model demonstrated good fit to the data: χ^2 ($40df$) $= 58.13, p < .05$, RMSEA $= .061$), so we averaged the four factors to create our measure of overall CQ. We assessed EQ with 19 items (Brackett, Rivers, Shiffman, Lerner, & Salovey, 2006) and obtained archival data on general mental ability (the SHL Critical Reasoning Test Battery, 1996) and Big-Five personality (Donnellan, Oswald, Baird, & Lucas, 2006). These controls are important because prior research shows CQ is related to EQ (Moon, 2010), general mental ability (Ang et al., 2007), and personality (Ang, Van Dyne, & Koh, 2006). We also controlled for previous leadership experience (number of years of full-time job experience with the Swiss Military), international experience (num-ber of countries participants had lived in), and age because prior research shows relationships with leadership effectiveness.

Results

CFA analysis supported the discriminant validity of the 10 constructs (χ^2 ($186df$) $= 255.12, p < .05$, RMSEA $= .046$) and the proposed 10-factor model provided a better fit than plausible alternative models. Table 1 presents descriptive statistics and correlations. Table 2 summarizes hierarchical regression and relative weight analyses (Johnson & LeBreton, 2004).

As predicted, IQ was positively related to general leadership effectiveness ($\beta = .23, p < .05$) and cross-border leadership effectiveness ($\beta = .18, p < .05$), even after controlling for age, leadership experience. international experience, Big-Five personality, EQ, and CQ. Thus, general mental ability had implications for both aspects of leadership effectiveness.

In addition and consistent with our predictions, EQ was positively related to general leadership effectiveness ($\beta = .27, p < .05$) but not to cross-border leader-ship effectiveness ($\beta = -.07$, n.s.), after controlling for age, leadership experience, international experience, Big-Five personality, IQ, and CQ. Relative weight analy-sis demonstrated that EQ predicted 25.7% of the variance in general leadership ef-fectiveness but only 3.5% of the variance in cross-border leadership effectiveness. Thus, EQ has special relevance to leadership effectiveness in domestic contexts but not to leadership effectiveness in cross-border contexts.

Finally, CQ was positively related to cross-border leadership effectiveness ($\beta = .24, p < .05$) but not to general leadership effectiveness ($\beta = -.11$, n.s.), after accounting for the controls. Relative weight analysis showed that CQ predicted 24.7% of the variance in cross-border leadership effectiveness and only 4.7% of the variance in general leadership effectiveness. Thus, results demonstrate the unique importance of CQ to cross-border leadership effectiveness.

Results also show that previous international experience predicted both general ($\beta = .30, p < .01$) and cross-border leadership effectiveness ($\beta = .35$,

Table 1. Means, Standard Deviations, and Correlations

Variable	M	SD	1	2	3	4	5	6	7	8	9	10	11	12
1. General leadership effectiveness[a]	5.13	0.66	(.91)											
2. Cross-border leadership effectiveness[a]	4.41	0.70	.56**	(.93)										
3. General intelligence[b]	22.06	5.69	.23**	.14	–									
4. Emotional intelligence[c]	4.82	0.62	.26**	.15	.23**	(.76)								
5. Cultural intelligence[c]	5.01	0.71	.17	.33**	.15	.62**	(.89)							
6. Agreeableness	4.38	0.64	.01	.04	.00	.11	.06	(.62)						
7. Conscientiousness	4.77	0.56	−.06	.02	.02	−.05	−.08	.02	(.77)					
8. Emotional stability	4.53	0.63	.01	.01	.13	.16	−.06	.29**	.18*	(.66)				
9. Extraversion	4.52	0.61	.07	.09	.10	.17	.15	.20*	.06	.18*	(.77)			
10. Openness to experience	4.08	0.65	.06	.14	−.06	.09	.20*	.02	.09	−.03	.37**	(.80)		
11. Age (in years)	29.07	3.96	−.08	.11	−.21*	.02	.09	.14	−.13	.03	−.19*	.10	–	
12. Leadership experience (in years)	6.44	4.79	−.13	−.04	−.28**	−.03	.01	.10	.15	.04	−.10	.12	.55**	–
13. Prior international experience	1.45	0.91	.23**	.38**	−.20*	.01	.25**	.09	−.02	−.21*	.00	.09	.11	.06

Note. $N = 126$.
[a]Observer report.
[b]Performance based.
[c]Self-report.
*$p < .05$, **$p < .01$.

Table 2. Hierarchical Regression Results ($N = 126$)

	General leadership effectiveness			Cross-border leadership effectiveness		
	Step 1	Step 2	RW	Step 1	Step 2	RW
Age (in years)	−.06	−.05	2.3%	.17	.16	5.6%
Leadership experience (in years)	−.11	−.04	4.0%	−.16	−.11	2.4%
Prior international experience	.25**	.30**	32.9%	.38***	.35***	48.1%
Agreeableness	−.02	−.03	0.3%	−.04	−.04	0.2%
Conscientiousness	−.07	−.06	1.8%	.02	.02	0.1%
Emotional stability	.07	.01	0.7%	.07	.07	0.9%
Extraversion	.03	.00	0.7%	.07	.03	1.3%
Openness to experience	.05	.06	1.4%	.08	.06	3.6%
General intelligence		.23*	25.5%		.18*	9.5%
Emotional intelligence		.27*	25.7%		−.07	3.5%
Cultural intelligence		−.11	4.7%		.24*	24.7%
F	1.32	2.39**		3.24**	3.61***	
	(8,117)	(11,114)		(8,117)	(11,114)	
ΔF	1.32	4.89**		3.24**	3.94**	
	(8,117)	(3,114)		(8,117)	(3,114)	
R^2	.08	.19		.18	.26	
ΔR^2	.08	.11		.18	.08	
Adjusted R^2	.02	.11		.13	.19	

Note. RW = relative weights in percentage of R^2 explained.
$^*p < .05$, $^{**}p < .01$, $^{***}p < .001$.

$p < .001$). Surprisingly, previous leadership experience did not predict general leadership effectiveness ($\beta = -.04$, n.s.) or cross-border leadership effectiveness ($\beta = -.11$, n.s.) in our study. While this result is inconsistent with earlier research that has demonstrated experience can be an important predictor of leadership success (Fiedler, 2002), it is also consistent with recent theoretical arguments that experience may not necessarily translate into effectiveness (Ng, Van Dyne, & Ang, 2009).

Discussion

This study responds to a recent call for research on the unique aspects of global leadership and the competencies that predict global leadership effectiveness (Avolio et al., 2009). As hypothesized, results of our rigorous multisource research design show differences in predictors of general leadership effectiveness compared to cross-border leadership effectiveness. Cross-border leaders must work simultaneously with systems, processes, and people from multiple cultures.

Thus, cultural intelligence—the capability of functioning effectively in multicultural contexts (Earley & Ang, 2003)—is a critical competency of effective global leaders.

Theoretical Implications

Our findings have important theoretical implications. First, as Chiu, Gries, Torelli, and Cheng (2011) point out, the outcomes of globalization are uncertain. Some academics predict a multicultural global village and others expect clashes between civilizations. As the articles in this issue attest, contextual and psychological factors influence the extent to which intercultural contact activates exclusionary or integrative reactions. For example, Morris, Mor, and Mok (2011) highlight the adaptive value and creative benefits of developing a cosmopolitan identity. Our findings complement this perspective by emphasizing the importance of cultural intelligence for leadership effectiveness—especially in high-stakes global encounters, such as cross-border military assignments. In addition, our study offers another perspective because we emphasize the value of theory and research on the competencies of global leaders that help them perform in global contexts, rather than focusing on psychological reactions to globalization. Focusing on competencies suggests exciting opportunities for future research on the dynamic interaction between globalization and global leaders.

A second set of theoretical implications is based on the context-specific relationships demonstrated in this study. Specifically, results suggest that EQ and CQ are complementary because EQ predicted general but not cross-border leadership while CQ predicted cross-border but not general leadership effectiveness. This contrasting pattern reinforces the assertion that domestic leader skillsets do not necessarily generalize to global leader skillsets (Avolio et al., 2009; Caligiuri, 2006). Hence, EQ and CQ are related but distinct forms of social intelligence (Moon, 2010), and each has context-specific relevance to different aspects of global leadership effectiveness. Thus, researchers should match types of intelligences to specifics of the situation to maximize predictive validity of effectiveness.

Practical Implications

Our findings also have practical implications for the selection and development of global leaders. First, the significant relationship between general intelligence and both forms of leader effectiveness reinforces the utility of intelligence as a selection tool for identifying leadership potential. In addition, the incremental validity of emotional and cultural intelligence as predictors of leadership effectiveness, over and above previous experience, personality, and general intelligence, confirms predictions that social intelligences also contribute to leadership effectiveness (Riggio, 2002). Accordingly, managers should consider multiple forms of intelligence when assessing leadership potential, especially when work roles include responsibility for coordinating complex social interactions.

Given the differential predictive validity of EQ and CQ relative to the two types of leadership effectiveness in our study, applying the notion of context similarity and matching types of intelligence with the leadership context should help organizations enhance their understanding of what predicts global leader effectiveness. This finding should also help organizations understand why leaders who are effective in domestic contexts may not be effective in cross-border contexts. These insights should help organizations tailor leadership development opportunities to the competency requirements of the situation. When leaders work primarily in domestic settings, organizations should place more emphasis on developing within-culture capabilities, such as EQ. In contrast, when leaders work extensively in international or cross-border settings, organizations should emphasize development of cross-cultural capabilities, such as CQ (Ng, Tan, & Ang, 2011).

Limitations and Future Research

Despite the strength of our multisource design and support for our predictions, this study has limitations that should help guide future research. First, our cross-sectional design prevents inferences about the causal direction of relationships. Thus, we recommend longitudinal field research that assesses capabilities and leadership effectiveness at multiple points in time.

Second, our study was conducted in a military context and all participants were male. Thus, we recommend caution in generalizing our findings to other settings until research can assess whether relationships can be replicated in other contexts. To address this need, we recommend future research on different types of intelligences and different aspects of leadership effectiveness in other vocational settings and different cultures (Gelfand, Erez, & Aycan, 2007).

Third, given that this is the first research, to our knowledge, that proposes and tests an integrated model of three types of intelligence and global leadership effectiveness, the model is necessarily incomplete. We did not consider the indirect effects of mediators or moderators. We recommend future research that "opens the black-box" by focusing on mediating mechanisms that link capabilities with global leader effectiveness. For example, Bass (2002) argued that multiple intelligences are a core element of transformational leadership. Previous research has demonstrated that emotional intelligence in domestic contexts (Rubin, Munz, & Bommer, 2005) and cultural intelligence in culturally diverse contexts (Elenkov & Manev, 2009) predict transformational leadership behavior. Judge and Piccolo (2004) provided meta-analytic evidence that transformational leadership behaviors predict leadership effectiveness. Thus, it is plausible that transformational leadership mediates the relationships of emotional and cultural intelligence with leadership effectiveness. Leader-member exchange (LMX) is another plausible mediator. For example, Riggio (2002) suggested that social and emotional intelligences most likely enhance the quality of leader–follower relationships, which then influence effective leadership. In sum, we recommend future research on mediators that link multiple intelligences with leadership effectiveness.

We also recommend future research on situational factors that moderate the relationships between multiple intelligences and leadership effectiveness. Judge et al.'s (2004) meta-analysis, for example, demonstrated that situational stressors influence relationships between general intelligence and leadership effectiveness. Thus, it is possible that situational stressors function as an important boundary condition that qualifies the relationships demonstrated in our study. Given that EQ (Mayer, Roberts, & Barsade, 2008) and CQ (Tarique & Takeuchi, 2008) are influenced by prior experiences, it is possible that EQ and CQ are especially important in high-stress situations. Alternatively, it is possible that global identity (Shokef & Erez, 2008) functions as a boundary condition that changes the nature of the relationships between leader competencies and leader effectiveness. In sum, we recommend field and experimental research on the extent to which situational stressors moderate the relationships demonstrated in our research.

Conclusion

In sum, this research begins to add to limited understanding of predictors of global leadership effectiveness and how the nomological networks of leadership effectiveness differ in different contexts. Most important, results demonstrate the critical importance of CQ in predicting leadership effectiveness in cross-border contexts. We recommend future research on IQ, EQ, and CQ as well as other intelligences in predicting different types of leadership effectiveness in both domestic and cross-cultural contexts.

References

Ang, S., & Ng, K. Y. (2007). Cultural and network intelligences: The twin pillars in leadership development for the 21st century era of global business and institutional networks. In K. Y. Chan, S. Singh, R. Ramaya, & K. H. Lim (Eds.), *Spirit and system: Leadership development for a third generation SAF* [Monograph] (pp. 46–52). Pointer: Journal of the Singapore Armed Forces.

Ang, S., & Van Dyne, L. (2008). Conceptualization of cultural intelligence: Definition, distinctiveness, and nomological network. In S. Ang & L. Van Dyne (Eds.), *Handbook of cultural intelligence: Theory, measurement, and applications* (pp. 3–15). Armonk, NY: M.E. Sharpe.

Ang, S., Van Dyne, L., & Koh, C. (2006). Personality correlates of the four-factor model of cultural intelligence. *Group and Organization Management, 31,* 100–123. doi:10.1177/1059601105275267

Ang, S., Van Dyne, L., Koh, C. K. S., Ng, K. Y., Templer, K. J., Tay, C., & Chandrasekar, N. A. (2007). Cultural intelligence: Its measurement and effects on cultural judgment and decision making, cultural adaptation, and task performance. *Management and Organization Review, 3,* 335–371. doi:10.1111/j.1740-8784.2007.00082.x

Ang, S., Van Dyne, L., & Tan, M. L. (2011). Cultural intelligence. In R. J. Sternberg & S. B. Kaufman (Eds.), *Cambridge handbook on intelligence* (pp. 582–602). New York: Cambridge University Press.

Avolio, J., Walumbwa, F. O., & Weber, T. J. (2009). Leadership: Current theories, research, and future directions. *Annual Review of Psychology, 60*, 421–449. doi:10.1146/annurev.psych.60.110707.163621

Bandura, A. (2002). Social cognitive theory in cultural context. *Applied Psychology: An International Review, 51*, 269–290. doi:10.1111/1464-0597.00092

Bartlett, C. A., & Ghoshal, S. (1992). What is a global manager? *Harvard Business Review* (September-October), 124–132. doi:10.1225/R0308F

Bass, B. M. (2002). Cognitive, social, and emotional intelligence of transformational leaders. In R. E. Riggio, S. E. Murphy, & F. J. Pirozzolo (Eds.), *Multiple intelligences and leadership* (pp. 105–118). Mahwah, NJ: Erlbaum.

Brackett, M. A., Rivers, S. E., Shiffman, S., Lerner, N., & Salovey, P. (2006). Relating emotional abilities to social functioning: A comparison of self-report and performance measures of emotional intelligence. *Journal of Personality and Social Psychology, 91*, 780–795. doi:10.1037/0022-3514.91.4.780

Caligiuri, P. M. (2006). Performance measurement in a cross-national context. In W. Bennett, C. E. Lance, & D. J. Woehr (Eds.), *Performance measurement: Current perspectives and future challenges* (pp. 227–244). Mahwah, NJ: Erlbaum.

Campbell, J. P., McCloy, R. A., Oppler, S. H., & Sager, C. E. (1993). A theory of performance. In N. Schmitt & W. C. Borman (Eds.), *Personnel selection in organizations* (pp. 35–70). San Francisco, CA: Jossey-Bass.

Caruso, D. R., Mayer, J. D., & Salovey, P. (2002). Emotional intelligence and emotional leadership. In R. E. Riggio, S. E. Murphy, & F. J. Pirozzolo (Eds.), *Multiple intelligences and leadership* (pp. 55–74). Mahwah, NJ: Lawrence Erlbaum.

Chen, G., Kirkman, B. L., Kim, K., Farh, C. I. C., & Tangirala, S. (2010). When does cross-cultural motivation enhance expatriate effectiveness? A multilevel investigation of the moderating roles of subsidiary support and cultural distance. *Academy of Management Journal, 53*, 1110–1130.

Chiu, C. Y., Gries, P., Torelli, C. J., & Cheng, S. Y. Y. (2011). Toward a social psychology of globalization. *Journal of Social Issues, 67*, 663–676. doi:10.1111/j.1540-4560.2011.01721.x

Deci, E. L., & Ryan, R. M. (1985). *Intrinsic motivation and self-determination in human behavior*. New York: Plenum.

Donnellan, M. F., Oswald, F. L., Baird, B. M., & Lucas, R. E. (2006). The mini-IPIP scales: Tiny-yet-effective measures of the Big Five factors of personality. *Psychological Assessment, 18*, 192–203. doi:10.1037/1040-3590.18.2.192

Earley, P. C., & Ang, S. (2003). *Cultural intelligence: Individual interactions across cultures*. Palo Alto, CA: Stanford University Press.

Eccles, J. S., & Wigfield, A. (2002). Motivational beliefs, values, and goals. In S. T. Fiske, D. L. Schacter, & C. Zahn-Waxler (Eds.), *Annual review of psychology* (Vol. 53, pp. 109–132). Palo Alto, CA: Annual Reviews. doi:10.1146/annurev.psych.53.100901.135153

Elenkov, D. S., & Manev, I. M. (2009). Senior expatriate leadership's effects on innovation and the role of cultural intelligence. *Journal of World Business, 44*, 357–369. doi:10.1016/j.jwb.2008.11.001

Fiedler, F. E. (2002). The curious role of cognitive resources in leadership. In R. E. Riggio, S. E. Murphy, & F. J. Pirozzolo (Eds.), *Multiple intelligences and leadership* (pp. 91–104). Mahwah, NJ: Erlbaum.

Gelfand, M. J., Erez, M., & Aycan, Z. (2007). Cross-cultural organizational behavior. *Annual Review of Psychology, 58*, 479–514. doi:10.1146/annurev.psych.58.110405.085559

Gregersen, H. B., Morrison, A. J., & Black, J. S. (1998). Developing leaders for the global frontier. *Sloan Management Review, 40*, 21–32. doi:10.1225/SMR039

Groves, K. S., & Feyerherm, A. (2011). Leader cultural intelligence in context: Testing the moderating effects of team cultural diversity on leader and team performance. *Group & Organization Management, 36*, 535–566. doi:10.1177/1059601111415654

House, R. J., Hanges, P. J., Javidan, M., Dorfman, P. W., & Gupta, V. (2004). *Culture, leadership, and organizations: The GLOBE study of 62 societies.* Palo Alto, CA: Sage.

Imai, L., & Gelfand, M. J. (2010). The culturally intelligent negotiator: The impact of cultural intelligence (CQ) on negotiation sequences and outcomes. *Organizational Behavior and Human Decision Processes, 112,* 83–98. doi:10.1016/j.obhdp.2010.02.001

Johns, G. (2006). The essential impact of context on organizational behavior. *Academy of Management Review, 31,* 386–408.

Johnson, J. W., & LeBreton, J. M. (2004). History and use of relative importance indices in organizational research. *Organizational Research Methods, 7,* 238–257. doi:10.1177/1094428104266510

Judge, T. A., Colbert, A. E., & Ilies, R. (2004). Intelligence and leadership: A quantitative review and test of theoretical propositions. *Journal of Applied Psychology, 89,* 542–552. doi:10.1037/0021-9010.89.3.542

Judge, T. A., & Piccolo, R. F. (2004). Transformational and transactional leadership: A meta-analytic test of their relative validity. *Journal of Applied Psychology, 89,* 755–768. doi:10.1037/0021-9010.89.5.755

Kanfer, R., & Heggestad, E. D. (1997). Motivational traits and skills: A person-centered approach to work motivation. *Research in Organizational Behavior, 19,* 1–56.

Kim, Y. J., & Van Dyne, L. (2011). Cultural intelligence and international leadership potential: The importance of contact for members of the majority. *Applied Psychology: An International Review.* Advance online publication. doi:10.1111/j.1464-0597.2011.00468.x

Mayer, J. D., Roberts, R. D., & Barsade, S. G. (2008). Human abilities: Emotional intelligence. *Annual Review of Psychology, 59,* 13.1–13.30. doi:10.1146/annurev.psych.59.103006.093646

Moon, T. (2010). Emotional intelligence correlates of the four-factor model of cultural intelligence. *Journal of Managerial Psychology, 25,* 876–898. doi:10.1108/02683941011089134

Morris, M. W., Mor, S., & Mok, A. (2011). From bicultural to global identity: Implications for responses to mixed-culture situations and cultural differences. *Journal of Social Issues, 67,* 760–773.

Mumford, M. D., Zaccaro, S. J., Harding, F. D., Jacobs, T. O., & Fleishman, E. A. (2000). Leadership skills for a changing world. Solving complex social problems. *Leadership Quarterly, 11,* 11–35. doi:10.1016/S1048-9843(99)00041-7

Ng, K. Y., Ang, S., & Chan, K. Y. (2008). Personality and leader effectiveness: A moderated mediation model of leadership self-efficacy, job demands, and job autonomy. *Journal of Applied Psychology, 93,* 733–743. doi:10.1037/0021-9010.93.4.733

Ng, K. Y., Tan, M. L., & Ang, S. (2011). Culture capital and cosmopolitan human capital: The impact of global mindset and organizational routines on developing cultural intelligence and international experiences in organizations. In A. Burton & J. C. Spender (Eds.), *The Oxford handbook of human capital* (pp. 96–119). Oxford: Oxford University Press. doi:10.1093/oxfordhb/9780199532162.003.0004

Ng, K. Y., Van Dyne, L., & Ang, S. (in press). Cultural intelligence: A review, reflections, and recommendations for future research. In A. M. Ryan, F. T. L. Leong, & F. Oswald (Eds.), *Conducting multinational research projects in organizational psychology.* Washington, DC: American Psychological Association.

Ng, K. Y., Van Dyne, L., & Ang, S. (2009). From experience to experiential learning: Cultural intelligence as a learning capability for global leader development. *Academy of Management Learning & Education, 8,* 511–526.

Offermann, L. R., Bailey, J. R., Vasilopoulos, N. L., Seal, C., & Sass, M. (2004). The relative contribution of emotional competence and cognitive ability to individual and team performance. *Human Performance, 17,* 219–243.

Offermann, L. R., & Phan, L. U. (2002). Culturally intelligent leadership for a diverse world. In R. E. Riggio, S. E. Murphy, & F. J. Pirozzolo (Eds.), *Multiple intelligences and leadership* (pp. 187–214). Mahwah, NJ: Lawrence Erlbaum.

Riggio, R. E. (2002). Multiple intelligence and leadership: An overview. In R. E. Riggio, S. E. Murphy, & F. J. Pirozzolo (Eds.), *Multiple intelligences and leadership* (pp. 1–6). Mahwah, NJ: Lawrence Erlbaum.

Rockstuhl, T., Hong, Y. Y., Ng, K. Y., Ang, S., & Chiu, C. Y. (2011). The culturally intelligent brain: From detecting to bridging cultural differences. *Neuroleadership Journal, 3,* 22–36.

Rockstuhl, T., & Ng, K. Y. (2008). The effects of cultural intelligence on interpersonal trust in multicultural teams. In S. Ang & L. Van Dyne (Eds.), *Handbook of cultural intelligence: Theory, measurement, and applications* (pp. 206–220). Armonk, NY: M.E. Sharpe.

Rubin, R. S., Munz, D. C., & Bommer, W. H. (2005). Leading from within: The effects of emotion recognition and personality on transformational leadership behavior. *Academy of Management Journal, 48,* 845–858.

Shin, S. J., Morgeson, F. P., & Campion, M. A. (2007). What you do depends on where you are: Understanding how domestic and expatriate work requirements depend upon the cultural context. *Journal of International Business Studies, 38,* 64–83. doi:10.1057/palgrave.jibs.8400247

SHL. (1996). *Critical reasoning test battery: Technical manual.* Thames Ditton, UK: Saville and Holdsworth Ltd. Occupational Psychologists.

Shokef, E., & Erez, M. (2008). Cultural intelligence and global identity in multicultural teams. In S. Ang & L. Van Dyne (Eds.), *Handbook of cultural intelligence: Theory, measurement, and applications* (pp. 177–191). Armonk, NY: M.E. Sharpe.

Spreitzer, G. M., McCall, M. W., & Mahoney, J. D. (1997). Early identification of international executive potential. *Journal of Applied Psychology, 82,* 6–29. doi:10.1037/0021-9010.82.1.6

Sternberg, R. J., & Detterman, D. K. (1986). *What is intelligence? Contemporary viewpoints on its nature and definition.* Norwood, NJ: Ablex.

Tajfel, H. (1981). *Human groups and social categories: Studies in social psychology.* Cambridge: Cambridge University Press.

Tarique, I., & Takeuchi, R. (2008). Developing cultural intelligence: The roles of international nonwork experiences. In S. Ang & L. Van Dyne (Eds.), *Handbook of cultural intelligence: Theory, measurement, and applications* (pp. 56–70). Armonk, NY: M.E. Sharpe.

Torelli, C. J., Chiu, C. Y., Tam, K. P., Au, K. C., & Keh, H. T. (2011). Psychological reactions to foreign cultures in globalized economy: Effects of simultaneous activation of cultures. *Journal of Social Issues, 67,* 716–742.

Triandis, H. C. (2006). Cultural intelligence in organizations. *Group and Organization Management, 31,* 20–26. doi:10.1177/1059601105275253

Turner, J. C. (1987). *Rediscovering the social group: A self-categorization theory.* Oxford: Basil Blackwell.

Van Dyne, L., Ang, S., & Koh, C. (2008). Development and validation of the CQS: The cultural intelligence scale. In S. Ang & L. Van Dyne (Eds.), *Handbook of cultural intelligence: Theory, measurement, and applications* (pp. 16–38). Armonk, NY: M.E. Sharpe.

Viswesvaran, C., Schmidt, F. L., & Ones, D. S. (2002). The moderating influence of job performance dimensions on convergence of supervisory and peer ratings of job performance: Unconfounding construct-level convergence and rating difficulty. *Journal of Applied Psychology, 87,* 345–354. doi:10.1037//0021-9010.87.2.345

Yeung, A., & Ready, D. (1995). Developing leadership capabilities of global corporations: A comparative study in eight nations. *Human Resource Management, 34,* 529–547. doi:10.1002/hrm.3930340405

THOMAS ROCKSTUHL is a PhD candidate and a research associate at the Center for Innovation Research in Cultural Intelligence + Leadership (CIRCQL) at Nanyang Business School, Nanyang Technological University, Singapore. His research interests include measurement of cultural intelligence and leadership in multicultural teams.

STEFAN SEILER received a PhD from University of Fribourg, CH. He is the Department Head of Leadership and Communication Studies at the Swiss

Military Academy at ETH Zurich. His research interests are intercultural leadership, leadership development, moral decision making, and leadership ethics.

SOON ANG received a PhD from Minnesota. She is Goh Tjoei Kok Chaired Professor in Management and Executive Director, Center for Innovation Research in Cultural Intelligence + Leadership (CIRCQL) at Nanyang Business School, Nanyang Technological University, Singapore. She specializes in cultural intelligence, global leadership, and outsourcing.

LINN VAN DYNE received a PhD from University of Minnesota. She is Professor at Michigan State University. She has two major research programs: proactive employee behaviors involving initiative and cultural intelligence.

HUBERT ANNEN received a PhD from University of Zurich, CH. He is the Department Head of Military Psychology and Military Pedagogics at the Swiss Military Academy at ETH Zurich. His main research interests are in management assessment, motivation, and stress.

Journal of Social Issues, Vol. 67, No. 4, 2011, pp. 841–853

Toward a Psychological Science of Globalization

Michele J. Gelfand*, Sarah L. Lyons, and Janetta Lun
University of Maryland

A psychological perspective has been largely absent in the multidisciplinary discourse surrounding globalization. In this commentary, we highlight the unique contributions that the articles in this special issue have made in advancing a new psychological science of globalization. We discuss the critical role that psychological theory plays in understanding reactions to globalization, and in turn, how globalization research provides a new context that challenges, refines, and extends psychological theory. We offer suggestions as to how psychology can take an active role in the future of globalization research, in particular in specifying the psychological dimensions on which globalization is construed (e.g., morality, power) and the implications these construals have for reactions to globalization. Building on research discussed in this special issue on psychological dynamics involved in responses to globalization, we offer some observations on factors that might play a role in positive and negative reactions to globalization.

Contributors to this volume have collectively paved the way for a new frontier in the study of globalization, adding a long overdue neglected dimension: The psychological dimension. Globalization, the rapid diffusion of economic, political, and cultural practices across national borders has a long past, with trade flourishing among people of different cultures as early as the 2nd century BC along the Silk Road that stretched from Rome to China (Elisseeff, 2000). Nevertheless, while globalization is not a new phenomenon, it has increased in unprecedented proportions in recent decades (Steger, 2009). Indeed, it is hard to find a phenomenon that has received more widespread discourse inside and outside the walls of academe. There is the *economic* dimension of globalization; the *political* dimension; the *sociological* dimension; the *technological* dimension, the *environmental* dimension; and the *marketing* dimension, all of which seek to capture the complex elephant

*Correspondence concerning this article should be addressed to Michele J. Gelfand, Department of Psychology, 3147c Biology/Psychology Building, University of Maryland, College Park, College Park, MD 20742 [e-mail: Mgelfand@psyc.umd.edu].

This research is based upon work supported by the US Army Research Laboratory and the U. S Army Research Office under Grant Number W911NF-08–1-0144.

that is globalization (Lecher & Boli, 2008; Steger, 2009). Now, finally, with this special issue on the Social Psychology of Globalization we at last have the beginnings of a *psychological dimension* to add to the cacophony of intellectual voices on a topic that is arguably one of the most important revolutionary trends in the history of mankind (Giddens, 2010).

While other disciplines have been busy debating, explaining, and predicting the future of globalization and its invariably positive and negative impacts, psychology has been largely left out of this intellectual discourse (cf. Arnett, 2002). On the one hand, mainstream psychology has ignored globalization, being largely been preoccupied with research on Western samples (Arnett, 2008), people who have been described as "the WEIRDest people in the world" (*W*estern, *E*ducated, *I*ndustrialized, *R*ich, and *D*emocratic; Henrich, Heine, & Norenzayan, 2010; p. 61). On the other hand, cultural, cross-cultural, and indigenous psychologies— while championing the importance of culture—have tended to focus on how individuals are impacted by the cultures in which they are embedded, and have been much less concerned with how the global context affects human behavior. And while other disciplines implicitly make assumptions about psychological reactions in discussing the social consequences of globalization and policies for managing it (Lecher & Boli, 2008; Steger, 2009), there has been a paucity of psychological research to back them up. The result is a series academic lacuna on the psychological underpinnings of globalization that risks not only having an incomplete understanding of the phenomenon but also one that is potentially misleading.

This special issue begins to address this void, and marshals in a new psychological science of globalization. The collection of articles draws upon existing psychological theory, employs a diverse set of methods, and samples a wide range of cultures, to address such fundamental questions as: How do people make meaning of globalization—how it is perceived and experienced—similarly and differently across cultures? Are there universals in how people construe globalization? What might explain unique cultural construals and responses to globalization (Chiu, Gries, & Torelli, 2011; Kashima et al., 2011)? What are the dynamics of psychological reactions to globalization? What conditions foster exclusionary and ethnocentric reactions to globalization and a "closing of the mind" toward globalization? What conditions foster inclusionary processes, those that facilitate integrative thinking and an opening of the mind which can result in learning, creativity, and cross-border intercultural effectiveness (Cheng, Leung, & Wu, 2011; Gries, Crowson, & Cai, 2011; Morris, Mok, & Mor, 2011; Norasakkunkit & Uchida, 2011; Rockstuhl, Seiler, Ang, van Dyne, & Anne, 2011; Tong, Hui, Kwan, & Peng, 2011; Torelli, Chiu, Tam, Au, & Keh, 2011)? Above all, these articles get at what has been missing in the globalization literature— what is going on "inside the head" in understanding, experiencing, and reacting to globalization.

In this commentary, we take a bird's eye view of the special issue and highlight the unique contributions that the authors have made in advancing a new psychological science of globalization. We discuss the critical role that psychological theory plays in understanding reactions to globalization, and in turn, how globalization research provides a new context that challenges, refines, and extends psychological theory. Drawing on the insights from the volume, we also discuss a number of important areas for future research, including specifying additional dimensions on which globalization is construed—particularly with respect to the psychology of power, status, and morality—and the implications of these psychological dimensions for reactions to globalization. And building on a foundation set forth on psychological dynamics involved in responses to globalization, we offer some observations on factors that might play a role in positive and negative reactions to globalization.

The Two-Way Street: How Psychological Theory Informs Globalization Research and How Globalization Research Informs Psychological Theory

The articles collectively offer numerous insightful analyses that not only expand globalization research in other disciplines but also expand and refine existing psychological theory. For example, psychology has long been argued to be a discipline of meaning (Kashima & Gelfand, in press), and many have advanced lay theories on a wide range of psychological phenomena (e.g., Chiu, Hong, & Dweck, 1997; Dweck, 1999; Furnham & Rees, 1988; Hong, Levy, & Chiu, 2001; Heider, 1958; Malle, 2010; Kruglanski, 1989; Sternberg, 1985; Wegener & Petty, 1998). This volume also makes clear that individuals across the globe also hold *lay theories about globalization* with important implications for the types of experiences and reactions to this phenomenon. Yang et al.'s (2011) impressive cluster analysis, for example, illustrated for the first time that people in different samples conceptualize the elements of globalization in very similar ways, involving global business enterprises/brands, information technology, geographic mobility, global disasters, and international trade regulators. Kashima et al. (2011) likewise showed that people in many societies also have lay theories about the trajectories of globalization; whether it is PRC, Japan, or Australia, people generally think that development levels have increased from the past to the present and expect them to continue increasing into the future. In addition to identifying universal aspects of lay theories of globalization, the articles also highlight how the specific circumstances of cultures entering the global market can result in notable differences in how people make meaning of globalization. For example, both Yang et al. (2011) and Kashima et al. (2011) describe how the unique cultural histories of Australia and Pacific Rim countries affect their folk theories about globalization and lay theories of social change, and Norasakkunkit & Uchida (2011) further illustrate that the way in which globalization is experienced varies dramatically even within any particular society. In all, the articles not only make a contribution to the interdisciplinary study of globalization by revealing that individuals hold lay theories about this trend, they also expand the psychological literature on lay theories that has yet to be applied to globalization.

The collection of articles in this volume illustrate that psychological theory provides important insight into when people have positive (inclusionary) versus negative (exclusionary) reactions to globalization. While economists, sociologists, and political scientists have long debated about the positive and negative impacts of globalization at a macro level (Giddens, 2010; Lecher & Boli, 2008; Steger, 2009), there has been little attention paid to how and when individuals experience globalization as an enhancement versus a threat. This volume illustrates how psychology adds another important voice to this interdisciplinary debate. For example, consistent with a long tradition of research on social categorization, the articles show that globalization can trigger an "us versus them" negative mentality when people view the juxtaposition of highly iconic representations of different groups (Chiu et al., 2011; Tong et al., 2011). Yet social psychology, with its penchant for studying how the power of the situation can dramatically affect social perception, can be fruitfully applied to understand *when* individuals react negatively to such social categorizations. For example, a key insight gleaned from these articles is that exposure to another foreign culture does not in and of itself cause negative outcomes. Torelli et al. (2011) showed that negative effects did not occur when Americans were exposed to just Chinese people or Chinese were exposed to just Americans; defensive processes only occurred when they were exposed to the two cultures simultaneously. Likewise, Tong et al. (2011) found that categorization in and of itself does not invariably lead to negative reactions. Rather, the effects of a categorization mindset were particularly strong when individuals perceive the two different cultural groups as highly dissimilar and also highly identify with their own local culture. Morris et al. (2011) similarly illustrate that people who typically have "exclusionary attitudes" (i.e., who do not identify with foreign cultures), are not necessarily threatened by foreign cultures per se, but the mixing of cultures that triggers the need for epistemic certainty and security. Interestingly, on the flip side, others have shown that under certain conditions, cultural mixing can have highly positive effects. In Cheng et al.'s (2011) article, creativity was sparked not simply when viewing a different group; it was the mixing that mattered for the generation of new ideas that pave the way for innovation. This research makes important contributions to the interdisciplinary study of globalization by illustrating how subtle differences in how people categorize other cultures vis-à-vis their own has a dramatic effect on their reactions. And in turn, this research also makes important contributions to basic psychological theory on social categorization by expanding the focus on "my group" versus "their group" to explore the psychological consequences of an exciting new paradigm on "cultural mixing" involving the direct juxtaposition of symbols of one group with another.

Yet another example of the "two-way" street of globalization and psychology research is in research that uses psychological theory to understand the factors that facilitate or inhibit cross-cultural understanding. For example, Gries et al. (2011) fruitfully applied intergroup contact theory (Allport, 1954) to understand American's attitudes toward other governments and their citizens, with important implications for public policy debates. At the same time, the article challenges age-old assumptions that increased contact, when rewarding, improves intergroup attitudes. To the contrary, Gries et al. find that that in some cases increased contact through media exposure and objective knowledge of another group actually caused more "negative" reactions (e.g., toward Chinese governments), resulting in recommendations for much tougher foreign policies toward China. Indeed, based on the other articles in this volume (e.g., Morris et al., 2011; Torelli et al. 2011), we might speculate that these effects would be even more pronounced for individuals that are high on local identification, have high uncertainty, have mortality salience, and/or perceive the two cultures as highly dissimilar. More generally, this work illustrates that classic theories in psychology are critical for understanding international relations, and at the same time, the psychological theories need to be refined and expanded when applied to the globalization context.

Hidden Psychological Dimensions of Globalization

While the articles in this special issue are diverse in their content, a key theme that cuts across the articles is that people make meaning—they socially construct—issues of globalization and pave the way for additional research on the hidden psychological dimensions underling globalization. For example, scholars in numerous disciplines have debated whether globalization invariably reflects modernization, westernization, or Americanization, with hotly contested economic, political, cultural and ethical implications. Articles in this volume provide a much needed psychological perspective on this debate. Yang et al. (2011) show for the first time that people can clearly distinguish between globalization with modernization and westernization. At the same time, they also illustrate that there might be wide variability in how globalization is conceptualized. Indeed, a close look at the data illustrate that perceived associations between globalization and westernization and Americanization ranged widely in the four regions studied. Future research is needed to explain and predict variability in these construals, and to examine the conditions under which individuals conflate globalization with Americanization and with what consequence. For example, to the extent that individuals, conflate globalization psychologically with westernization or Americanization does this promote more exclusionary reactions and more negative views of American citizens and its government? Moreover, drawing on other articles in this volume, might such exclusionary reactions be exacerbated when individuals perceive their country as very dissimilar and/or identify highly with their local culture (cf. Tong et al., 2011) and/or have high degrees of mortality salience (cf. Torelli et al., 2011)?

Likewise, while Yang et al. illustrated the issues that people most strongly associate with globalization (i.e., international trade, global consumption, technology, human mobility), future research with even broader sampling across different countries, socioeconomic groups, ages, and occupations might very well reveal additional meaningful dimensions, and/or differences in how people weigh different dimensions in defining globalization. For example, might the list of concepts that were identified as related to globalization by Yang et al. (2011) look different if individuals who hold more negative views of the phenomenon (e.g., members of Al Qaeda, the Taliban, anti-globalization activists) were sampled? Taking the dynamic perspective advanced in this volume, how individual and/or situational differences affect the specific globalization issues that are activated, the way they are categorized, and/or the weights people place on them is an exciting frontier in the psychological science of globalization.

Research in this volume has also begun to unearth implicit dimensions on which people evaluate globalization issues, pioneering an important area for future research. Yang et al. (2011), for example, showed that people across the four regions they studied perceive globalization as increasing competence and to some degree warmth, and have generally favorable evaluations of many globalization issues. This work provides a "rosy" view of evaluations of globalization, and future research is needed to examine the psychological factors that might cause more dour implicit evaluations. Do experiences with threat, need for closure, mortality salience, or cultural tightness (discussed below) affect the degree to which people see globalization as reflecting competence and warmth (or a lack thereof)? How do individuals' lay theories of social change (i.e., where one's country has been and where it is going; Kashima et al., 2011), affect their evaluation of the competence and warmth of their own and other societies, as well as their attitudes toward different globalization issues?

Future research is also needed to unearth other underlying psychological dimensions on which globalization is evaluated. One interesting psychological candidate in is that of morality. Moral foundations theory (Haidt, 2008; Haidt & Graham, 2007) in particular can be fruitfully applied to a psychological science of globalization. Haidt and Graham identified five fundamental moral values that relevant for the study of globalization including the morality of *care* (protecting others from harm), the morality of *fairness* (justice, treating others equally), the morality of the *ingroup* (loyalty to one's group, nation), the morality of *authority* (respect for tradition), and the morality of *purity* (avoiding contamination from things, foods, actions). Drawing on this work, we would suspect that there could be underlying "moral conflict" about different dimensions of globalization. For example, some might see unbridled geographic mobility (e.g., immigration) as violating morality of ingroup, tradition, or purity, whereas others might see it through the lens of a morality of fairness and justice. Other dimensions of globalization identified by Yang et al. (2011), whether it is global business enterprises, information technology, global disasters, or international trade, might likewise be imbued with very different moral foundations across the globe. As well, the conditions under which "cultural mixing" (Chiu et al., 2011; Morris et al., 2011; Torelli et al., 2011) violates fundamental moral and sacred values has important implications for exclusionary reactions, and in the extreme, for conflict and the support for violence (Ginges, Atran, Medin, & Shikaki, 2007). For example, the moral outrage of many Muslims in Saudi Arabia as Americans set up military bases in their Islamic holy land during the Iraqi-Kuwait conflict (see Morris et al., 2011). These and other accounts of "taboo tradeoffs" (Tetlock, Kristel, Elson, Green, & Lerner, 2000) illustrate the critical importance of studying the moral foundations of globalization.

Power is also another important psychological dimension that individuals use to construe globalization. Throughout history, the drive for obtaining status and power has been thought of as a fundamental motivator of human behavior (e.g., Adler, 1966; Frieze & Boneva, 2001; Kipnis, 1976; McClelland, 1975, 1987; Winter, 1973). As the philosopher Hobbes (1651) put it simply: "I put for a general [sic] inclination of all mankind, a perpetual and restless desire of power after power that ceaseath only in Death" (p. 161). To have power is to have control over resources, to have the ability to influence others' behavior, and to be able to act on your own volition (see Dahl, 1957; Galinsky, Gruenfeld, & Magee, 2003). Relatedly, status is related to the position that one holds within a social network or hierarchy and the respect that an individual is conferred to by others (Magee & Galinsky, 2008; Sell, Lovaglia, Mannix, Samuelson, & Wilson, 2004). Power and status are major dimensions upon which humans evaluate themselves and others (Osgood, May, & Miron, 1975; Galinsky et al., 2003), and globalization should be of no exception. To what extent does cultural mixing make one feel less powerful and have lower status, creating "status conflicts" (Bendersky & Hays, in press) across cultural groups vis-a-vis globalization? Does the cultural mixing of Starbucks and the Great Wall, the juxtaposition of Chinese and American brands, or the merging of two different countries activate threats to one's status or power? As well, how might power and status be implicated in folk theories about the historical trends of one's society (Kashima et al., 2011)? Put differently, to what extent do individuals, through narratives and other cultural products that have been passed down, assess the degree to which their societies have more or less power or status, and what implication does this have for their reactions to cultural mixing and ultimately exclusionary or inclusionary processes (Chiu et al., 2011)? While many articles in this volume discuss the notion that globalization might elicit threats—whether to one's cultural identity, to maintaining categories, or to maintaining an economic advantage (Morris et al., 2011)—we suspect that power and status threats are important to add to this "psychological mix."

Psychological Dynamics and Globalization: The Good, the Bad, and the Ugly

The articles in this volume illustrate an irony in reactions to globalization. On the one hand, globalization increases one's exposure to multiple cultures and can result in heightened perspective taking—and opening of the cultural mind—and associated positive consequences such as creativity (Chiu et al., 2011; Cheng, et al., 2011; Leung & Chiu, 2010; Maddux & Galinsky, 2009; Maddux, Leung, Chiu, & Galinsky, 2009). On the other hand, exposure to multiple cultures can also produce diametrically opposite results—the closing of the cultural mind, low perspective taking, and high ethnocentrism. Articles in this volume make great strides in charting out the conditions under which such inclusionary versus exclusionary reactions are exacerbated or attenuated. For example, we now know that factors that predict exclusionary reactions include existential anxiety (Torelli et al., 2011) and identification with one's local culture (Tong et al., 2011), and we would add other likely candidates such as cognitive load (Gilbert & Hixon, 1991; Sweller, 1988), need for closure (Kruglanski, Webster & Klem, 1993), political conservativism (Jost, Glaser, Kruglanski, & Sulloway, 2003), low relational and residential mobility (Oishi, 2010; Schug, Yuki, & Maddux, 2010, Schug, Yuki, Horikawa, & Yakemura, 2009), and cultural tightness (Gelfand et al., 2011). By contrast, factors that predict positive reactions include need for cognition (Torelli et al., 2011), identification with a foreign culture (Morris et al., 2011), multicultural experiences (Maddux & Galinsky, 2009; Maddux et al., 2009), cultural intelligence (Rockstuhl, et al., 2011) and perhaps factors such as general trust, high relational and residential mobility (Schug et al., 2009; 2010), and cultural looseness (Gelfand et al., 2011). By charting out the contextual and psychological processes that activate positive versus negative reactions to globalization, this volume helps to explain and predict when globalization will produce positive or negative responses.

A important principle identified across the articles is that while cultural mixing causes exclusionary reactions when one strongly identifies with one's own culture or when one faces existential threats (e.g., mortality salience), it can be reduced when the perceiver is motivated to engage in thoughtful elaboration about cultural complexities (Chiu et al., 2011; Cheng et al., 2011; Torelli et al., 2011). This analysis opens the exciting possibility of looking at interactions among other factors that might simultaneously foster attachment to one's group and the motivation to engage with others and their impact on reactions to globalization.

For example, many articles touched upon the role of identification with one's own culture (Tong et al., 2011; Torelli et al., 2011) versus the role of identification with a foreign culture (Morris et al, 2011), yet adopting a foreign or global identity needs not mean sacrificing one's local or cultural identity. Accordingly, we can consider the benefits of accepting global influence while simultaneously protecting one's local, cultural identities. Indeed, our own research (Lyons, Lun, & Gelfand, 2010, 2011) suggests that having either a global *or* a local identity activated in isolation might not be ideal for psychological reactions to globalization; rather, having both identities activated produces more positive responses because it enhances feelings of both inclusion and distinctiveness. More specifically, we theorized that although adopting a shared identity can reduce intergroup bias by decreasing the salience of subgroup differences (Gaertner, Mann, Murrell, & Dovidio, 1989), social identity research lends theoretical support also to the benefit of maintaining *both* cultural/subgroup and shared identities. According to optimal distinctiveness theory (Brewer, 1991), individuals experience tension between the need for group inclusiveness and the need for distinctiveness. In this view, while adopting a shared global identity fulfills the need for inclusiveness, and can reduce intergroup bias by decreasing the salience of subgroup differences (Gaertner, Dovidio, Nier, Ward, & Banker, 1999), it can at the same time deny an individual the distinct identity offered by one's subgroup national identity in intercultural contexts. Research has indeed shown that such conditions can lead individuals to identify more strongly with their subgroup and result in even more intergroup bias than when only subgroup identities are activated (cf. Hornsey & Hogg, 2000).

Accordingly, we theorized that if an individual adopts a shared identity while holding onto a subgroup identity, both the need for inclusiveness and the need for distinctiveness can be fulfilled, resulting in more inclusionary responses to outgroups (Lyons, et al., 2010, 2011). Data collected in the field and in the laboratory support this general notion. Using data from the 2005 World Values Survey, Americans who were high on both global and national identities were more trusting of people of other nationalities than those who were high on one identity or the other, or low on both, and this effect was also found in other samples including China, Australia, Indonesia, and Morocco. Moreover, high dual global-national identification predicted other measures of openness in other countries. For example, in Indonesia, high global-national identification predicted willingness to be neighbors with immigrants/foreign workers and people of a different race. In Lebanon, high global-national identification predicted willingness to be neighbors with Americans and support for inclusive attitudes within Lebanon itself (Lyons, Lun, & Gelfand, 2010). Other experimental research in which we primed shared and cultural identities also illustrated more cooperative reactions to outgroups when both subgroup and global identity were made salient. This suggests that one way to promote inclusionary reactions to globalization is to not only to uphold a global mindset, but also to simultaneously make concerted efforts to protect local, cultural identities. Under these conditions, individuals have the confidence to assert their local interests while being motivated to cooperate on a larger, global level.

While we have discussed how the interplay of having a high cultural and high global identification can produce positive responses to globalization, it is also interesting to speculate on the effects of just the opposite condition—having a low cultural identity and a low global orientation—and its impact on responses to globalization. Such individuals do not identify with either identity and can be described having "identity confusion" (Arnett, 2002; see also Berry, 1970 for related work). As Arnett (2002) aptly put, for these individuals, "the images, values, and opportunities they perceive as being part of the global culture undermine their belief in the value of local culture practices. At the same time, the ways of the global culture seem out of reach to them, too foreign to everything they know from their direct experience. Rather than being bicultural, they may experience themselves as excluded from both their local culture and global culture, truly belonging to neither" (p. 778). Having low cultural and low global identification may put people at risk for anomie, social isolation, and health problems. Indeed, the insightful analysis by Norasakkunkit and Uchida (2011) in this volume of the NEETs population in Japan (i.e., not in employment, education, or training) is a case in point. Constituting hundreds of thousands of people in the population, NEETs face little prospects of securing desirable employment and participating in the global workforce, and have become marginalized from society. According to their data, they ultimately also lose their own cultural identity and become "cultural deviants" who differ widely in their attitudes from those in the local culture. Future research needs to look at the consequences of such identity confusion in the context of globalization, and how being marginalized affects psychological, social, and health outcomes across different cultures. As the authors note, while in some countries marginalization might take the form of passive withdrawal, in others it might result in active protests and even support for violence.

Conclusion

Globalization has increased dramatically in its scope and reach in the last several decades. The effects of globalization have been glamorized by its supporters and demonized by its opponents. Globalization has facilitated international trade and technological advances, and exposure to different cultures, which can promote learning and creativity. Yet at the same time, it has been criticized for eroding important cultural characteristics of societies, and as such globalization has met resistance from those who feel threatened by foreign influence, breeding distrust and suspicion throughout local communities. There have been numerous perspectives advanced on these issues in the interdisciplinary walls of academe over the last several decades. Psychology is a new on this interdisciplinary block to offer its insights into globalization, and as this special issue attests, provides novel perspectives on the way individuals make meaning of globalization and the factors that give way to integrative processes related to globalization while reducing exclusionary reactions to foreign cultures. The articles in this special issue have collectively paved the way for a psychological science of globalization that is a much needed perspective for theory and practice alike.

References

Adler, A. (1966). The psychology of power. *Journal of Individual Psychology, 22*, 166–172.

Allport, G. W. (1954). *The nature of prejudice*. Reading, MA: Addison-Wesley.

Arnett, J. J. (2002). The psychology of globalization. *American Psychologist, 57*, 774–783. doi:10.1037/0003-066X.57.10.774

Arnett, J. J. (2008). The neglected 95%: Why American psychology needs to become less American. *American Psychologist, 63*, 602–614. doi:10.1037/0003-066X.63.7.602

Bendersky, C., & Hays, N. (in press). Status conflict in groups. *Organization Science*.

Berry, J. W. (1970). Marginality, stress and ethnic identification in an acculturated aboriginal community. *Journal of Cross-Cultural Psychology, 1*, 239–252. doi:10.1177/135910457000100303

Brewer, M. (1991). The social self: On being the same and different at the same time. *Personality and Social Psychology Bulletin, 17*, 475–482. doi:10.1177/0146167291175001

Cheng, C.-Y., Leung, A., & Wu, T.-Y. (2011). Going beyond the multicultural experience–creativity link: The mediating role of emotions. *Journal of Social Issues, 67*, 806–824. doi:10.1111/j.1540-4560.2011.01731.x

Chiu, C.-Y., Gries, P., Torelli, C. J., & Cheng, Y. Y. (2011). Toward a social psychology of globalization. *Journal of Social Issues, 67*, 663–676. doi:10.1111/j.1540-4560.2011.01721.x

Chiu, C.-Y., Hong, Y., & Dweck, C. S. (1997). Lay dispositionalism and implicit theories of personality. *Journal of Personality and Social Psychology, 73*, 19–30. doi:10.1037/0022-3514.73.1.19

Dahl, R. (1957). The concept of power. *Behavioral Science, 2*, 201–215.

Dweck, C. S. (1999). *Self-theories: Their role in motivation, personality, and development*. New York, NY: Psychology Press.

Elisseeff, V. (2000). *The silk roads: Highways of culture and commerce*. Oxford/New York: UNESCO Publishing/Berghahn Books.

Frieze, I. H., & Boneva, B. S. (2001). Power motivation and motivation to help others. In Y. Lee Chai & J. A. Bargh (Eds.), *The use and abuse of power: Multiple perspectives on the causes of corruption* (pp. 75–89). Philadelphia, PA: Psychology Press/Taylor & Francis.

Furnham, A., & Rees, J. (1988). Lay theories of schizophrenia. *International Journal of Social Psychiatry, 34*, 212–220. doi:10.1177/002076408803400307

Galinsky, A., Gruenfeld, D., & Magee, J. (2003). From power to action. *Journal of Personality and Social Psychology, 85*, 453–466. doi:10.1037/0022-3514.85.3.453

Gaertner, S. L., Dovidio, J. F., Nier, J. A., Ward, C. M., & Banker, B. S. (1999). Across cultural divides: The value of a superordinate identity. In D. A. Prentice, D. T. Miller, D. A. Prentice, D. T. Miller (Eds.), *Cultural divides: Understanding and overcoming group conflict* (pp. 173–212). New York, NY: Russell Sage Foundation.

Gaertner, S., Mann, J., Murrell, A., & Dovidio, J. (1989). Reducing intergroup bias: The benefits of recategorization. *Journal of Personality and Social Psychology, 57*, 239–249. doi:10.1177/1368430205051066

Gelfand, M., Raver, J. L., Nishii, L., Leslie, L. t., Lun, J., Lim, B., . . . Yamaguchi, S. (2011). Differences between tight and loose cultures: A 33-nation study. *Science, 332*(6033), 1100–1104. doi:10.1126/science.1197754

Giddens, A. (2010). *Runaway world: How globalization is reshaping our lives*. New York: Routledge.

Gilbert, D. T., & Hixon, J. G. (1991). The trouble of thinking: Activation and application of stereotypic beliefs. *Journal of Personality and Social Psychology, 60*, 509–517.

Ginges, J., Atran, S., Medin, D., & Shikaki, K. (2007). Sacred bounds on rational resolution of violent political conflict. *Proceedings of the National Academy of Science, 104*, 7357–7360. doi:10.1073/pnas.0701768104

Gries, P. H., Crowson, H. M., & Cai, H. (2011). When knowledge is a double-edged sword: Contact, media exposure, and American China policy preferences. *Journal of Social Issues, 67*, 787–805. doi:10.1111/j.1540-4560.2011.01728.x

Haidt, J. (2008). Morality. *Perspectives on Psychological Science, 3*, 65–72. doi:10.1111/j.1745-6916.2008.00063.x

Haidt, J., & Graham, J. (2007). When morality opposes justice: Conservatives have moral intuitions that liberals may not recognize. *Social Justice Research, 20*, 98–116. doi:10.1007/s11211-007-0034-z

Heider, F. (1958). *The psychology of interpersonal relations.* New York: Wiley.

Henrich, J., Heine, S. J., & Norenzayan, A. (2010). The weirdest people in the world? *Behavioral and Brain Sciences, 33,* 61–135. doi:10.1017/S0140525×0999152X

Hobbes, T. (1991 [1651]). *Leviathan.* Cambridge: Cambridge University Press.

Hong, Y., Levy, S. R., & Chiu, C. (2001). The contribution of the lay theories approach to the study of groups. *Personality and Social Psychology Review, 5*(2), 98–106. doi:10.1207/S15327957PSPR0502_1

Hornsey, M., & Hogg, M. (2000). Subgroup relations: A comparison of mutual intergroup differentiation and common ingroup identity models of prejudice reduction. *Personality and Social Psychology Bulletin, 26,* 242–256. doi:10.1177/0146167200264010

Jost, J. T., Glaser, J., Kruglanski, A. W., & Sulloway, F. J. (2003). Political conservatism as motivated social cognition. *Psychological Bulletin, 129,* 339–375. doi:10.1037/0033-2909.129.3.339

Kashima, Y., & Gelfand, M. J. (in press). A history of culture in psychology. In A. W. Kruglanski & Stroebe (Eds.), *Handbook of the history of social psychology.* Taylor & Francis Group.

Kashima, Y., Shi, J., Tsuchiya, K., Cheng, S. Y. Y., Chao, M. M.-M., Kashima, E., & Shin, S.-h. (2011). Globalization and folk theory of social change: How globalization relates to societal perceptions about the past and future. *Journal of Social Issues, 67,* 696–715. doi:10.1111/j.1540-4560.2011.01723.x

Kipnis, D. (1976). *The powerholders.* Chicago: University of Chicago Press.

Kruglanski, A. W. (1989). *Lay epistemics and human knowledge: Cognitive and motivational bases.* New York: Plenum Press.

Kruglanski, A. W., Webster, D. M., & Klem, A. (1993). Motivated resistance and openness to persuasion in the presence or absence of prior information. *Journal of Personality and Social Psychology, 65,* 861–876, doi:10.1037/0022-3514.65.5.861

Lecher, F. J., & Boli, J. (2008). *The globalization reader* (3rd ed.). New York: Blackwell Publishing.

Leung, A. K.-y., & Chiu, C.-Y. (2010). Multicultural experience, idea receptiveness, and creativity. *Journal of Cross-Cultural Psychology, 41,* 723–741. doi:10.1177/0022022110361707

Lyons, S. L., Lun, J., & Gelfand, M. J. (2010). *The interplay of cultural and shared identities in intercultural negotiations.* Presented at the Annual Meeting of the International Association of Conflict Management (IACM), Boston, MA.

Lyons, S. L., Lun, J., & Gelfand, M. J. (2011). *The interplay of cultural and shared identities in intercultural negotiations.* Presented at the Annual Meeting of the Academy of Management, San Antonio, TX.

Maddux, W. W., & Galinsky, A. D. (2009). Cultural borders and mental barriers: The relationship between living abroad and creativity. *Journal of Personality and Social Psychology, 96,* 1047–1061. doi:10.1037/a0014861

Maddux, W. W., Leung, A. K.-y., Chiu, C.-y., & Galinsky, A. (2009). Toward a more complete understanding of the link between multicultural experience and creativity. *American Psychologist, 64,* 156–158. doi:10.1037/a0014941

Magee, J. C., & Galinsky, A. (2008). Social hierarchy: The self-reinforcing nature of power and status. In J. P. Walsh & A. P. Brief (Eds.), *Academy of management annals* (Vol. 2, pp. 351–398). London, UK: Taylor & Francis.

Malle, B. F. (2010). Intentional action in folk psychology. In T. O'Connor & C. Sandis (Eds.), *Blackwell companion to the philosophy of action.* Oxford, UK: Blackwell.

McClelland, D. (1975). *Power: The inner experience.* New York: Irvington.

McClelland, D. (1987). *Human motivation.* Cambridge: Cambridge University Press.

Morris, M. W., Mok, A., & Mor, S. (2011). Cultural identity threat: The role of cultural identifications in moderating closure responses to foreign cultural inflow. *Journal of Social Issues, 67,* 760–773. doi:10.1111/j.1540-4560.2011.01726.x

Norasakkunkit, V., & Uchida, Y. (2011). Psychological consequences of post-industrial anomie on self and motivation among Japanese youth. *Journal of Social Issues, 67,* 774–786. doi:10.1111/j.1540-4560.2011.01727.x

Oishi, S. (2010). The psychology of residential mobility: Implications for the self, social relationships, and well-being. *Perspectives on Psychological Science, 5,* 5–21. doi:10.1177/1745691609356781

Osgood, C. E., May, W. H., & Miron, M. S. (1975). *Cross-cultural universals of affective meaning.* Urbana, IL: University of Illinois.

Rockstuhl, T., Seiler, S., Ang, S., van Dyne, L., & Annen, H. (2011). Beyond general intelligence (IQ) and emotional intelligence (EQ): The role of cultural intelligence (CQ) on cross-border leadership effectiveness in a globalized world. *Journal of Social Issues, 67*, 825–840. doi:10.1111/j.1540-4560.2011.01730.x

Schug, J., Yuki, M., & Maddux, W. W. (2010). Relational mobility explains between- and within-culture differences in self-disclosure toward close friends. *Psychological Science, 21*, 1471–1478. doi:10.1177/0956797610382786

Schug, J. R., Yuki, M., Horikawa, H., & Takemura, K. (2009). Similarity attraction and actually selecting similar others: How cross-societal differences in relational mobility affect interpersonal similarity in Japan and the United States. *Asian Journal of Social Psychology, 2*, 95–103. doi:10.1111/j.1467-839X.2009.01277.x

Sell, J., Lovaglia, M. J., Mannix, E. A., Samuelson, C. D., & Wilson, R. K. (2004). Investigating conflict, power, and status within and among groups. *Small Group Research, 35*(1), 44–72. doi:10.1177/1046496403259813

Steger, M. B. (2009). *Globalization: A very short introduction.* New York: Oxford University Press.

Sternberg, R. J. (1985). Implicit theories of intelligence, creativity, and wisdom. *Journal of Personality and Social Psychology, 49*, 607–627. doi:10.1037/0022-3514.49.3.607

Sweller, J. (1988). Cognitive load during problem solving: Effects on learning. *Cognitive Science, 12*, 257–285. doi:10.1016/0364-0213(88)90023-7

Tetlock, P. E., Kristel, O. V., Elson, S. B., Green, M. C., & Lerner, J. S. (2000). Taboo trade-offs, forbidden base rates, and heretical counterfactuals. *Journal of Personality and Social Psychology, 78*, 853–870. doi:10.1037/0022-3514.78.5.853

Tong, J. Y.-Y., Hui, P. P.-Z., Kwan, L., & Peng, S. (2011) National feelings or rational dealings? The role of procedural priming on the perceptions of cross-border acquisitions. *Journal of Social Issues, 67*, 743–759. doi:10.1111/j.1540-4560.2011.01725.x

Torelli, C. J., Chiu, C.-Y., Tam, K.-P., Au, K. C., & Keh, H. T. (2011). Exclusionary reactions to foreign cultures: Effects of simultaneous exposure to cultures in globalized space. *Journal of Social Issues, 67*, 716–742. doi:10.1111/j.1540-4560.2011.01724.x

Wegener, D. T., & Petty, R. E. (Eds.). (1998). Special issue: Naive theories and social judgment. *Social Cognition, 16*(1), 1–198.

Winter, D. (1973). *The power motive.* New York: The Free Press.

Yang, D., Chen, X., Cheng, S. Y. Y., Kwan, L., Tam, K.-p., & Yeh, K.-H. (2011). Lay psychology and its social impact. *Journal of Social Issues, 67*, 677–695. doi:10.1111/j.1540-4560.2011.01722.x

MICHELE J. GELFAND is Professor of Psychology and Distinguished University Scholar Teacher at the University of Maryland, College Park. She received her Ph.D. in Social/ Organizational Psychology from the University of Illinois. Gelfand's work explores cultural influences on conflict, negotiation, justice, revenge, and forgiveness; workplace diversity and discrimination; and theory and methods in cross-cultural psychology.

SARAH L. LYONS is a Ph.D. student in the Social and Organizational Psychology program at the University of Maryland. Her research interests include multicultural identities, acculturation, and intergroup processes.

JANETTA LUN is a post-doctoral research associate in the Department of Psychology at the University of Maryland at College Park. She received her Ph.D. from the University of Virginia in Social Psychology. Her research interests include culture, shared understanding, and intercultural negotiation.

Statement of Ownership, Management, and Circulation
(All Periodicals Publications Except Requester Publications)

1. Publication Title	2. Publication Number	3. Filing Date
Journal of Social Issues	0 0 1 _ 6 5 2	10/1/11

4. Issue Frequency	5. Number of Issues Published Annually	6. Annual Subscription Price
Quarterly	4	$932.00

7. Complete Mailing Address of Known Office of Publication (Not printer) (Street, city, county, state, and ZIP+4®)	Contact Person
Wiley Subscription Services, Inc., 111 River Street, Hoboken, NJ 07030	E. Schmidichen
	Telephone (Include area code) (201) 748-6346

8. Complete Mailing Address of Headquarters or General Business Office of Publisher (Not printer)

Wiley Subscription Services, Inc., 111 River Street, Hoboken, NJ 07030

9. Full Names and Complete Mailing Addresses of Publisher, Editor, and Managing Editor (Do not leave blank)

Publisher (Name and complete mailing address)

Wiley Subscription Services, Inc., 111 River Street, Hoboken, NJ 07030

Editor (Name and complete mailing address)

Sheri R. Levy, Department of Psychology, Stony Brook University, 142 Psychology - B Bldg. Stony Brook, NY 11794

Managing Editor (Name and complete mailing address)

None

10. Owner (Do not leave blank. If the publication is owned by a corporation, give the name and address of the corporation immediately followed by the names and addresses of all stockholders owning or holding 1 percent or more of the total amount of stock. If not owned by a corporation, give the names and addresses of the individual owners. If owned by a partnership or other unincorporated firm, give its name and address as well as those of each individual owner. If the publication is published by a nonprofit organization, give its name and address.)

Full Name	Complete Mailing Address
The Society for the Psychological Study of Social Issues	1901 Pennsylvania NW Ste 901
	Washington, DC 20006

11. Known Bondholders, Mortgagees, and Other Security Holders Owning or Holding 1 Percent or More of Total Amount of Bonds, Mortgages, or Other Securities. If none, check box → ☑ None

Full Name	Complete Mailing Address

12. Tax Status (For completion by nonprofit organizations authorized to mail at nonprofit rates) (Check one)
The purpose, function, and nonprofit status of this organization and the exempt status for federal income tax purposes:
☐ Has Not Changed During Preceding 12 Months
☐ Has Changed During Preceding 12 Months (Publisher must submit explanation of change with this statement)

PS Form **3526**, September 2006 PSN 7530-01-000-9931 **PRIVACY NOTICE:** See our privacy policy on www.usps.com

13. Publication Title	14. Issue Date for Circulation Data
Journal of Social Issues	September 2011

15. Extent and Nature of Circulation		Average No. Copies Each Issue During Preceding 12 Months	No. Copies of Single Issue Published Nearest to Filing Date
a. Total Number of Copies (Net press run)		2067	1900
b. Paid Circulation (By Mail and Outside the Mail)	(1) Mailed Outside-County Paid Subscriptions Stated on PS Form 3541(Include paid distribution above nominal rate, advertiser's proof copies, and exchange copies)	1622	1560
	(2) Mailed In-County Paid Subscriptions Stated on PS Form 3541 (Include paid distribution above nominal rate, advertiser's proof copies, and exchange copies)	0	0
	(3) Paid Distribution Outside the Mails Including Sales Through Dealers and Carriers, Street Vendors, Counter Sales, and Other Paid Distribution Outside USPS®	0	0
	(4) Paid Distribution by Other Classes of Mail Through the USPS (e.g. First-Class Mail®)	0	0
c. Total Paid Distribution (Sum of 15b (1), (2),(3), and (4))		1622	1560
d. Free or Nominal Rate Distribution (By Mail and Outside the Mail)	(1) Free or Nominal Rate Outside-County Copies lincluded on PS Form 3541	55	47
	(2) Free or Nominal Rate In-County Copies Included on PS Form 3541	0	0
	(3) Free or Nominal Rate Copies Mailed at Other Classes Through the USPS (e.g. First-Class Mail)	0	0
	(4) Free or Nominal Rate Distribution Outside the Mail (Carriers or other means)	0	0
e. Total Free or Nominal Rate Distribution (Sum of 15d (1), (2), (3) and (4)		55	47
f. Total Distribution (Sum of 15c and 15e) ▶		1677	1607
g. Copies not Distributed (See Instructions to Publishers #4 (page #3)) ▶		390	293
h. Total (Sum of 15f and g) ▶		2067	1900
i. Percent Paid (15c divided by 15f times 100) ▶		96.72	97.08

16. Publication of Statement of Ownership

☑ If the publication is a general publication, publication of this statement is required. Will be printed in the December 2011 issue of this publication. ☐ Publication not required.

17. Signature and Title of Editor, Publisher, Business Manager, or Owner	Date
Elizabeth Konkle, Associate Financial Manager	10/1/11

I certify that all information furnished on this form is true and complete. I understand that anyone who furnishes false or misleading information on this form or who omits material or information requested on the form may be subject to criminal sanctions (including fines and imprisonment) and/or civil sanctions (including civil penalties).

PS Form **3526**, September 2006